Learners' Resource Ce

St. HARTLEPOOL TS24 7NT Tel

FROM PALM TO PINE

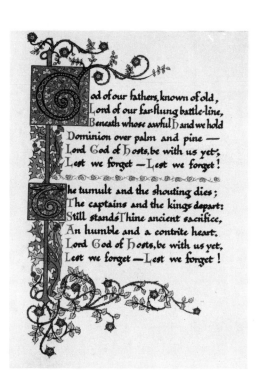

God of our fathers, known of old,
Lord of our far-flung battle-line,
Beneath whose awful Hand we hold
Dominion over palm and pine —
Lord God of Hosts, be with us yet,
Lest we forget — Lest we forget!

The tumult and the shouting dies;
The captains and the kings depart:
Still stands Thine ancient sacrifice,
An humble and a contrite heart.
Lord God of Hosts, be with us yet,
Lest we forget — Lest we forget!

From Palm To Pine

Rudyard Kipling
Abroad and At Home

Marghanita Laski

SIDGWICK & JACKSON

LONDON

To my daughter,
Rebecca Lydia Howard

First published in Great Britain in 1987
by Sidgwick & Jackson Limited
1 Tavistock Chambers, Bloomsbury Way
London WC1A 2SG

ISBN 0-283-99422-3

Picture Research by Deborah Pownall

Text set by SX Composing Limited, Rayleigh, Essex, England
Illustrations originated by Bridge Graphics Limited, Hull, England
Printed and bound by Graficas Estella, S.A., Estella, Spain

Dep. Leg.: NA. 1.472-1986

Half-title: 'Recessional' was one of several of Kipling's poems to be inspirationally illuminated. In this version of 1914 by Henrietta Wright, the decoration features the rose, the shamrock, and the thistle. Title-page: A portrait of Rudyard Kipling from a series of famous writers published in the 1890s.

CONTENTS

FOREWORD

T HE year 1986, during which this book was written, represents something of a hinge period in Kipling studies. Ten years earlier, on 26 May 1976, Rudyard Kipling's last surviving child, Elsie Bambridge, had died at the age of eighty. She had safeguarded her father's reputation with a ferocity that tantalized and maddened all those who wanted to work on his life and his writing; who wanted to be able to read more than the authorized canon published in this country and the little more that had been pirated in America; who wanted to know more of Kipling's life than the one authorized biography, that by Charles Carrington, though it remains, to this date, the most useful there is.

No one could know, in the years between Kipling's death and hers, just what material by and about Kipling Mrs Bambridge was holding, and, worse, what might have been destroyed. Today Kipling's work is out of copyright. It is the National Trust now, not an over-protective daughter, which has the responsibility for releasing unpublished Kipling material; and what has already been published may be republished by anyone at will.

So in the coming decades we are likely to learn a great deal about Kipling, about both the work and the man. Already hitherto unpublished 'pieces' and verses have been published, and there is much more to come. Already a distinguished scholar, Thomas Pinney, is working on the Kipling letters.

Rudyard Kipling was, however, as regards his private life, one of the most reticent of writers. If his daughter had needed any justification for her fierce exclusiveness, she could always call on filial piety and on her father's wishes, which we the public know best from his poem 'The Appeal', first published in 1939 and now standing at the end of the Definitive Edition of his collected verse:

> If I have given you delight
> By aught that I have done,
> Let me lie quiet in that night
> Which shall be yours anon:
>
> And for the little, little, span
> The dead are borne in mind,
> Seek not to question other than
> The books I leave behind.

It might have been thought decently pious in us too to abide by Kipling's wish for continuing privacy but it would be inconceivably priggish, in today's climate, not to look at a writer's life as well as his work, just because he had asked us not to do so in some touching verses.

But we must be cautious. Though it may not be possible to refrain entirely from speculation about relations between Kipling and his work, it would be foolish to make guesses that may soon be disproved by evidence.

I have, therefore, largely confined myself to what is already known about Kipling, both from his own work and from the works of critics and biographers who have relied on fact rather than speculation; though there must be provisos about Kipling's apparent self-revelations, and I shall discuss these in Chapter Three. The picture is, therefore, at present, of limited dimensions and there are many patches of darkness. It will be wonderfully interesting when these are lit.

The dates given in the text for works are those of first publication, which are not necessarily the dates of the books in which they were collected; these will be found on page 186. Where there are omissions in a quotation, or where less than a whole poem is quoted, the omissions are indicated by three dots.

It remains to offer my warm thanks to the people who have helped me.

I must first thank Helen Fry for the perfectionism she brought to the three series of BBC Radio programmes that we made together: 'Kipling's English History', 'Kipling's India', and 'Round the World with Rudyard Kipling'; my thanks, too, to the readers who made of poetry read aloud an acceptable art. I should like to thank in advance Pamela Howe of BBC Bristol with whom I am making a fourth series.

Especially warm thanks to Catherine Freeman who invited me to see a part of India under the best possible auspices. I must also thank Dr R. J. Bingle, Curator of European Manuscripts in the India Office Records at the British Library for exceptionally interesting information on John Lockwood Kipling's career in India and its emoluments, together with the facts I sought on the fall of the rupee; my friend John Grey Murray for his trusting loan of the rare 1882 Murray's *Guide to the Punjab and Rajputana*; J. H. Price, Editor of Thomas Cook's Timetables, for esoteric information about transport in the Suez Peninsula; Norman Entract, Secretary of the Kipling Society; and John Shearman, former Secretary of the Kipling Society.

Decorative capitals were one of Lockwood Kipling's many specialities. Those in this book have been taken from The Second Jungle Book.

INTRODUCTION

Winds of the World, give answer! They are whimpering to and fro –
And what should they know of England who only England know? –
The poor little street-bred people that vapour and fume and brag,
They are lifting their heads in the stillness to yelp at the English Flag! . . .

from 'The English Flag'

O F all our great English writers, Rudyard Kipling came to have the widest geographical range. He visited every continent, traversed almost every sea, and wrote stories, verses, essays, about almost every place he had visited and some he had not. He travelled in time as well as in space, and ranged imaginatively from the Old Stone Age to a future that was further away from him than it is from us, the two-thousandth century AD. Himself without orthodox belief – he said once that Freemasonry was the nearest thing to a religion that he knew – he could often enter into the skin of people alien to him and so convincingly that whether he got it right or not, no reader would want to say him nay: the twelfth-century Jew Kadmiel of the story 'The Treasure and the Law', the Calvinist ship's engineer of the long poem 'McAndrew's Hymn'; the Indian child of the story 'Little Tobrah' who killed his blind sister for what seemed to him, and to the Englishman's servants who listened to the story, perfectly satisfactory reasons. And this kind of imaginative foray has hardly ever disturbed any of Kipling's readers.

Where varying degrees of distrust have assailed Rudyard Kipling's readers from about 1890 to the present day are, quite simply, when he writes about a certain range of subjects on which some people then and most people now have other outlooks than his.

It is no part of my business to write an Apology for Kipling, but it is fair to observe that such criticism often comes from critics who are ignorant of much of his work and of the climate in which it was written; and, less excusably, from critics who are unable to respond imaginatively to any high-mindedness other than their own, not realizing that whatever its immediate focus, English middle-class high-mindedness is just as admirable and just as silly wherever and whenever it is exercised. Kipling puts forward many views for which such critics condemn him; but there are hardly any (except on what he called 'the Immoderate Left'), which the knowledgeable Kipling reader cannot qualify with modifiers, and sometimes even with diametrically opposite opinions. For Kipling was, like most writers, a chameleon, and could change his skin to his imagination's needs; or, as he himself put it, he had two separate sides to his head.

8

As to those who cannot stomach Kipling's ideals, it is they who are the losers in wider understanding, for if Kipling's ideals as expressed in his writings are often unfashionable, they are not ignoble. If we believe in self-government even for those palpably unready for it, it is not ignoble to believe in a duty of disinterested tutelage. If we believe in our version of democratic government, it is not ignoble to believe in benevolent autocracy. If we believe, with E. M. Forster, that we should betray our country rather than our friends, it is still not ignoble to ask, as Kipling did in his poem 'The Children's Song', better known as 'Land of our Birth',

> Teach us to look in all our ends
> On Thee for judge, and not our friends . . .

If we recoil now from a specifically White Man's burden, it is surely just such a burden that the world's richer nations, whatever their colour, feel a duty to shoulder in the face of such disasters as the recent famines in Africa:

> Take up the White Man's burden –
> The savage wars of peace –
> Fill full the mouth of Famine
> And bid the sickness cease . . .

And it was, in its time, rather out of date than ignoble to look to a Commonwealth of white, equal, sister-nations to maintain the structure of the world.

But it has to be admitted that little of Kipling's finest writing is about the ideals set out in the paragraph above, and almost none of it about the last of these. Most of the material quoted in this book will come from Kipling's better work, but not all of it can or should.

Why Kipling's work can differ so amazingly in quality is something I shall consider in Chapter Three. For the present, and before we start on his travels and his work as a grown-up writer, I want to place him in his family, a homeless child born of homeless parents and on both sides homeless grandparents, yet firmly ensconced among the best of England's cultural traditions. But small wonder that the earlier decades of his adult life were dominated by the search for a place to which he could really belong.

John Lockwood Kipling, of whom Fred Macdonald said, 'gentle, kindly, and wise, everyone liked him'; and Alice, who at twenty-six had feared being a family burden, but now, wrote Aggie, was 'better than I have seen her for years'. (The Macdonald Sisters)

CHAPTER ONE

THE CHILD IN HIS FAMILY

Father, Mother, and Me,
Sister and Auntie say
All the people like us are We,
And every one else is They . . .

from 'We and They'

THERE is an old reservoir in Staffordshire known as Lake Rudyard. Here, at a picnic party in 1863, John Lockwood Kipling met Alice Macdonald, both of them twenty-four years old. On 18 March 1865 they married and on 30 December of that year their first child, a son, was born. He was christened Joseph Rudyard: Joseph a Kipling family name, and Rudyard for the reservoir where his parents had first met.

So far as social background went, John and Alice were well matched. Both their fathers were Methodist ministers. John's father was a Yorkshireman, and Rudyard would sometimes claim to be a Yorkshireman himself, though he did little to take up that inheritance. Of John Kipling's family we hear little. He had two sisters and a brother, but the Kipling family seems to have played little or no part in Rudyard's life. John's widowed mother, born Frances Lockwood, was dismissed by her wickedly witty daughter-in-law as a mere 'sock-knitter'. As often happens in marriages, one family was dominant: and that family was the extraordinary Macdonalds.

'My Father with his sage Yorkshire outlook and wisdom; my Mother, all Celt –' wrote Rudyard.[1] This branch of the Macdonald clan came from Skye, set off for America after the Jacobite rising of 1745, and stopped off in Ireland. Rudyard's maternal great-grandfather, another Methodist minister, came to England in 1795. His youngest child, George Browne Macdonald, married his second wife, Hannah Jones, in Manchester in 1833 and by her he had eleven children – his first wife had died childless. Of these eleven children, three died in infancy, one in childhood. The older surviving son, Henry or Harry, emigrated to America after he left Oxford. The younger son, Fred, went into the Ministry and became, in 1899, President of the Wesleyan Methodist Conference. But none of the five daughters stayed in that persuasion. The four who married all did so in the Church of England, and not all retained any faith at all.

But those defections did not mar a family life which was exceptionally close and loving. By every account, George Macdonald and his wife Hannah were very fine people, deeply religious yet understandingly tolerant of young people and their needs, and they gave their attractive daughters a degree of freedom unusual in the mid-nineteenth century. Indeed, they gave their daughters everything that was good, except for good health.

In the early years of this century, a German psychologist, Ernst Kretschmer, put up a theory that genius erupted in families just before they toppled into madness and decay. There are enough examples to the contrary to shoot the theory down, but the Macdonald family would have been grist to Kretschmer's mill. A family legend of a mad ancestor may not have been true, but it is certain that the family was plagued with physical ill health, and the kind of sensitive nervous systems that exacerbated physical symptoms. Both George Macdonald and his daughter, Louisa suffered from agonizingly painful backs, and in Hannah Macdonald and all her daughters, frenetic gaiety alternated with depression. Alice was seldom entirely well. In 1870 she bore a stillborn child in Bombay, and neither of her surviving children was noticeably healthy. The daughter, some years after her marriage, became periodically insane. Rudyard himself was both physically and mentally frail, and sometimes feared madness. Two of Rudyard's own children died too young for adult life, one from sickness, one in war. The surviving daughter, Elsie, was, to say the least, pathologically over-protective of her father's memory. She had no children, and the Kipling family died out.

A Methodist minister must make his home's stability inside the family, not in the dwelling-place, for every three years he moves on. This stability the Macdonald parents achieved, and it was from the absolute security of home that the Macdonald daughters, during this peripatetic existence, managed to build a lively social life, mostly in London and in what then could have been called a Bohemian set. Only Edith, the youngest – sharp-tongued Aunt Edie – remained unmarried. Each of the others chose a man who was to prove of exceptional quality.

Georgiana – Georgie – who married first, in 1860, chose Edward Jones, soon to be known in the family as Ned, and eventually to the world as Sir Edward Burne-Jones, Bart. Agnes – Aggie – married Edward Poynter, a more fashionable and conventional painter than Ned Jones and eventually President of the Royal Academy and another baronet. And in a double wedding with Aggie in 1866, Louisa married Alfred Baldwin, the son of a Methodist ironmaster.

Alice, the oldest surviving Macdonald daughter, was intelligent, witty, creative, vivacious and an incorrigible flirt. It was said by her sister Edie that 'Alice never seemed to go on a visit without becoming engaged to some wild cad of the desert', and she did have rather a lot of engagements: once with the poet William Allingham, one of the Rossettis' set and best known today for his verses 'Up the airy mountain/Down the rushy glen...', and twice with William Fulford, another member of the same group, who eventually became ordained. But when Alice met John Lockwood Kipling, with his long golden beard and grey-blue eyes, impressive for all his small stature, this time the engagement stuck.

Left: Louisa Macdonald: to her Lockwood Kipling wrote from Bombay in 1865, 'If somebody – a potential masculine or feminine somebody – turns out as he should, would you object to god-mothering the name of Joseph Rudyard?' She accepted.
Right: Agnes Macdonald was a fine pianist and had a good mezzo-soprano voice, but above all, wrote her sister Edie, 'In friendship she was fidelity itself, inspiring lifelong devotion.'

John, as he was called in the family (Lockwood in his professional life) had started his working career in art in Burslem, designing dinner-plates. It was there that Fred Macdonald, on his first circuit in Burslem, had met John, who had by then moved back to the South Kensington Museum (our Victoria and Albert) where he had been a student and now had a post as sculptor which could have been permanent. But so highly was he esteemed by his boss, Sir Philip Cunliffe-Owen, that when young men were being looked for to help create the new school of art at Bombay, his strongest recommendation was of young Lockwood Kipling, then twenty-seven years old. The Bombay post of Architectural Sculptor, with a salary of 400 rupees (approximately £36) per month, was accepted. On 12 April 1865, three weeks after their wedding, the Kiplings sailed for India in the P&O steamer *Ripon*, taking, perforce, the overland route across the Suez Peninsula. Trains had run from Alexandria to Cairo since 1854, but only after 1858 had they replaced the six-seater, mule-drawn coaches between Cairo and Suez, a year before work on the Canal began and a year too late to carry reinforcements to India to help quell the Mutiny; these had to go round the Cape.

Left: Alice and Rudyard in 1866. 'Ruddy is a great lark,' Lockwood wrote to Edie. 'It's the quaintest thing in the world to see him eating his supper, intensely watched by the three dogs.'
Right: In 1871 there had arrived at Southsea a sturdy child of nearly six, and here he is. 'In 1877 when the rescue came,' wrote A.W. Baldwin, 'the boy was half-blind, and crazed to the point of suffering from delusions.'

In Bombay Rudyard was born. His first experience of India, which is to say, his first five years, broken only by one visit to England, was entirely favourable. Bombay, cleansed by sea breezes, was comparatively healthy, and Ruddy, like most white children in India, was the pampered and spoilt king of a domain attended by the many servants whose availability was often such a potent motive in persuading middle-class Englishwomen to go to India. Ruddy loved his ayah dearly, as he did his Hindu bearer Meeta, with whom he spoke the vernacular that, to his surprise, he remembered when he came back to India after eleven years away.

But Rudyard and his sister Alice, nicknamed Trix, who had been born on that visit to England in 1868, must go back home for most of their childhood. This was the common lot of middle- and upper-class white children in India. It was not only that the climate was in many places intolerable; in many places it was perfectly endurable, and there were, in any case, those schools in the healthy Hills, of which Rudyard later wrote contemptuously that the children sent there 'picked up curious accents and learned a great deal too much of life'.[2] English children must go Home because they must belong to Home and not to India. India was where their fathers

14

worked, where the sons themselves might come back to work and the daughters to marry, but their breeding, their culture, their ideals, and their voices, must be English, or, as it might be, Scottish or Irish or Welsh; but in those days English, not British, was the portmanteau word that covered the lot.

No mystery in Kipling's life remains still so impenetrable as the circumstances of Ruddy and Trix being sent Home and their first five years there. The India Office Records show that John Lockwood Kipling took Sick Leave from 15 April to 14 December 1871, during which time his salary was halved to only about £18 a month, out of which it cannot have been easy to pay the fares Home and, for the adults, back again. Perhaps this illness (could it have been Alice's?) explains why the children were taken Home so much earlier than was usual.

Most Anglo-Indian parents (Anglo-Indian was then used of English people living in India) as well endowed as the Kiplings were with family in England would, both for love and economy, have sent the children to one or other relative, and it is strange that Alice and Lockwood did not. It is true that the Macdonald grand-parents had been appalled by the little boy's behaviour on the earlier visit, noisy, tempestuous, arrogant: 'Out of the way, out of the way, there's an angry Ruddy coming!' he is said to have shouted down the Bewdley street, where the grandpa-rents and Edie were now living so as to be near the Baldwins. Indeed Louisa Baldwin said of that visit that: '[Alice's] children turned the house into such a bear-garden, & Ruddy's screaming tempers made Papa so ill, we were thankful to see them on their way'.[3]

Still, when the Kiplings decided they must leave the children at Home, with Ruddy only five-and-a-half years old and Trix not yet three, the family rallied. The Alfred Baldwins offered to take Trix, just a few months younger than their Stanley, while Ruddy was to have been shared between his godfather Fred and the Burne-Jones family until he was old enough for day school; and the children would always spend their holidays together. Lord Birkenhead in his biography of Kipling, adds that Grandmother Kipling, who lived with her unmarried daughter Ruth – 'a sweet young woman', said Trix later – had also offered them a home.

But Alice would have none of these kindly plans. She had never thought of sending her children to her family, she said in later years; she had seen this done and it never worked. From a newspaper advertisement she picked the Holloways of Lorne Lodge, 4 Campbell Road, Southsea, a retired naval officer – Uncle Harry – and his wife – Auntie Rosa – reportedly experienced in boarding children from India. For, no doubt, the best of motives, the Kiplings told the children nothing of the impending separation, simply took them to Southsea and left them there.

Rudyard later wrote three versions of the time at Southsea: with some fictional licence in his novel *The Light that Failed*; seemingly more authentically, in his short story of 1888, 'Baa, Baa, Black Sheep'; and finally in his autobiography *Something of Myself*, written shortly before his death in 1936. According to his accounts, life at Southsea was tolerable so long as 'Uncle Harry' was alive. But after his death, the

Philip and Margaret Burne-Jones (right and left) and May and Jenny Morris (centre) collaborated with Ruddy in a family magazine, the Scribbler, *in which, in 1879, he was first published.*

Woman (as he named her), though kind and loving to Trix, made Ruddy's life a hell on earth, and her son Harry, a few years older than Ruddy, gleefully abetted her. The House of Desolation was his later name for Lorne Lodge. Almost his every action was a transgression, and for every transgression he was punished, whether by beatings, or worse, once he had learned to read, by taking away his only consolation, his books. Inevitably he learned deceit and, when found out, was punished again, once by being sent to school with a placard reading 'LIAR' stitched to his coat. Both children squinted. Ruddy's eyesight deteriorated, the more so, he believed, because he had to do his reading furtively in bad light. This was not diagnosed till almost the end of his time at Southsea. When at last, in 1877, Alice came back, it was to find that the sturdy little son she had left had grown into a near-blind nervous wreck who, when she first bent over his bed to kiss him, cowered for fear of a blow.

It is a miserable story, and so Kipling believed it till the end of his life. But is it entirely true? We must remember, when Rudyard Kipling seemingly tells us something about himself, that concealment about himself was his second nature (perhaps he learned this at Auntie Rosa's), that he was a consummate story-teller, and that it was his practice to allow his pen to run away with him.

It was at Oxford that Ned Jones and William Morris met, and thereafter their family lives were close. Georgie, especially, was influenced by Morris's social and political views.

So when considering the Southsea episode, there are some facts outside Kipling's own accounts that should be remembered. Some nine months after the children went to Southsea, Grandmother Macdonald and Aggie spent a week or so in lodgings there to see for themselves, and later Georgie and Louie did the same. None saw anything to make them apprehensive. 'They seem to be attached to Mrs H., and she seems very fond of them,' the grandmother wrote.[4] Happy holidays were spent in London with Georgie and her children, and no misery at Southsea was ever revealed. 'Children tell little more than animals', was Rudyard's later reason for this reticence, together with fear of retribution. We cannot help remembering that David Copperfield at school had to wear a similar placard to Ruddy's. Oddest of all, if the substance of Ruddy's later accounts were accepted as true at the time, is that Trix was left with Mrs Holloway for several more years; and Ruddy, apparently spontaneously, would visit her there. Indeed it was at Mrs Holloway's in 1880 that he met and fell in love with Florence Garrard, a later boarder there, but that, in a phrase Kipling was to make famous, is another story.

Whatever the exact facts of the case, it is clear that Ruddy was unhappy enough and unhealthy enough at Southsea for his mother to take him away for a country holiday and for some happy months in London before leaving him with three kind,

In the centre of this group of boys at the United Services College, second row back, sits sixteen-year-old Rudyard, with prominent moustache.

elderly, 'cultured' sisters, the Misses Craik and the widowed Mrs Winnard, who lived near Addison Road. There he passed contentedly the few months before he was to go to public school in January 1878, at the age of twelve; and for some of his school holidays he went back to the 'Little House of the Dear Ladies', as he later called it.

Now Rudyard was fortunate indeed, for the cheap school, which was all that his parents could afford, was excellent. It was the United Services College at Westward Ho! on Bideford Bay in Devon, and it had been founded in 1874, only four years before Rudyard went there. The prime mover in its foundation, and its first headmaster, was Cormell Price, an old friend of the family. He had been at King Edward's School, Birmingham, with Ned Jones and with Alice's brother Harry; and at Oxford 'Crom' Price's friends were Ned Jones and William Morris, and through these the Rossettis and Holman Hunt and Ford Madox Brown, and Swinburne and the American critic Charles Eliot Norton, the painters and writers and designers who were to play their large part in shaping young Kipling's imaginative life.

Unusually for a headmaster of those days, Price was not a clergyman, and this must have been congenial to Lockwood Kipling, a disbeliever in religion. The school – 'twelve bleak houses by the shore', wrote Kipling – was run with the utmost economy and austerity, but the atmosphere was congenial, and the education first class. Here Kipling, always to be short like his father, and now fitted out with big round spectacles, was known as Giglamps or Giggers, after the bespectacled 'Gigadibs, the literary man' of Robert Browning's collection of poems called *Men and Women*. At Westward Ho! he met the Irish boy George Beresford and Lionel Dunsterville, the three of them the originals for Beetle, M'Turk, and Stalky of Kipling's school stories *Stalky & Co*.

The United Services College had been intended for boys who would go into the Army, to prepare them for the competitive entrance exams which even the Army had required since 1871, but whose parents could not afford the crack school Haileybury. Price's boys would not, of course, try for such top regiments as the Guards or the Hussars, for which a private income was essential, but for county regiments, regiments of the line, or perhaps, if there was a family connection, for the Indian Army. Obviously there could be no question of an Army career for the short, unathletic, myopic Rudyard. It is rather surprising that the headmaster did not seek out ways of sending him to the university, so that he might try for the Indian Civil Service, that élite corps of only some 800 men whom Philip Mason, himself an Indian Civil Servant as well as a writer, fairly calls in the title of his authoritative book, 'The Men Who Ruled India'. This career, with its comparatively high pay, was open to the talents; Rudyard's uncle Harry Macdonald, had passed the ICS exam, though frustrated marital hopes took him off to America instead.

The career that Crom Price trained Rudyard for, and in the event rightly, was journalism. The level of creativity in the family was high. Grandmother Macdonald wrote poetry and so did most of her daughters. Alice had had stories and poems published in magazines, and she wrote songs and composed music. Lockwood Kipling was an admirable writer as well as an artist of considerable quality. So Price cannot have been surprised at Rudyard's obvious creative potential.

He appointed Rudyard editor of the school magazine, a job that entailed correcting proofs and overseeing printing. He gave Rudyard the run of his own magnificently heterodox library with the result that Rudyard had probably read more widely than any other great English writer. Then, in 1882, when this precocious boy was not yet seventeen, his father's intervention led to the offer of a job: cub reporter on the *Civil and Military Gazette* of Lahore at, Rudyard said later, 100 silver rupees a month, but this was a mistake, for in fact his first monthly salary was 150 rupees, about £13.50.

If ever a young man was ready for his literary destiny, it was Rudyard Kipling at sixteen. But he was not at all sure that he wanted to seek that destiny in India and for several reasons, only one of which was that London, not Lahore, was the centre of the literary world. But the opportunity lay waiting in Lahore and, more, the beloved parents were now there. So on 20 September 1882, Rudyard Kipling sailed from Tilbury in the P & O steamer *Brindisi*, passing, this time, through the Suez Canal, which had been opened in 1869.

CHAPTER TWO

KIPLING'S OWN INDIA

Keep ye the Law – be swift in all obedience –
Clear the land of evil, drive the road and bridge the ford.
Make ye sure to each his own
That he reap where he hath sown;
By the peace among Our peoples let men know we serve the Lord! . . .

from 'A Song of the English'

IPLING'S own India, the India he lived and worked in from 1882 till 1889 was not a great deal of the sub-continent. It was mostly one province, the Punjab, and in the Punjab mostly one town, the capital, Lahore.

Lockwood and Alice Kipling had come to Lahore in 1875. His appointment there as Principal of the Mayo School of Industrial Art and Curator of the Museum brought him a doubling of salary by 1882 to 1,000 rupees *per mensem* – about £80 a month in 1882 with the rupee falling steadily. His task was to promote the study and execution of native forms and designs, it having been noticed, as Murray's *Guide* put it, that: 'Injury has been done to some of the native arts of the Punjab, as of other parts of India, by unwise copying of European designs.'

Rudyard's starting salary on the *Civil and Military Gazette* of 150 rupees a month was, presumably, just enough for a young man on his own to lodge and feed himself and pay for some service, but these problems were not Rudyard's, for he lived with his family in the 'tied' bungalow in the Museum grounds, nicknamed Bikanir House after the Indian desert, because the Kiplings had cut down all trees and bushes round the bungalow, hoping to diminish the fly menace. Bikanir House was decorated by Alice in up-to-the-aesthetic-movement style:

> The dado round the room was in the form of an Indian panel design in rich colours: the material the design was painted on was cheap, coarse cotton, bought in the bazaar. A soft green colour-wash covered the walls. John had cut out and framed in narrow black some of Walter Crane's full-page illustrations of nursery rhymes and these made up most of the pictures above the dado.[1]

For the five years that Rudyard was in Lahore, he lived in Bikanir House. So he could afford a sufficiency of good service, his own personal servant Kadir Baksh (son of Lockwood's bearer, Mauz Baksh), who would shave him before he woke up, his *sais* or groom, his Dog Boy who looked after his fox terrier, Vixen.

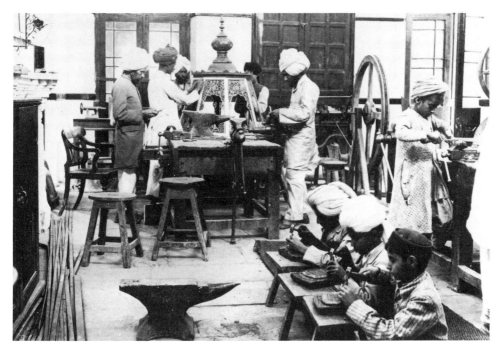

A workroom in the Mayo School of Industrial Art at Lahore. From 1875 until his retirement in 1893 Lockwood Kipling was its head, as well as being Curator of the Lahore Museum.

Lahore at that time had some 130,000 inhabitants. It was, as Kipling says in *Kim*, 'a large manufacturing city', of telegraph wires, electric lights, horse-drawn tram-cars, medical schools, and an ice-making factory, as well as of bazaars and sacred cows. The English civilians mostly lived in Donald Town, the district of the city south of the Grand Trunk Road. Through Donald Town ran the Mall, and on it were the Englishmen's Punjab Club and the Lawrence Gardens where the English would promenade in suitable weather, and, on Saturday evenings, listen to the Police Band. The other English enclaves, military not civil, were the Fort in the old city, and the Mian Mir cantonment, or barracks, some 5 miles to the south-east. Most of the Eurasians must have lived near the workshop of the North-Western railways which covered 125 acres and employed some 2,000 workmen with twenty-five European foremen. Lahore was an important junction, and the working of India's railways has long been an Eurasian prerogative. The Lahore Indians lived in the old town inside the walls or in and around the Anarkali Bazaar outside them.

These four lots of people, the white civilians, the Army, the Eurasians, and the Indians, were the inhabitants of Kipling's India. Not many white civilians had Kipling's knowledge of all of them. He owed this in part to his own 'satiable curiosity (as insatiable as his Elephant Child's), in part to his journalistic work, and in part because his parents, most unusually, invited Indians to their home.

21

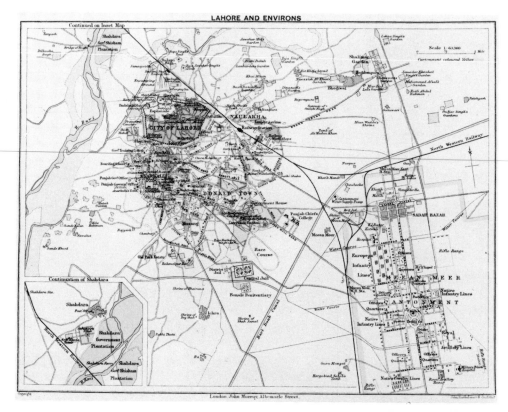

LAHORE AND ENVIRONS

Rudyard's paper, the *Gazette*, was a subsidiary of the *Pioneer* of Allahabad, a national newspaper. The *Gazette* circulated only locally, and though it employed 170 printing hands, it had only two white men on its staff: the Editor, who in 1882 was Stephen Wheeler, and the Assistant Editor, Rudyard Kipling.

Office hours, Rudyard wrote to a friend in 1882, were from 10 a.m. till 4.15 p.m., though by 1936, he had come to remember them as from 8.30 a.m. to 6 p.m., and, he added, 'I never worked less than ten hours and seldom more than fifteen.'[2] Holidays were thirty days a year, 'if no one is sick', Rudyard wrote drily, presumably referring to Wheeler, whose health was poor. Rudyard did not much like Wheeler, who was a hard taskmaster, but he appreciated Wheeler's professionalism and the chance of learning the trade.

The White Civilians

High noon behind the tamarisks – the sun is hot above us –
    As at Home the Christmas Day is breaking wan.
They will drink our healths at dinner – those who tell us how they love us,
    And forget us till another year be gone! . . .

from 'Christmas in India'

Rudyard's first social life in India was inevitably with people of his parents' social circle; and the kinds of white people they would know depended, even more in India than at Home, on their jobs and salary levels. The people young Kipling would meet at the Punjab Club were the men from the Canals and from the Forestry Department, from Engineering and Railways, doctors and lawyers and bank managers and senior policemen; but not the missionaries, whom Kipling had little time for, or the commercial travellers; and not the Lieutenant-Governor or others of the highest ranks.

Only very incidentally do we hear from Kipling of English women who worked in India. He knew of the nursing service that the new Vicereine, Lady Dufferin, had set up for service in the *zenanas*, the secluded women's quarters, for he paid it the tribute of a poor poem. In the story, 'Garm – a Hostage', there is a casual reference to a respected woman doctor. And there were the Salvation Army lassies of whom he complained to General William Booth on the P&O boat from Adelaide to Colombo in 1891.

Opposite above: On either side of Upper Mall Road lie the Lawrence Gardens and the Punjab Club. The Art School and Museum are to the south-west of the Anarkali bazaar. The Naulakha lies north of the Railway Station.
Opposite below: The Indian tram-horses, usually Kábulis, were 'among the few horses in the world that wear hats as a protection . . . from sunstroke and headache, to which an animal from a comparatively cold climate is liable'. (Beast and Man)

Left: The Salvation Army's pioneer party in India in 1882.
Right: William Booth founded the Salvation Army (the Skeleton Army, shocked Anglicans called it)
in 1877. Its evangelizing fervour and cheerful music brought converts from among the poorest.

'Why,' I asked, 'can't you stop your Salvation lassies from going out to India, and living alone native-fashion among natives?' I told him something of village conditions in India. The despot's defence was very human.

'But what *am* I to do?' he demanded. 'The girls *will* go, and one *can't* stop 'em.'[3]

There were in fact several white women in India, married and unmarried, who worked with and for the native Indians, and whom Rudyard might well have admired as, later, he did Mary Kingsley. He did not meet them. With the almost single exception of the voluntary service in famine given by the girl he calls William in the story 'William the Conqueror' (and she was based on an American woman), the white women of his social world played purely social roles. And in general he did not think much of them, to judge from a piece he wrote for the *Gazette* in 1887, ostensibly from a visiting tourist:

If they were prettier, the Englishwomen in India would be delightful. I admit that their 'belles' startle one rather. They would be out of consideration in a small country town in England . . . Women of from forty to fifty and upwards – I'm not exaggerating, I assure you – are the Lillie Langtrys of India.[4]

Some seventy white residents made up the society that centred on the Punjab Club, enough for there to be some choice of social life, and here white Lahore was fortunate. In his cruel story 'A Wayside Comedy' of 1888, Kipling tells of an isolated out-station of two married couples and a bachelor, where all but one husband, jovially ignorant, hated each other and with good reason; but social life had to go on as before because, as the Major, the ignorant husband, says: 'in a little Station we must all be friendly'.

    *   *   *

So long as Rudyard was in India, his life, like that of everyone else, was dominated by the weather, and of all India, the weather of the Punjab is the most extreme. From mid-September until mid-April, Lahore is pleasantly cool and even, in January, frosty. In mid-April the hot weather begins, dry heat until the end of June with the thermometer up to 120°F in the shade. Then, with the monsoon rains, comes the most unhealthy season of the year, the great heat continuing until mid-August when the thermometer begins to fall.

 For Rudyard's first hot-weather in 1883 Lockwood had asked his wife to stay down in the Plains for longer than usual, until she left for England to collect Trix. Lockwood went to the Hills, and Rudyard had his thirty days there, but he was down again at Lahore for malarial August.

> There are six other months when no one ever comes to call and the thermometer walks inch by inch to the top of the glass, and the office is darkened to just above reading-light, and the press-machines are red-hot of touch, and nobody writes anything but accounts of amusements in the Hill-stations or obituary notices. Then the telephone becomes a tinkling terror, because it tells you of the sudden deaths of men and women that you knew intimately, and the prickly-heat covers you with a garment . . .
>
> Then the sickness really breaks out, and the less recording and reporting, the better for the peace of the subscribers. But . . . the people at the Hill-stations in the middle of their amusements say: 'Good gracious! Why can't the paper be sparkling? I'm sure there's plenty going on up here.' That is the dark half of the moon.
>
> from 'The Man Who Would Be King'

Working during the great heats was nearly unendurable. But stopping work, which could hardly be called leisure, was as bad. A very few women stayed down in the Plains from poverty or from decency, but the general rule was that the men were on their own, and for social life must manage as best they could:

> Four men . . . sat at a table playing whist. The thermometer marked – for them – one hundred and one degrees of heat . . . A tattered, rotten punkah of whitewashed calico was puddling the hot air and whining dolefully at every stroke . . . It was as though the earth was dying of apoplexy . . .
>
> The four, stripped to the thinnest of sleeping-suits, played whist crossly, with wranglings as to leads and returns. It was not the best kind of whist, but they had taken some trouble to arrive at it. Mottram of the Indian Survey had ridden thirty and railed one hundred miles from his lonely post in the desert since the night before; Lowndes of the Civil Service, on special duty in the political department, had come as far to escape for a moment the miserable intrigues of an impoverished native State . . . Spurstow, the doctor of the line, had left a cholera-stricken camp of coolies to look after itself for

forty-eight hours while he associated with white men once more. Hummil, the assistant engineer, was the host. He stood fast and received his friends thus every Sunday if they could come in. When one of them failed to appear, he would send a telegram to his last address, in order that he might know whether the defaulter were dead or alive. There are very many places in the east where it is not good or kind to let your acquaintances drop out of sight even for one short week. The players were not conscious of any special regard for each other. They squabbled whenever they met; but they ardently desired to meet as men without water desire to drink. They . . . understood the dread meaning of loneliness. They were all under thirty years of age.   from 'At the End of the Passage'

Rudyard's health was never robust after he came to Lahore. He was often ill there, with recurrent dysentery and fever. Typhoid was endemic at all seasons. And in one of those worrying errors that lead to always suspended belief in the autobiographical *Something of Myself*, Kipling tells us, as fact, that in an outbreak of typhoid at Lahore, the men of his group tended the men and the women the women, because there were no professional nurses there. But this episode had appeared in a story of 1887, 'By Word of Mouth', set in a small station. In his late sixties, Kipling must have forgotten it, and forgotten that Lahore in his day had two hospitals, the largest medical school in India, a training home for nurses, and a well-staffed prison hospital.

At last, for the men in the burning summer Plains came the annual releases. Kipling describes the journey up to the Hills in the story 'Garm – a Hostage', the Narrator travelling with friends and with two dogs, Garm a bull-terrier, and his own fox-terrier Vixen. First, the train to Umballa, and then the dawks, the two-horse carriages, up to Kalka.

After Kalka the road wound among the hills, and we took a curricle with half-broken ponies, which were changed every six miles. No one dreamed of a railroad to Simla in those days, for it was seven thousand feet up in the air. The road was more than fifty miles long, and the regulation pace was just as fast as the ponies could go . . . A cool breath from the snows met us about five miles out of Kalka, and she [Vixen] whined for her coat . . .

Now and then we would meet a man we knew going down to his work again, and he would say: 'What's it like below?' and I would shout: 'Hotter than cinders. What's it like up above?' and he would shout back: 'Just perfect!'

In earlier years, Lockwood and Alice had gone to the cheaper Hill-stations. Now they could afford Simla, since 1804 the summer capital of India, with the Viceroy living in an overgrown, overcrowded shooting-lodge called Peterhoff. There is hardly a foot of level ground in Simla – 'Here if one sees ten yards level, one screams out, "What a site for a house!"', wrote Lady Canning, wife of the first Viceroy, in 1860.[5] In the summer of 1885, the Viceroy was Lord Dufferin, and he lifted the Kiplings up from middle-class society into his own circle, for, he said, 'Dullness and Mrs Kipling cannot exist in the same room.'[6] But social differences were not forgotten and when the Viceroy's son fell for Trix Kipling, he suggested, 'Don't you

Simla's European town on the ridge; below it, 'the crowded rabbit-warren' where 'are discussed by courtesans the things which are supposed to be the profoundest secrets of the India Council'. (Kim)

think, Mrs Kipling, that your daughter should be taken to another hill-station?'

'Don't you think, your Excellency,' retorted Alice, 'that your son should be sent home?' and so he was.

Though many of the stories in *Plain Tales from the Hills* are set in days before young Rudyard went there, they still give an excellent picture of social life in the Simla of the 1880s, of the balls, the picnics, the intrigues, both political and sexual, the flirtations and the adulteries, the gaieties and the tragedies, of this annual tribal migration. In Simla, *par excellence*, those older women whom Rudyard has identified as India's belles, her Lillie Langtrys, were the social queens. Some of them were bitches mitigated by streaks of decency, like Mrs Hauksbee 'who was sometimes nice to her own sex', some were bitches of unmitigated wickedness like Mrs Reiver, 'bad from her hair – which started life on a Brittany's girl's head – to her boot-heels, which were two and three-eighth inches high.' In the story 'The Rescue of Pluffles', Mrs Reiver has attached silly young Pluffles to her 'rickshaw wheels, and seems hell-bent on ruining him; and Mrs Hauksbee chooses to save him. It was Mrs Hauksbee in 'Consequences' who passed the misrouted Government papers on to the buccaneer Tarrion who was thereby able to blackmail the Government into giving him the cushy job he wanted. The 'Venus Annodomini', however (we never learn her true name), differed from Mrs Hauksbee and Mrs Reiver in that 'she never

27

lifted a finger to attract anyone'; but, like Ninon de Lenclos, all men were attracted to her. But when 'Very Young' Gayerson fell for her, she released him by revealing a nineteen-year-old daughter and calling up to Simla 'Very Young' Gayerson's papa, who had been devoted to the Venus Annodomini a generation earlier. And there can be little doubt that among the models for Rudyard's bitch women of Simla, pretty, witty Alice Kipling should be counted.

Trix Kipling aged seventeen, not yet enjoying her first Simla season. 'My prettiest frocks and sashes/Don't help to fill my programme-card,' her brother wrote in 'My Rival'.

All these stories, and many more, were collected in *Plain Tales from the Hills* – one of Kipling's cleverest titles – published from Calcutta in 1888. But when it came to choosing a dedicatee for the book, Rudyard must have been in something of a dilemma, and the phrase he chose, 'To the wittiest woman in India', was a cunning way out of it. Given the choice of words, given the strength of the Family Square, as the Kiplings called the unit of Lockwood, Alice, Rudyard, and Trix, given Alice's expectation of homage from her son, it was unthinkable that anyone but Alice should be intended. But there exists a letter from Kipling to a Mrs Burton at Peshawar, asking her to accept this dedication. So far as we know, she did not reply, though she received a presentation copy.

Rudyard had been given the chance to write these stories when Stephen Wheeler retired from the *Gazette* in 1886, and the new Editor was Rudyard's friend E. Kay Robinson, from the Allahabad *Pioneer*. He encouraged Rudyard to supply the *Gazette* with stories as well as articles, and these constituted some two-thirds of the stories in *Plain Tales*.

Plain Tales was not, however, Kipling's only book published while he was in India. Apart from some family and local trivia, the *Gazette* offices had printed in 1886, *Departmental Ditties* 'in the form of an envelope with flap; tied with red tape'. Most of the society verses fail to outlast their time, but a few were rather better, like 'My Rival', surely inspired by Alice and Trixie? Here are the first and last verses:

> I go to concert, party, ball –
>   What profit is in these?
> I sit alone against the wall
>   And strive to look at ease.
> The incense that is mine by right
>   They burn before Her shrine;
> And that's because I'm seventeen
>   And she is forty-nine . . .
>
> But even She must older grow
>   And end Her dancing days,
> She can't go on for ever so
>   At concerts, balls, and plays.
> One ray of priceless hope I see
>   Before my footsteps shine;
> Just think, that She'll be eighty-one
>   When I am forty-nine!

In 1917, when Trix was forty-nine, she was in one of the lapses from sanity that had assailed her since she was thirty; and Alice was dead.

Most people who have read this little book remember, too, the cruel verses called 'The Story of Uriah', about Jack Barrett, sent down from cool Simla to burning Quetta, because his wife had another fish to fry. Jack Barrett died at Quetta, and his wife put on a show of mourning for 'Five lively months at most'. This title, another good one like most of Kipling's, refers to King David's captain Uriah, in the second book of Samuel, sent to be killed in the forefront of the battle, because David coveted Uriah's wife. And the poem 'Arithmetic on the Frontier' (*see page 32*) already foreshadowed the wealth of creation to come, though this poem was unnoticed in Kipling's first English review.

This was from Andrew Lang, folklorist and man of letters, who, in *Longman's Magazine* of October 1886, wrote:

There is a special variety of English *Vers de Societé*, namely the Anglo-Indian species. A quaint and amusing example of this literature has just reached me, named *Departmental Ditties*. The modest author does not give his name . . . On the whole, these are melancholy ditties, Jobs, and posts, and pensions, and the wives of their neighbours appear (if we trust the satirist) to be much coveted by Her Majesty's Oriental civil Servants . . .[7]

Kipling's last publications in India were the first paper-bound volumes of the Indian Railway Library issued in 1888, the covers designed in Lockwood's Art School. There were six of these, various in kind. *Soldiers Three* contained seven soldier tales; *The Story of the Gadsbys* was would-be sophisticated dialogue; *In Black and White* contained eight stories about Indians; *Under the Deodars* contained six stories about whites, one of them in dialogue, two of them about Mrs Hauksbee; *The Phantom Rickshaw* contained four longer stories, including 'The Strange Ride of Morrowbie Jukes' about an Englishman trapped in a morass of sand – this story gave Angus Wilson his title: *The Strange Ride of Rudyard Kipling*; and *Wee Willie Winkie* contained four stories about children (*discussed in Chapter Nine*).

In 1892 the first three Railway Books were published together in one volume and the last three in another. Their titles were eventually established as *Soldiers Three and Other Stories* for the first volume, *Wee Willie Winkie and Other Stories* for the second.

Some of Kipling's finest Indian stories are in these volumes, and certainly one of the very finest is 'The Man Who Would be King' (originally published with *The Phantom Rickshaw*), one of Kipling's few stories about white civilians in India who are outside the social pale. They are two rogues, Dravot and Carnehan, who set off to the north to make a kingdom, over the border to Kafiristan, then barely entered by Westerners; and there are betrayed by lust. The story ends in the newspaper office on an intolerably hot night, 'when there crept to my chair what was left of a man . . . [a] rag-wrapped, whining cripple who addressed me by name, crying that he was come back.' This was the remnant of Peachey Carnehan who, at the end of his tale,

> brought out a black horsehair bag embroidered with silver thread, and shook therefrom, on to my table – the dried, withered head of Daniel Dravot! The morning sun that had long been paling the lamps struck the red beard and blind sunken eyes; struck, too, a heavy circlet of gold studded with raw turquoises, that Carnehan placed tenderly on the battered head . . .
> 'Poor old Daniel that was a monarch once!'

Among the most interesting of Kipling's writings on India, because a lasting strain in his art, are the stories he wrote about men of his own kind, the white professional middle classes, at work. Finlayson of 'The Bridge-Builders' can stand for them. He had half-built his bridge over the Ganges when the floods came, early that year, too early for his calculation. There was nothing Finlayson could do but sit and wait:

> He took no count of time, for the river was marking the hours, inch by inch and foot by foot, along the embankment, and he listened, numb and hungry, to the straining of the

stone-boats, the hollow thunder under the piers, and the hundred noises that make the full note of a flood . . . There were no excuses in his service. Government might listen, perhaps, but his own kind would judge him by his bridge, as that stood or fell.

In autumn 1887 Kipling was transferred from the *Gazette* at Lahore to the parent paper, the *Pioneer* at Allahabad, where he lodged first at the Club there, and then with Aleck Hill, a meteorologist, professor of science at the Muir College, and his American wife Edmonia, known as Ted. Their bungalow was called Belvedere and its neglected garden modelled the home of Riki-tiki-tavi, the mongoose in *The Jungle Book*. He was to spend one more hot-weather in Lahore while Kay Robinson was on leave, and one more summer in Simla. Kipling had been asked why he did not leave India, where he was never really well or happy. His reply was that he thought it proper to work his seven years hard there, and so he nearly did.

Kipling's Soldiers

> We aren't no thin red 'eroes, nor we aren't no blackguards too,
> But single men in barricks, most remarkable like you;
> An' if sometimes our conduck isn't all your fancy paints,
> Why, single men in barricks don't grow into plaster saints . . .
>
> from 'Tommy'

Twenty years after the Mutiny, in 1877, the English Prime Minister Disraeli created our Indian Empire, with Queen Victoria its Queen Empress. Its armies were constantly being reshaped. In Kipling's time, the soldiers in India could be divided into roughly four kinds.

There were the native regiments of sepoys, no longer the soldiers of the East India Company but the Queen's; they had Indian non-commissioned officers and some commissioned officers, but the higher ranking officers were all British. There were the forces we allowed the Native Princes to maintain, sometimes very grand and sometimes not, as in the land of a King who lived on the road to Tibet, with a Kingdom 4 miles square and most of them up-ended; and on his revenue of £400 a year, says Kipling in the charming story 'Namgay Doola' he maintained '. . . one elephant and a standing army of five men'. There were also still some irregular troops, often, in the first instance, raised by some enterprising individual. Lastly, and best known to Kipling, there were the British regiments recruited in Britain, entirely manned and officered by the British.

In Kipling's days, the British soldiers at the Mian Mir cantonments in Lahore were the 2nd Fifth Fusiliers 'with whom I dined in awed silence a few weeks after I came out';[8] later, the 30th East Lancashires, newly formed from the 30th and Mulvaney's 'ould' 50th, and in his last years the 31st East Surrey, 'a London recruited confederacy of skilful dog-stealers'. There was also an infantry detachment at the eerie Fort Lahore, and with its subalterns Kipling sometimes dined.

31

In general, the Army and the civilians did not mix – 'These people do not join Lahore society in dances, garden parties etc.,' Lockwood Kipling wrote in a letter home, but through his work (and a flirtation too), Rudyard got to know Mian Mir. At first, it was the officers he knew and wrote about and especially the young officers for whom his admiration was adoration. In 'The Drums of the Fore and Aft' he wrote, 'God has arranged that a clean-run youth of the British middle classes shall, in the matter of backbone, brains, and bowels, surpass all other youths.' And in 'Arithmetic on the Frontier', probably the best of the Departmental Ditties:

The flying bullet down the Pass,
That whistles clear: 'All flesh is grass.' . . .

A scrimmage in a Border Station –
    A canter down some dark defile –
Two thousand pounds of education
    Drops to a ten-rupee jezail –
The Crammer's boast, the Squadron's pride,
    Shot like a rabbit in a ride!

No proposition Euclid wrote
    No formulae the text-books know,
Will turn the bullet from your coat,
    Or ward the tulwar's downward blow.
Strike hard who cares – shoot straight who can –
    The odds are on the cheaper man . . .

A jezail is an Afghan rifle. A tulwar is a sabre. And the Pass is the Khyber Pass, the Pass just the other side of the Border, which is the North-West Frontier, India's frontier with Afghanistan, down which it was expected that the Russians, from the far side of Afghanistan, would one day pour. Guarding the North-West Frontier was the principal preoccupation of the Army in India.

Kipling went up to the Frontier only once, in 1885, when his paper sent him to cover the Viceroy's reception for the Ameer of Afghanistan. He boldly walked a short distance over the Frontier and a hidden tribesman took a pot shot at him – the only time in India he heard a shot fired in anger, and it may have been in play. The fact is that for all Kipling's convincing accounts of soldiers in India in action, there were no wars there between 1882 and 1889, hardly so much as a Border skirmish. But here, in the Irish tongue of Mulvaney is his account of the Regiments coming back to the Border-town of Peshawar after an engagement on the Frontier:

We came through in the early mornin' . . . Mother av Glory, will I iver forget that comin' back? The light was not fair lifted, and the first we heard was 'For 'tis my delight av a shiny night' frum a band that thought we was the second four companies av the Lincolnshires. At that we was forced to sind them a yell who we was, an' thin up wint 'The wearin' av the Green'. It made me crawl all up my backbone . . . Then right smash into our rear came fwhat was left of the Jock Elliott's – wid four pipers an' not half a kilt among thim, playin' for the dear life . . . The Fly-by-Nights was waitin' for their second battalion, and whin ut came out, there was the Colonel's horse led at the head – saddle-empty . . . They waited till the remnint av the battalion was up, and then – clane against ordhers – for who wanted *that* chune that day? – they wint back to Peshawar slow-time . . . wid 'The Dead March' . . . The carpse was wid them, and they'd ha taken ut so through a Coronation.

from '"Love-o'-Women"'

Kipling has often been condemned for his common soldiers: whether for using the working classes (as Shakespeare did) for comic relief, or for giving them a written 'funny talk' that distances them from superior people. Neither accusation stands up. Kipling's common soldiers are often, and often with superb effectiveness, tragic not comic; and the written dialect was a serious literary experiment of the time, used, not for distancing, but to try to bring a wider range of people into serious treatment in literature. And to those who say that Kipling got the dialects wrong, that, for instance (as Edith Somerville of the Irish writing pair, Somerville and Ross, maintained), no Irishman ever spoke like Mulvaney, one need only play a recording of an imaginative Irishman reading aloud the words Kipling gave to Mulvaney.

All Kipling's best army work is about common soldiers for whom his respect and affection came to be unstinted. He was appalled by the only very casual care that the authorities took over the soldiers' health and sanitary conditions, and especially by the fact that 9,000 men a year were laid up with venereal disease. And he was outraged by the contempt with which most civilians regarded them – for most of the time:

> For it's Tommy this, an' Tommy that, an' 'Tommy,
>   wait outside';
> But it's 'Special train for Atkins' when the trooper's on the tide – . . .

from 'Tommy'

We know from other sources that in a decent regiment the Colonel's wife would see to it that she and the other officers' wives did what they could to help the soldiers' wives, both official wives and those married without permission. Kipling does not seem to have met many such Colonels' ladies. 'She said "my regiment" and the world knows what that means,' he reports of one of them, and in 'The Daughter of the Regiment', the story of a troop-train in the summer heats halted because of the cholera that has broken out on it, he specifies that not only was there no doctor on the train, but no officers' ladies who might help. There is no one to help the sick, frightened men but the Colour Sergeant's fat wife 'Ould Pummeloe', who had lost four of her five children in the past fourteen months for '"av our childher die like sheep in these days, they died like flies thin."'

'"Are ye goin' to let the bhoys die while you're picknickin', ye sluts?"' cries Ould Pummeloe to the other soldiers' wives, sheltering under the trees. '"'Tis wather they want. Come on an' help."'

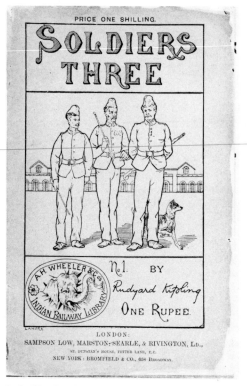

Left: The first English edition of vol. 1 of the Indian Railway Library: from left, Ortheris, Mulvaney, and Learoyd. On the title page 'We be Soldiers Three – /pardonnez moy, je vous en prie.'
Right: As they grew in Kipling's achievement, each of his 'soldiers three' emerged as a basically tragic character, with Mulvaney, (here realized by Lockwood), the most fully created.

All the hot day Ould Pummeloe and the other women carried water to the men from a nearby well, till suddenly she said, '"Hould me up, bhoys! I'm feelin' bloody sick!" 'Twas the sun, not the cholera, did ut. She misremembered she was only wearin' her ould black bonnet, an' she died . . .'

So much for a Sergeant's good wife. For a bad one, a refrain will do:

> Cheer for the Sergeant's weddin' –
> Give 'em one cheer more!
> Grey gun-'orses in the lando,
> An' a rogue is married to a whore.

from 'The Sergeant's Weddin''

The Irish voice that tells many of the soldiers' tales and verses is that of Terence Mulvaney, who, with Jack Learoyd from Yorkshire and Stanley Ortheris the Cockney, make up Kipling's Soldiers Three. We first meet them in the story 'The Three Musketeers' in *Plain Tales*, and they stand with Shakespeare's Nym and

Bardolph and Pistol as the most famous soldiers in literature. They had no real existence. What Kipling could make from a chance meeting, an overheard sentence, an anecdote, or a dusty report in the files was the stuff of his genius, and from such scraps he made his Soldiers Three. He used them, at worst, for japes and practical jokes. More often and better, he used them for fundamentally tragic ends to do with the various hells of the common soldier's life in India. Here is a hot-weather night at the main gate of Fort Amora, 'most desolate and least desirable of all fortresses in India'. Mulvaney

> was stripped to the waist; Learoyd on the next bed-stead was dripping from the skinful of water which Ortheris, clad only in white trousers, had just sluiced over his shoulders; and a fourth private was muttering uneasily in the glare of the great guard-lantern. The heat under the bricked archway was terrifying . . .

The fourth private rouses for a moment, says, '"*I'm* damned and I can't die."' 'Who's that?' the Narrator asks, and Mulvaney – '"Gentleman born . . . dhrinks like a fish. He'll be gone before the cowld weather's here."'

To join the Army as a ranker was one of the conventional recourses of disgraced gentlemen. (After P. C. Wren's novel, *Beau Geste* of 1924, they tended to go into the French Foreign Legion.) Kipling usually wrote well about rogues, and often with a dry cynicism that can be ultimately comic, as in his poem about the Prodigal Son who went back to the hogs rather than stay with the unctuous disapproval that greeted him on his return home; or tragic:

> To the legion of the lost ones, to the cohort of the damned,
>   To my brethren in their sorrow overseas,
> Sings a gentleman of England cleanly bred, machinely crammed,
>   And a trooper of the Empress, if you please.
> Yes, a trooper of the forces who has run his own six horses,
>   And faith he went the pace and went it blind,
> And the world was more than kin while he held the ready tin,
>   But to-day the Sergeant's something less than kind . . .
>
>   Gentlemen-rankers out on the spree,
>   Damned from here to Eternity,
>   God ha' mercy on such as we,
>   Baa! Yah! Bah! . . .   from 'Gentlemen-Rankers'

Syphilis, typhoid, dysentery, cholera, heatstroke, the tulwar, kukri, and jezail – so many ways of death for the British soldier in India. There was another, essentially a hot-weather death, when nerves were ragged and temper hair-trigger. This was murder, as Kipling told of in probably his best poem, 'Danny Deever':

> 'What are the bugles blowin' for?' said Files-on-Parade.
> 'To turn you out, to turn you out,' the Colour-Sergeant said.
> 'What makes you look so white, so white?' said Files-on-Parade.
> 'I'm dreadin' what I've got to watch,' the Colour-Sergeant said.

35

For they're hangin' Danny Deever, you can hear the Dead March play,
The Regiment's in 'ollow square – they're hangin' him to-day;
They've taken of his buttons off an' cut his stripes away,
An' they're hangin' Danny Deever in the mornin'.

'What makes the rear-rank breathe so 'ard?' said Files-on-Parade.
'It's bitter cold, it's bitter cold,' the Colour-Sergeant said.
'What makes that front-rank man fall down?' said Files-on-Parade.
'A touch o' sun, a touch o' sun,' the Colour-Sergeant said.
They are hangin' Danny Deever, they are marchin' of 'im round,
They 'ave 'alted Danny Deever by 'is coffin on the ground;
An' 'e'll swing in 'arf a minute for a sneakin' shootin' hound –
O they're hangin' Danny Deever in the mornin'!

''Is cot was right-'and cot to mine,' said Files-on-Parade.
''E's sleepin' out an' far to-night,' the Colour-Sergeant said.
'I've drunk 'is beer a score o' times,' said Files-on-Parade.
''E's drinkin' bitter beer alone,' the Colour-Sergeant said.
They are hangin' Danny Deever, you must mark 'im to 'is place,
For 'e shot a comrade sleepin' – you must look 'im in the face;
Nine 'undred of 'is county an' the Regiment's disgrace,
While they're hangin' Danny Deever in the mornin'.

'What's that so black agin the sun?' said Files-on-Parade.
'It's Danny fightin' 'ard for life,' the Colour-Sergeant said.
'What's that that whimpers over'ead?' said Files-on-Parade.
'It's Danny's soul that passin' now,' the Colour-Sergeant said.
For they're done with Danny Deever, you can 'ear the quickstep play,
The Regiment's in column, an' they're marchin' us away;
Ho! the young recruits are shakin', an' they'll want their beer to-day,
After hangin' Danny Deever in the mornin'!

Lord Baldwin in his book on the Macdonald family was surely right to suggest that the rhythm of 'Danny Deever' derives from a terrifying folk-poem that Grandmother Macdonald used to recite to her children, and they, surely, to theirs:

'Pray where are you going child?' said Meet-on-the-Road.
'To school, sir, to school, sir,' said Child-as-it-stood.
'What have you in that basket?' said Meet-on-the-Road.
'Some pudding, sir, some pudding, sir,' said Child-as-it-stood . . .

A frequent theme of Kipling's is that of the soldier who has served overseas and is ever after sick for the land of his service – for Burma, for South Africa, or, if he is a Roman soldier, for Britain. But he never gives us a soldier who is homesick for India; only soldiers in India who are sick for Home. Here is the Cockney, Ortheris:

Now I'm sick to go 'Ome – go 'Ome – go 'Ome! . . . I'm sick for London again; sick for the sounds of 'er and the sights of 'er and the stinks of 'er; orange-peel and hasphalte an' gas comin' in over Vaux'all Bridge. Sick for the rail goin' down to Box 'Ill, with your gal on your knee an' a new clay pipe in your face. That' an' the Stran' lights where you knows ev'ry one, an' the Copper that takes you up is an old friend that tuk you up before, when you was a little, smitchy boy lying loose 'tween the Temple an' the Dark Harches . . . An' I lef' all that for to serve the Widder beyond the seas . . .

from 'The Madness of Private Ortheris'

And Learoyd:

I reckon you've never heard tell o' Greenhow Hill . . . Moors an' moors an' moors, wi' never a tree for shelter, an' grey houses wi' flagstone rooves an' pewits cryin', an' a windhover goin' to an' fro just like those kites.   from 'On Greenhow Hill'

And Mulvaney: '"Eyah! Cork's own city an' the blue sky above it and the times that was – the times that was."'

Why had they joined? Desperation, mostly, a desperate need to get away from, maybe poverty, maybe the police, maybe a girl, and probably easiest to forget them in the hard times the Army gave, the breaking in, the training for fighting, the training for dying:

> When you're wounded and left on Afghanistan's plains,
> And the women come out to cut up what remains,
> Jest roll to your rifle and blow out your brains
>   An' go to your Gawd like a soldier.

from 'The Young British Soldier'

It has been said that Queen Victoria greatly disliked the nickname 'The Widow at Windsor' which Kipling used and said the soldiers used. But when he used it, it was to great and often grim effect; as in 'The Widow's Party':

> 'Where have you been this while away,
>   Johnnie, Johnnie?'
> Out with the rest on a picnic lay.
>   Johnnie, my Johnnie, aha! . . .
>
> 'What was the end of all the show,
>   Johnnie, Johnnie?'
> Ask my Colonel, for I don't know,
>   Johnnie, my Johnnie, aha!
> We broke a King and we built a road –
> A court-house stands where the Reg'ment goed.
> And the river's clean where the raw blood flowed
>   When the Widow give the party.

For those who survived, then sometimes, to the victor the spoils. Readers who cannot separate the quality of Kipling's work from its content are appalled by the poem 'Loot', but there is no reason to suppose that it represents Kipling's own attitude, and much to suggest it does not: for instance, the religious and aesthetic sacrilege implied in the verse quoted would have been abhorrent to him. He was simply writing, and writing well, of things-as-they-are:

37

Now remember when you're 'acking round a gilded Burma god
    That 'is eyes is very often precious stones;
An' if you treat a nigger to a dose o' cleanin'-rod
    'E's like to show you everything 'e owns.
When 'e won't prodooce no more, pour some water on the floor
    Where you 'ear it answer 'ollow to the boot
When the ground begins to sink, shove your baynick down the chink,
    An' you're sure to touch the – Loot! loot! loot!

from 'Loot'

Many soldiers of all ranks died in India. But when the numbers were totted up, the end for most of them was just back to civilian life again, and so it was for Kipling's Soldiers Three:

Ortheris – landed at last in the 'little stuff' bird-shop' for which your soul longed; Learoyd – back again in the smoky, stone-ribbed North, amid the clang of the Bradford looms; Mulvaney . . . sweltering on the earthwork of a Central India Line '. . . an my heart's sick in my ribs for a wink at anything wid the Quane's uniform on ut.'

from 'Private Learoyd's Story'

The Interface and the Borderline

If you go straight away from Levées and Government House Lists, past Trades' Balls – far beyond everything and everybody you ever knew in your respectable life – you cross, in time, the Borderline where the last drop of White blood ends and the full tide of Black sets in . . . One of these days, this people . . . will turn out a writer or a poet: and then we shall know how they live and what they feel.

from 'His Chance in Life'

Kipling's job as a journalist often forced him to work at the interface between ruler and ruled, but as a creative writer he was never sure where he stood. Where, as a Freemason, he ought to stand, he knew – though it may be significant that he distanced himself by making the speaker a Cockney:

We'd Bola Nath, Accountant,
    An' Saul the Aden Jew,
An' Din Mohammed, draughtsman
    Of the Survey Office too;
There was Babu Chuckerbutty,
    An' Amir Singh the Sikh,
An' Castro from the fittin'-sheds,
    The Roman Catholick! . . .

from 'The Mother-Lodge'

For Kipling, as for most Englishmen of his kind, Jews were definitely on the borderline. But – and as always with Kipling we must be willing to distinguish the creator from the man – he wrote some sympathetic stories about Jews, and one of them an Indian story, 'Jews in Shushan', about a tiny colony in an Indian city who could never amass the ten males needed to set up a congregation.

Similarly with the Indians. To do Kipling justice, he would never have shared the contempt many of the working-class English in India felt for the few Indians they came into touch with. The Drummer Boy, ordered to keep an eye on Kim, is typical: 'He styled all natives "niggers"; yet servants and sweepers called him abominable names to his face, and, misled by their deferential attitude, he never understood.'

'Nigger' was the ordinary, casual rudery of Mulvaney when speaking of Indians, and sometimes 'heathen'. 'Ask the heathen if he iver saw a man tame an elephint – anyways – a white man.' ('My Lord the Elephant') But what Kipling could accept in Mulvaney, he found inexcusable in an officer: 'The Captain Commanding the Fort . . . was not a nice man. He called all natives "niggers", which, besides being extreme bad form, shows gross ignorance.' ('On the City Wall')

Men who made serious endeavours to come close to Indian life Kipling admired but mistrusted. Such a man is Strickland, whom we first meet in 'Miss Youghal's Sais'. He 'held the extraordinary theory that a Policeman in India should try to know as much about the natives as the natives themselves'. Strickland could pass as most kinds of Indian, had attended many an esoteric religious ceremony, had even 'helped once, at Jagadhri, at the Painting of the Death Bull, which no Englishman must look upon'. But no one in white authority approved of Strickland's ways.

Trejago was another Englishman who 'took too deep an interest in native life'. So when he heard a pretty laugh through a barred window in a dark gulley, he whispered a verse of 'The Love Song of Har Dyal'.

> Can a man stand upright in the face of the naked Sun; or a Lover
> in the Presence of his Beloved?
> If my feet fail me, O Heart of my Heart, am I to blame, being
> blinded by the glimpse of your beauty?'

It was capped by the pretty voice beyond the grating. Next morning an old woman threw a packet into his dogcart. It contained

> the half of a broken glass-bangle, one flower of the blood-red *dhak*, a pinch of *bhusa* or cattle-food, and eleven cardamons . . . Trejago knew far too much about these things . . . No Englishman should be able to translate object-letters.

But Trejago could, and the results were tragic. This story is significantly called 'Beyond the Pale'.

The affair of Trejago and little Bisesa could never have come to good. Lasting amatory relationships between sahibs and Indian women were indeed beyond the pale; the converse, memsahib with Indian, was unthinkable. But the men were often lonely and the women exquisitely lovely. Kipling's most moving story of an inter-racial relationship is 'Without Benefit of Clergy'. John Holden and Ameera love each other in their house overlooking the walled city, where Ameera bears a son who is their pride and joy, and where – how else could it end? – baby and mother die. Holden goes back to his own people, and the little house rots away in the Rains.

But for white men not of the top echelon and for some Kipling regarded as not first class, intermarriage was not unthinkable. Phil Garron, in '"Yoked with an Unbeliever"' is a failure, sent out by a despairing family to grow tea, who began to look on India as his home. 'Some men fall this way, and they are of no use afterwards.' Phil 'did what many planters had done before him – that is to say, he made up his mind to marry a Hill-girl and settle down . . . So he married Dunmaya by the forms of the English church', was well cared for by her, and 'saved from perdition'.

And there is Georgie Porgie, that competent administrator in Burma, who bought there a wife so enchanting and so admirable that he decided that a white wife must be even better. So, with the careful savings of Georgina, as he called her, and promising a speedy return, Georgie Porgie went to England, came back with an English wife to Bombay, and asked for a posting in India which, for his good work in Burma, he received. Georgina waited and waited, and at last set off for India and eventually, through the window of their bungalow, saw Georgie Porgie and the Bride. 'What is that noise down there?' asked the Bride, a little later that evening. It was not, as her husband casually suggested, some hillman beating his wife, but 'Georgina crying, all by herself, down the hillside, among the stones of the watercourse where the washermen wash the clothes.' This is the very end of the story 'Georgie Porgie' and it leaves us in no doubt that Kipling's view was that Georgie Porgie had behaved abominably.

The English lower classes in India were allowed by Kipling to take their inter-racial matings more cheerfully, as in his jolly poem 'The Ladies', which ends with the famous lines: *For the Colonel's Lady an' Judy O'Grady/Are sisters under their skins!'* The third verse runs:

> I was a young un at 'Oogli,
>   Shy as a girl to begin;
> Aggie de Castrer she made me,
>   An' Aggie was clever as sin;
> Older than me, but my first un –
>   More like a mother she were –
> Showed me the way to promotion an' pay,
>   An' I learned about women from 'er!

Whether undertaken lightheartedly or in anguish, from these matings had sprung the Eurasians of Kipling's day, to whom the name Anglo-Indian has now been handed on. Most of those Kipling wrote about were not Anglo at all, but came from far older relationships between Indians and Portuguese – the names Aggie de Castro above and 'Castro from the fittin'-sheds' indicate such families. But if a common man could sleep with a Eurasian girl, a gentleman could not marry her.

> Understand clearly, there was not a breath of a word to be said against Miss Castries – not a shadow of a breath. She was good and very lovely – possessed what innocent people at Home call a 'Spanish' complexion, with thick blue-black hair growing low down on the forehead, into a 'widow's peak,' and big violet eyes under eyebrows as black and as straight as the borders of a *Gazette Extraordinary* when a big man dies. But – but – but – Well, she was a *very* sweet girl and very pious, but for many reasons she was 'impossible'. Quite so. All good Mammas know what 'impossible' means. It was obviously absurd that Peythroppe should marry her. The little opal-tinted onyx at the base of her finger-nails said this as plainly as print.   from 'Kidnapped'

So, with the encouragement of Mrs Hauksbee and for his own good, Peythroppe was taken away and beaten up by men of his own kind until he agreed to give up the marriage.

Kipling's most offensive story on this theme, though kindly meant, is 'His Chance in Life'. Miss Vezzis the nursemaid, 'black as a boot', came of a family who lived on the Borderline in

> – a big rabbit-warren of a house full of Vezzises, Pereiras, Ribieras, Lisboas, and Gonsalveses, and a floating population of loafers; besides fragments of the day's market, garlic, stale incense, clothes thrown on the floor, petticoats hung on strings for screens, old bottles, pewter crucifixes, dried *immortelles*, pariah puppies, plaster images of the Virgin, and hats without crowns.

The Vezzises had their pride. They traced their descent from a 'mythical' plate-layer who had worked on the earliest Indian railways 'and they valued their English origin'. Of Miss Vezzis's fiancé, Michele D'Cruze (connected – O shame! – with a black Jew from Cochin, and a cook), the Vezzis family demanded that he earn 50 rupees a month before marriage; and Michele, a Telegraph Signaller at 35 rupees a month, had no hope of *that*.

But in the little sub-station of Tibasu, where Michele had been sent, a Hindu-Moslem riot broke out. There was no white man to take charge, and the Indian authorities panicked. The Native Police Inspector came to the Telegraph Office and 'afraid, but obeying the old race-instinct which recognizes a drop of White blood as far as it can be diluted, said, "What orders does the *Sahib* give?"

'The "*Sahib*" decided Michele. Though horribly frightened, he felt that, for the hour, he, the man with the Cochin Jew and the menial uncle in his pedigree, was the only representative of English authority in the place.'

So he led the seven policemen to face the mob and dispersed it with a single volley, then took charge of the town until next morning when the white Assistant Collector rode in. Michele told his story, bursting into hysterical tears as he ended it. 'It was the White drop in Michele's veins dying out.'

41

St Xavier's at Lucknow, was the famous school in Kim. As Father Victor said, 'the best schooling a boy can get in India is, of course, at St Xavier's in Partibus at Lucknow'. The school was inspired by La Martinière College at Lucknow, shown here.

The Englishman understood. Michele got a new post at 65 rupees a month, and married Miss Vezzis.

Kipling did not mean to be offensive. He had nothing against Eurasians in their right places – which were not in Sahibs' social lives or their jobs. But again, where only men are involved, and generally, not men of the top social order, the case may be altered. Kipling's attitude to young Ottley, who clearly had an Indian mother (but not too clearly, for the story is in *Land and Sea Tales for Scouts and Guides*), is one of admiration for a young chap who had learned enough from his elders to get a damaged locomotive moving when its Indian driver had panicked. And there is respect in his account of the 'sallow-hued' boys who went to school with Kim at St Xavier's in Lucknow, 'cadets of the old Eurasian houses', Pereiras, De Souzas, and D'Silvas, from railway yards, abandoned cantonments, tea gardens, from large estates, mission-stations, and 'cinchona plantations south of all', whose adventures on their road to and from school 'would have crisped a Western boy's hair'.

These boys would grow up to their own places in Indian society. They were less likely to threaten the Sahibs than were the educated Indians with whom the Indian Government intended eventually to replace the white men. Such ideals were unacceptable to the kind of white man Kipling knew best, and never does he show an Indian set in authority over white men and wielding that authority wisely and courageously. 'Never forget,' he wrote in 'His Chance in Life', 'that unless the outward and visible signs of Our Authority are always before a native he is as incapable as a child of understanding what authority means' – and for Kipling these signs must always be White.

Yet there was one situation in which, as Kipling saw it, Englishman and Indian could meet on – nearly – equal terms, and this was as brave men. In 'The Ballad of East and West' the son of the Colonel of the Guides rides boldly up the Khyber Pass to retrieve his father's stolen horse from the brigand chief Kamal; and so gains Kamal's respect that he rides back with not only the mare but also Kamal's son, to be enlisted into the Guides:

> The Colonel's son he rides the mare and Kamal's boy the dun,
> And two have come back to Fort Bukloh where there went forth but one.
> And when they drew to the Quarter-Guard, full twenty swords flew clear –
> There was not a man but carried his feud with the blood of the mountaineer.
> 'Ha' done! ha' done!' said the Colonel's son. 'Put up the steel at your sides!
> 'Last night ye had struck at a Border thief – to-night 'tis a man of the Guides!'
>
> *Oh, East is East, and West is West, and never the twain shall meet,*
> *Till Earth and Sky stand presently at God's great Judgment Seat;*
> *But there is neither East nor West, Border, nor Breed, nor Birth,*
> *When two strong men stand face to face, though they come from the ends of the earth!*

There was another, if rare, relationship that a white man could have with natives, and this was the almost paternal relationship of men of several generations' service in India with those they served. Such in 'The Tomb of His Ancestors' is the Devonshire family Kipling calls the Chinns, with service in Central India since the capture of Seringapatam in 1799:

> The Chinns are luckier than most folk, because they know exactly what they must do. A clever Chinn passes for the Bombay Civil Service, and gets away to Central India, where everyone is glad to see him. A dull Chinn enters the Police Department or the Woods and Forests, and sooner or later he too appears in Central India, and that . . . gave rise to the saying, 'Central India is inhabited by Bhils, Mairs, and Chinns, all very much alike.'

And the eldest sons of the Chinns go into the Army, and they too come back to Central India to serve the little Bhils, one of India's aborigine races, who love the Chinns as totally as the Chinns love them.

But by Kipling's day, this kind of Englishman, who seemed more like another caste than an alien, was dying out. The old Indian gentlewoman in *Kim* has been exchanging happy insults with an English District Superintendent of Police. When he has ridden away, she tells Kim: 'These be the sort to oversee justice. They know the land and the customs of the land. The others, all new from Europe, suckled by white women and learning our tongues from books, are worse than the pestilence.'

India of the Indians

This is a handful of cardamons,
This is a lump of *ghi*:
This is millet and chillies and rice,
A supper for thee and me!

from *Kim*

For Kipling's best writing about India, the English presence is – almost – blotted out. It is in this writing that he expresses his extraordinary sense of the visual beauty of this most beautiful country. He, this short-sighted young man, could see Indian landscapes, people, artefacts, with, sometimes, the enamelled brilliance of the Mogul court painters, sometimes with the delicacy of such an English water-colourist of India as Edward Lear. For the brilliance:

– a palanquin of unchastened splendour – evidently in past days the litter of a queen. The pole whereby it swung between the shoulders of the bearers was rich with the painted *papier-mâché* of Cashmere. The shoulder-pads were of yellow silk. The panels of the litter itself were ablaze with the loves of all the gods and goddesses of the Hindu Pantheon – lacquer on cedar. The cedar sliding doors were fitted with hasps of translucent Jaipur enamel and ran in grooves shed with silver. The cushions were of brocaded Delhi silk, and the curtains which once hid any glimpse of the beauty of the King's palace were stiff with gold.

Through one of Kipling's horrid practical jokes, Mulvaney has been reduced to a drunken stupor, and mistakenly carried off in the palanquin to a temple in Benares. (But Mulvaney here is only a device for telling the story in the Irish voice which enhances its strange beauty.) The bearers set down the palanquin behind a pillar, and, when the praying starts, Mulvaney dares to peep out:

– the doors av all the palanquins slid back, an' the women bundled out . . . 'Twas more glorious than transformations at a pantomime, for they was in pink an' blue an' silver an' red an' grass green, wid dimonds an' imeralds an' great red rubies all over thim. But that was the least part av the glory. O bhoys, they were more lovely than the like av any loveliness in hiven; ay, their little bare feet were better than the white hands av a lord's lady, an' their mouths were like puckered roses, an' their eyes were bigger an' darker than the eyes av any living woman I've seen . . . I niver saw the like, an' niver I will again.

from 'The Incarnation of Krishna Mulvaney'

These were the wives and daughters of the kings of India at a big Queens' Praying. Such a sight Kipling could never have seen. Had he ever seen a girl like John Holden's Ameera?

Ameera wore all that she valued most. The diamond nose-stud that takes the place of the Western patch in drawing attention to the curve of the nostril, the gold ornament in the centre of the forehead studded with tallow-drop emeralds and flawed rubies, the heavy circlet of beaten gold that was fastened round her neck by the softness of the pure

44

metal, and the chinking curb-patterned silver anklets hanging low over the rosy ankle-bone. She was dressed in jade-green muslin as befitted a daughter of the Faith, and from shoulder to elbow and from elbow to wrist ran bracelets of silver tied with floss silk, frail glass bangles slipped over the wrist in proof of the slenderness of the hand.

from 'Without Benefit of Clergy'

Or were the only beautiful Indian women Kipling had really seen the sometimes lovely prostitutes? His likely associations with them are discussed in Chapter Six.

It was in prose rather than in verse that Kipling wrote best about the Indians, but some jingling verses give a fine impression of the first of the year's *kafilas*, or camel caravans, trudging south to trade in India:

> When spring-time flushes the desert grass,
> Our kafilas wind through the Khyber Pass.
> Lean are the camels but fat the frails,
> Light are the purses but heavy the bales,
> As the snowbound trade of the North comes down
> To the market-square of Peshawur town.
>
> In a turquoise twilight, crisp and chill,
> A kafila camped at the foot of the hill.
> Then blue smoke-haze of the cooking rose,
> And tent-peg answered to hammer-nose;
> And the picketed ponies, shag and wild,
> Strained at their ropes as the feed was piled;
> And the bubbling camels beside the load
> Sprawled for a furlong adown the road;
> And the Persian pussy-cats, brought for sale,
> Spat at the dogs from the camel-bale;
> And the tribesmen bellowed to hasten the food;
> And the camp-fires twinkled by Fort Jumrood;
> And there fled on the wings of the gathering dusk
> A savour of camels and carpets and musk,
> A murmur of voices, a reek of smoke,
> To tell us the trade of the Khyber woke . . .

from 'The Ballad of the King's Jest'

With the caravan of that poem, written in 1890, is a muleteer called Mahbud Ali. Some ten years later, when Kipling was writing *Kim*, he made Mahbud Ali a substantial horse-trader, and an Afghan lynch-pin of the Secret Service operations that Kipling calls the Great Game.

Kim, white orphan, Indianized street-urchin, has befriended the Lama from Tibet, whom he found by the great gun Zam-Zammah that stands outside the Lahore Museum, the Wonder House, as the Indians call it. Kim, drawn to the Lama, decides to look after him; and the Lama readily accepts Kim as his *chela*, or disciple, who will help him to find the Sacred River he is seeking. Now Kim needs

'An old lady who is more or less curtained and hid away in a bullock-cart.' Such pilgrimages, says Kipling in Kim, *often suit both a strong-tongued, iron-willed dowager and her long-suffering family.*

help, so he goes to look for Mahbud Ali at the Kashmir Serai, 'that huge open square over against the railway station . . . where the camel and horse-caravans put up on their return from Central Asia'.

Mahbud Ali helps them, both from fondness for Kim, 'the Little Friend of all the World', and to further the Great Game. Kim and the Lama take the train to Umballa where they start walking. An old sepoy sergeant guides them to the road, the Grand Trunk Road, which runs from the Khyber to Calcutta:

> 'See, Holy One – the Great Road which is the backbone of all Hind. For the most part it is shaded, as here, with four lines of trees: the middle road – all hard – takes the quick traffic. In the days before rail-carriages the Sahibs travelled up and down here in hundreds. Now there are only country-carts and such like. Left and right is the rougher road for the heavy carts – grain and cotton and timber, bhoosa, lime and hides. A man goes in safety here – for at every few *kos* is a police-station . . . All castes and kinds of men move here. Look! Brahmins and chumars, bankers and tinkers, barbers and bunnias, pilgrims and potters – all the world going and coming.'

On the road, Kim and Teshoo Lama make the acquaintance of the sharp-tongued good-natured old Indian gentlewoman who is on a pilgrimage as nearly secular as that of Chaucer's Wife of Bath. It is in the safety of her little caravan, her travelling group, that Kim awakes to morning on the Road:

> The diamond-bright dawn woke men and crows and bullocks together. Kim sat up and yawned, shook himself . . . this was life as he would have it – bustling and shouting, the buckling of belts, and beating of bullocks and creaking of wheels, lighting of fires and cooking of food, and new sights at every turn of the approving eye. The morning mist swept off in a whorl of silver, the parrots shot away to some distant river in shrieking green hosts: all the mill-wheels within earshot went to work. India was awake, and Kim was in the middle of it.

These pictures of dawn and of evening on the Road, are Kipling's water-colours, though this next one, he said, he owed to his father:

> A line of stalls selling very simple food and tobacco, a stack of firewood, a police-station, a well, a horse-trough, a few trees . . . are all that mark a *parao* on the Grand Trunk . . . the sun was driving broad golden spokes through the lower branches of the mango trees; the parakeets and doves were coming home in their hundreds . . . and shufflings and scufflings in the branches showed that the bats were ready to go out on the night-picket. Swiftly the light gathered itself together, painted for an instant the faces and the cart-wheels and the bullocks' horns as red as blood. Then the night fell, changing the touch of the air, drawing a low, even haze, like a gossamer veil of blue, across the face of the country, and bringing out, keen and distinct, the smell of wood-smoke and cattle and the good scent of wheaten cakes cooked on ashes.

Kim is an ecumenical book, and in it many castes, many beliefs, are sympathetically shown. However, the Indian religions that Kipling most respected, in so far as he understood them (which was not entirely) were those practised by good men and in the Hills.

One such man was Sir Purun Dass, the high-caste Brahmin of the story 'The Miracle of Purun Bhagat' who, at the height of his career, honoured by British and Indians alike, resigned position, palace, and power, and took up the begging-bowl and ochre-coloured dress of the holy man:

> He was a Sunnyasi – a houseless, wandering mendicant, depending on his neighbours for his daily bread; and so long as there is a morsel to divide in India, neither priest nor beggar starves. He had never in his life tasted meat, and very seldom eaten even fish. A five-pound note would have covered his personal expenses for food through any one of the many years in which he had been absolute master of millions of money. Even when he was being lionized in London, he had held before him his dream of peace and quiet – the long, white, dusty Indian road, printed all over with bare feet . . .

For Kipling, perhaps for many an Englishman who had known the burning Plains in the heats, the Hills seemed to promise spiritual cleansing, detachment from the world. It was to the Hills that the Sunnyasi, once Sir Purun Dass, made his way:

> He followed the Himalaya-Thibet road, the little ten-foot track that is blasted out of solid rock, or strutted out on timbers over gulfs a thousand feet deep . . . When he first started, the roar of the world he had left still rang in his ears . . . but when he had put the Mutteeanee Pass behind him that was all done . . .

He came to a deserted shrine on a high pass, some fifteen hundred feet above a little village whose simple villagers would welcome him as their own holy man, and gladly feed him. '"Here shall I find peace," said Purun Bhagat.'

It was from hills even higher that Teshoo Lama had come, from Tibet, the Roof of the World, but it was in the Plains that he at last found his River, the River into which the Lord Buddha had shot an arrow, and which therefore became the River of Ultimate Healing. But, at the last, Kipling was a Westerner. The best for two characters he loved as dearly as he did the Lama and the Sunnyasi could not be what they themselves sought, which was self-loss in the Great Soul. The best must be that Christian-born ideal of all Westerners, Christian or not, which is love of creatures, and it was for this love that the Sunnyasi left his eyrie to save human life,* and the Lama wrenched himself back from the Great Soul for love of Kim.

Kim is one of those novels both rightly and wrongly called picaresque: rightly, because it is – partly – about rogues, which is what picaresque means; wrongly, because picaresque does not mean a story about journeying. Journeying novels must have their own criteria, and be judged accordingly. Given Kipling's deep admiration for Mark Twain, it seems probable that he thought of Huck Finn when making his own little vagabond. Given, too, that *Huckleberry Finn* is one of the greatest of American novels, *Kim* does not stand up too badly against it. And just as Mark Twain's book is a marvellous evocation of life on the Mississippi, so is *Kim* of one area of India. And at the level at which Kim travelled through it, that part of Northern India, which was Kipling's own India, has not greatly changed, though some of it has now become Pakistan.

Kipling's Indian Journeys

Just as all beginners on local papers, Kipling must learn to cover local events before he could be sent afield: the formal and ceremonial events, the amateur theatricals (adverse criticisms *not* required), and the 'Weeks' held in the cold-weather season by the larger stations, a week of socializing with dances and sports, when all the English from the out-stations not impossibly far away would ride or drive in to relax with their own kind.

Stephen Wheeler held Rudyard to the grindstone of this sort of work for a couple of years, and fairly enough. But it was only natural that the kind of young man that Rudyard was should make what escapes he could, and the more readily since he was not, it seems, popular at first in the Punjab Club, being precocious, bumptious, and dirty-mouthed, though it cannot have been easy to be such a young apprentice *and* a would-be intellectual among experienced and practical men.

Once, indeed, young Kipling was hissed on his entrance into the Club, but this was through no fault of his own. In 1883, the *Gazette* supported a Bill that would implement the decision of the Liberal Government in England to allow Indian judges to try white people in the courts. Kipling's own sympathies were with the hissers. By 1882, when he went out to India, the best of England's public servants, both in India and at home, had come to believe that the right intention of our

---

*The curious may care to notice that the Sunnyasi's decision is an exalted form of that made by Giffen, a 'broke' drunken British officer who went native but rose to a similar occasion. He is the subject of some verses in *Departmental Ditties*.

The Punjab Club in Lahore, 'where bachelors, for the most part, gathered to eat meals of no merit among men whose merits they knew well.' (Something of Myself)

Imperial mission should be to bring our subject peoples to fitness for self-government. This interpretation was as unwelcome to Kipling as it was to the older men at the Punjab Club. The Indian Civil Service, he wrote in his good story 'On the City Wall' of 1888, believed that India may eventually be capable of standing alone. But, Kipling maintained, it will never be capable of standing alone; yet his story offered the most sympathetic understanding he ever achieved of Indian political aspirations. And sometimes he escaped from the Club, not only to the very different society of the military cantonments, but often to what was, for most of the Lahore English, the alien and best-left-unvisited territory of the Indian city.

Not many of the discoveries made in these explorations appeared in the paper. They were to be transmuted later. *Gazette* readers would not wish to hear of the evenings their reporter spent in the prostitute's salon with disaffected Indians of all kinds and from everywhere; they would prefer to read the story that resulted, 'On the City Wall'.

One report from the native city that did get into the *Gazette* was an exploration, undertaken with a protective policeman, into the conditions under which the milk was produced which found its way on to the English breakfast tables. The cattle stood

> – nearly up to their knees in filth; but the refuse was blue and rotten below the surface, and smelt beyond all description . . . Semi-circular depressions showed where the cows had been lying all night, and the blue black-veined slime was, of course, plastered

liberally over udders, stomach, and breast. The *gowala* [cow herd] and his family . . . were just awake; and came out of their huts wrapped in all manner of foul garments. One woman had on a specially unclean *chudder*, which, in the course of milking, flopped and dangled into the *lotahs*. Her children, when they saw the chance, dipped their fingers into the warm milk and licked them afterwards. These fingers were smeared with three distinct, albeit nameless, abominations.[9]

This, of 1885, is good investigative journalism of a kind that must have encouraged Wheeler to send his Assistant Editor further afield. He had already, the previous year, been to Patiala, to the north-west of Simla, for the State Visit of the Viceroy, Lord Ripon, to open a college there, and his description of the accumulated treasures of the Maharajah's palace made amusing reading: 'When His Highness bought anything he did it wholesale,' Kipling wrote, and he listed the 'things' through several paragraphs:

> Bolts, nuts, and screws in assorted cases . . . albums in Russia leather, malachite, ivory, mother-of-pearl, silver, onyx, and agate . . . riding whips, sausage-machines, champagne-tweezers, candle-sticks . . . twenty-seven brass parrot cages . . . stereoscopes, patent medicines, patent inks, and a flock of India-rubber decoy ducks –[10]

Kipling's pieces from Patiala pleased. Later that year he was sent to Amritsar, site of the Sikhs' Golden Temple and then one of the richest cities of India. The occasion was Amritsar's great Fair, whose main business was horse-trading, but with other such attractions as horse and cattle shows with prizes, sports, and fireworks. Then a year later, in the spring of 1885, Kipling was sent on his biggest assignment so far, to Rawalpindi, to Peshawar, and to the Frontier to cover the State Visit of the Ameer of Afghanistan to Lord Dufferin, the new Viceroy. (This was the occasion when Kipling took a few steps over the Border and was fired at.) The Ameer was unpunctual, the arrangements for his reception had constantly to be modified, and rain made a mess of much that had been prepared. Still, Kipling managed to send back some ten credible despatches to his paper, culminating in a description of one of those magnificent ceremonial parades which, forty years after the British departure, India still superbly mounts.

Even as a very young man, Rudyard was far from being an adventurous traveller, and was always to be keenly alive to discomfort, and resentful of it. In May of that same year, he went for a holiday trip from Simla with a young friend and the friend's newly wedded wife. This trip, with plenty of Hill-coolies to carry the baggage, was a common tourist excursion, six stages out from Simla, with the nights in Government-maintained bungalows. The couple were going on beyond Kotgargh, but Kipling turned back. He was out of condition – 'I feel as if hot irons were struck down my marrow bones,' he wrote in his diary – and he felt *de trop* with the honeymoon pair. But his mishaps with coolies and baggage on his way back touched up nicely for *Kim*, and the mountain landscape was evocatively re-created in several fictions, most notably in 'The Miracle of Purun Bhagat'.

Kipling's transfer to the *Pioneer* at Allahabad in 1887 made something of a roving correspondent of him. In November of that year he was sent off on the most substantial journey he was to have in India, a month's tour of the native states of Rajasthan, or, as it was then called, Rajputana.

Kipling's nineteen pieces from Rajputana were published in the *Pioneer* between December 1887 and February 1888. As *Letters of Marque* they were published in book form in 1899, in the first volume of the travel pieces called *From Sea to Sea*.

The Rajputana pieces have much interest in relation to Kipling's later work, though seldom for their own sake. Most of the writing is marred by the intrusive presence of the Narrator, that facetious, know-all Kipling *persona* which he was so often to don, and usually to ill effect; here Kipling, rather ashamedly, named him the Globe-Trotter. For the most part the journeys were on the regular tourist round: Agra and the Taj Mahal, Jaipur, Amber, Chitor, Udaipur. The bathing-*ghât* at the last did produce a nearly fine passage of descriptive writing, but marred by the entry of 'the Englishman', as he is there called, into the middle of it.

Kipling did, however, on this trip, make one venture off the beaten track, and took himself probably further from the safe and the known than he ever did again; that is if he really travelled alone, as he intimated he did, though to conceal a companion, as he sometimes did, was justifiable journalism. This side-trip was to Boondi in the centre of Rajasthan, unreachable by rail, the rough road as yet unmetalled, and, on arrival, nowhere to stay but a dusty, neglected guest-bungalow inefficiently served by an old and feeble *chowkidar*, or watchman. 'But,' wrote Kipling, quoting some earlier traveller (probably Tod, whose work on Rajputana seems to have been his principal guide) '"the *coup d'oeil* of the castellated Palace of Boondi, from whichever side you approach it, is perhaps the most striking in India. Whoever has seen the Palace of Boondi can easily picture to himself the hanging gardens of Semiramis."' And Kipling added in his own voice, 'This is true – and more too . . . the Palace of Boondi, even in broad daylight, is such a palace as men build for themselves in uneasy dreams – the work of goblins rather than of men.' Not only the Palace but the whole shabby circuitous city, with its Dispensary tended by a man now almost without English but trained, long ago, at the Lahore Medical School, shocked Kipling out of his self-conscious Globe-Trotter role, and what he wrote about Boondi was as a good writer.

The principal interest of the Rajputana trip is generally taken to be the effects it had on Kipling's later creative writing, such as the knowledge gained of native states which was used in *The Naulahka*. More importantly, it has been generally accepted that Amber, or, sometimes, Chitor must be the original for the lost city of Cold Lairs in *The Jungle Books*. Both assumptions are palpably wrong.

Amber is a palace, Chitor is a fort, Cold Lairs is, or was, a city. Amber and Chitor are in desert country, Cold Lairs is in jungle. Amber and Chitor, though deserted, have never been lost; already in Kipling's day, elephants waited at the foot of each hill to carry the Globe-Trotters up. But Cold Lairs –

You could still trace the stone causeways that led up to the ruined gates where the last splinters of wood hung to the worn, rusted hinges. Trees had grown into and out of the walls; the battlements were tumbled down and decayed, and wild creepers hung out of the windows of the towers on the walls in bushy hanging clumps. A great roofless palace crowned the hill . . . From the palace you could see the rows and rows of roofless houses that made up the city looking like empty honeycombs filled with blackness . . .

from 'Kaa's Hunting'

Angus Wilson, who also doubts the long-accepted attributions, suggests as a possibility Tughakabad near Delhi, but this is open to similar objections. Tughaka-bad is not in jungle, it is a fort and palace, but not a city, and it has long been well known. Why should not the original of Cold Lairs be in Central India, where all but one of the Mowgli stories are set? Kipling himself never went there. He took his information about this jungle country from Professor and Mrs Hill who took a trip there in 1888, made an album of their photographs, and no doubt talked to Kipling about the trip. It is surely most likely that the inspiration for Cold Lairs came from the same source.

For good writing as such, the most interesting journey Kipling made for the *Pioneer* was in 1888, briefly to Benares then on to Calcutta. For what he saw there, he used a title that was potent with him for a long time: 'The City of Dreadful Night'. Kipling took it from a poem so called by James Thompson and used it for an unimportant poem of his own, printed in the *Gazette*; and then for his pieces on Calcutta, eventually published in book form from Allahabad in 1891.

Kipling's first impression of Calcutta was, like most people's, the stench: 'Has anyone thoroughly investigated the Big Calcutta Stink? . . . It resembles the essence of corruption that has rotted for the second time – the clammy odour of blue slime. And there is no escape from it.'

In the last century, it was common for journalists to visit urban haunts of poverty and vice with a policeman for protector and guide. Dickens did it in London and Liverpool, Daniel Kirwan, a visiting American, did it in London, and Kipling for the cow-byres in Lahore. Now, in Calcutta, he hired a policeman to take him round the brothels. First, albeit in the slums, to the top end of the trade:

A glare of light on the stair-head, a clink of innumerable bangles, a rustle of much fine gauze, and the Dainty Iniquity stands revealed, blazing – literally blazing – with jewellery from head to foot . . . the Dainty Iniquity . . . prettily invites everyone to be seated, and proffers such refreshments as she conceives the palates of the barbarians would prefer. Her Abigails are only one degree less gorgeous than she.

The tour wound on and on and down and down, through alleys ever more filthily squalid, to a coffee-shop in a dirty shed.

Five pitiful draggle-tails are huddled together on a bench under one of the lamps, while the sixth is squirming and shrieking before the impassive crowd. She sings of love as understood by the Oriental – the love that dries the heart and consumes the liver.

'Hers was the face from which a man could write Lalla Rookhs *by the dozen, and believe every word that he wrote. Hers was the beauty that Byron sang of . . .' (*City of Dreadful Night, *chap. 6)*

And on and on and down and down to the lowest sink of all, the prostitutes' street:

> . . . the line of open doors, the flaring lamps within, the glimpses of the tawdry toilet-tables adorned with little plaster dogs, glass balls from Christmas trees, and – for religion must not be despised though women be fallen – pictures of the saints and statuettes of the Virgin.

When little Ruddy first came to England as a child, he was appalled to see a white woman at the menial task of making a fire. Now, he was shocked by the sight of a non-Indian prostitute. She is to be found on page 90.

But Kipling had seen prostitutes before, and we may wonder whether some of his professed shock may be journalist's licence. What *is* surprising is the readiness of such newspapers as the *Gazette* and the *Pioneer* with their respectable Anglo-Indian readership, to print much of the material Kipling wrote for them, not only such investigations as this but also the stories and verses predicated on adultery, drunkenness, cowardice, and, in general, the seamier side of the white rulers' lives.

Kipling saw no cause to register shock, whether his own or for readers, on a visit he made in 1888 to the Government's opium factory at Ghazipur on the Ganges.

An opium den, such as Kipling described in his early story 'The Gate of the Hundred Sorrows' – 'My friend, Gabral Misquitta, the half-caste, spoke it all . . . before he died.'

Here the Opium Department prepared and packed for export a product which brought *daily* to the Indian Government a sum equivalent to two-and-a-half years of the Viceroy's salary: 'a splendid income', wrote Kipling, impressed. The cake, his guide explained, had to be just so, not too moist, not too dry, or 'John Chinaman won't have it.' It was important that John Chinaman took the Indian opium, and not only for the huge profit. It had long been accepted that to encourage the Chinese addiction to opium was to reduce the potential threat of what was soon to be named the Yellow Peril.

Kipling made two more trips for the *Pioneer* before he left India: one to the coal-fields of Giridih and one to the huge railway workshops at Jamalpur, both roughly to the north-west of Calcutta. His accounts are of only mild interest.

*　　　　*　　　　*

From the time that Kipling went to Allahabad, events were moving him towards a decision to leave India; as he would have said later, the cards were dealt him, and he had only to play them. An unimportant novel, *All in a Garden Fair*, by Walter Besant, had struck him forcefully in 1886, and convinced him he was ripe to seek his literary fortune in London. In 1888 Trix had become engaged to John Fleming, a soldier seconded to the Survey Department, so the Family Square was breaking up. Most importantly of all, Mrs Hill, after dangerous meningitis, decided to go home to Pennsylvania to convalesce, and what to hinder Rudyard from going home that way? – so long as he could find the money. He sold the copyrights of the Indian Railway Books for £200, of *Plain Tales* for £50, and that of *Departmental Ditties* for some small sum he could not afterwards remember. (Fortunately he was able to buy his copyrights back a few years later.) With this and six months' pay – 4,200 rupees or about £275 – Rudyard Kipling left India, and, apart from a short visit in 1891, left it for ever. He left behind in India *Mother Maturin*, the manuscript of a projected novel he had started in 1885, about an old Irishwoman who kept an opium den in Lahore and sent her daughter to be educated in England – according to Mrs Hill who had read the draft. Back in England, Kipling sent for it, and, it is said, much later mined it for *Kim*.

These were the last of Kipling's travels in India during his working life there. But there was one more journey to come. Towards the end of 1891 he left his steamer from Adelaide at Colombo, and took the ferry from Colombo to Tuticorin, in the extreme south. There he was free of the great railway system of India, begun in the 1850s and still building in Kipling's day. For his journey to Lahore, four days and nights on trains, he probably took the eastern route, for it was this landscape which served him later for the famine story 'William the Conqueror', though the years of famine in the Madras district had been in the later 1870s, before his time in India.

Kipling arrived in Lahore a week before Christmas, local boy made good, and lionization awaiting him. But within the week a cable arrived from London telling him that his greatest friend had died on 5 December. Rudyard left almost immediately for Bombay, where, before boarding his steamer, he found time for a brief visit to his old Ayah. He is said to have taken only fourteen days on his journey, arriving back in London on 10 January; so he might – just – have had time to spend some part of Christmas Day with his family. A week after he landed, he was married.

Kipling never went back to India. It would be interesting to know if this was the result of negative or positive decision, and, if the latter, whether his own decision or his wife's.

*   *   *

Kipling himself raises a point about Englishmen's attitudes to Indians which could be interestingly explored in its relation to his own work. This is the 'Hindu or Musalman bent, which each Englishman's mind must take before he has been three years in the country'. Kipling's bent was unquestionably towards the Musalman, that is, the Moslem – 'A Hindu is an excellent person, but – but –'[11] Hardly a Hindu of Kipling's creation is an excellent person, with the important exception of Hurree Babu in *Kim*, who although ridiculous in his intellectual pretensions is first-class in the Great Game, and the braver because of his (as Kipling sees it) typically Bengali timidity.

The effect of Kipling's Musalman bent in Kipling's art is surely important and deserves exploration. But here it must remain just another possible story.

CHAPTER THREE

The Craftsman

Much I owe to the Lands that grew –
More to the Lives that fed –
But most to Allah who gave me two
Separate sides to my head . . .

from 'The Two-Sided Man'

THE word *craft* has probably changed as little over the centuries as any important word in English. When Chaucer, adapting a Latin tag, wrote 'the life so short, the craft so long to learn', he was speaking of his work in just the same spirit as Kipling's for whom craft was always to be respected, but art mistrusted:

When the flicker of London sun falls faint on the Club-room's green and gold,
The sons of Adam sit them down and scratch with their pens in the mould –
They scratch with their pens in the mould of their graves, and the ink and the
    anguish start,
For the Devil mutters behind the leaves: 'It's pretty, but is it Art?' . . .

from 'The Conundrum of the Workshops'

In Kipling's earliest professional work, art was hardly called for, but rather mastery of the craft of journalism, and this his stint on the *Civil and Military Gazette* certainly gave him. He learned that, no matter what, a newspaper must be filled, proof-corrected, put to bed. He learned the importance of looking things up, for his harshest critics, the men at the Punjab Club 'were not concerned with my dreams. They wanted accuracy and interest, but first of all accuracy.'[1] According to 'the Father' (this horrid nomenclature, 'the Mother', 'the Uncle', 'the Beloved Aunt' was Macdonald family practice), accuracy 'had *not* been my distinction on the little Civil and Military', and where accuracy entailed looking up and checking, it never was.

Though Kipling could soon afford to leave daily journalism for more leisured writing, journalism's training and its ways of thinking stayed with him all his life. As he wrote, some thirty years after he had left the paper:

The Soldier may forget his Sword,
    The Sailorman the Sea,
The Mason may forget the Word
    And the Priest his Litany:

Kipling's study at Bateman's. 'Left and right of the table were two big globes on one of which a great airman had once outlined in white paint those air-routes to the East and Australia which were well in use before my death.' (Something of Myself)

> The Maid may forget both jewel and gem,
>   And the Bride her wedding-dress –
> But the Jew shall forget Jerusalem
>   Ere we forget the Press!...

from 'The Press'

But though journalism and creative writing are cousins, they are not identical. It is the craft of Kipling the creative writer that must concern us most, and on some aspects of his craftsmanship in this field, Kipling might seem to have been – for him – unusually forthcoming. In Lahore, he tells us in *Something of Myself*, he used 'a slim, octagonal-sided, agate penholder with a Waverley nib'.[2] Then came stylos, and then fountain-pens. By choice he wrote on large blocks of 'off-white', blue sheets made specially for him, but in need on anything available. On his desk in his Sussex home, an array of gadgets: pen tray, wooden boxes, paper-weight, pen-wiper, an 'outsize office pewter ink-pot'.

But all this is merely a smokescreen of the mechanics of writing. It is completely irrelevant to what we really want to know which is, how is the miracle worked. How does creative writing come about and what determines its quality? What was distinctively peculiar in the case of Kipling?

Of course, these questions are unanswerable, but we do know something of how the process works in general, and even something of its particular workings in Kipling.

There is the collection of the material, which is often an unconscious process, no creative writer knowing, at that stage, what is going to be useful; and the letting it slip down into what Henry James, Kipling's and his family's friend, called 'the deep well of the unconscious'. There is the leaving it there to soak, to seethe, to 'macerate', in Robert Louis Stevenson's word. There is its emergence, not necessarily when called for, but when ready. Virginia Woolf said that the new work must come to feel like a ripened pear inside her, ready to drop. Next the writing, and Kipling's experiences here are typical. Then, finally, the process written about least, too often attended to least: the judging of what has emerged.

Kipling usually knew, and we can often see, where much of his material came from: from his prodigious reading, and most, perhaps, from the Bible, always ready to his pen, whether for a title, a reference, or the very subject of a story or a poem; no one unversed in the Bible can read Kipling well. Shakespeare, of course, he knew, and Shakespeare's contemporaries and he could write effective poems in their styles. He knew the moderns too: Browning, a profound influence on him – he had liked, as a schoolboy, to think of himself as Fra Lippo Lippi – and Swinburne and Robert Louis Stevenson whose work he respected almost that side of idolatry, and others whom he liked less, such as Ernest Dowson, or 'the suburban Toilet-Club school favoured by the late Mr. Oscar Wilde'.[3]

Popular literature went into the deep well as readily as the classics, and children's books fell in and emerged transformed: a sinister late story, 'Fairy-Kist', depends on a shell-shocked soldier's unconscious memory of Mrs Ewing's pretty story 'Mary's Meadow'; and we have already seen the probable source of the rhythm of 'Danny Deever' (*see pages 35-6*). Kipling's Introduction to the *Barrack-Room Ballads* offers a nice encapsulation of his – and most other writers' – normal ways of going on:

> When 'Omer smote 'is bloomin' lyre,
> He'd 'eard men sing by land an' sea;
> An' what 'e thought 'e might require,
> 'E went an' took – the same as me! . . .

Considerable study could productively be given to the influence on Kipling of popular song: hymn tunes, drawing-room songs, street ballads, and, above all, music-hall songs, and if we knew more of the relations of these to his finished work, we would be better readers of his popular verse. (Some biographers have made shots at 'matches', but alas, few with good enough ears for rhythm.)

In the early days, the material that went into the deep well often came directly from Kipling's journalism; and often re-emerged with surprising rapidity. The newspaper story of 1 January 1887 about the capture of a Burmese town by mother-naked British soldiers was out again in the paper as the short story, 'The Taking of Lungtungpen' on 11 April of that same year. Sometimes the material must have come from stories he was told, perhaps by his mother, of her life in India while he was a child in England; many of Kipling's Indian stories are of the 1870s and earlier, not of the 1880s. Sometimes the material came from soldiers' tales, or from the files, or from Army history. 'Gunga Din' (I cite Carrington[4]) was the name Kipling gave to Juma, the heroic water-carrier of the Guides at the siege of Delhi, during the Mutiny of 1857. In Kipling's version the poem's words are those of a wounded soldier whose life is saved by Gunga Din, as he names the water-carrier, at the expense of his own. Its last line 'You're a better man than I am, Gunga Din!' has passed into our language, a catch-phrase casually used by people who may have no idea of its source. But this is true of so many of Kipling's lines that one can fairly say that if, like Homer, "e went an' took' what he might need, he gave a very great deal back.

The end of the Indian Mutiny was only eight years away when Lockwood and Alice Kipling went out to India in 1865, and it is curious that it hardly ever enters Rudyard's work. Naturally, one did not speak of 'the Black Year' with Indians: when Khem Singh, the political prisoner of 'On the City Wall', told old stories to the Subaltern in charge of the Fort where he was held, 'he never told tales of '57 because, as he said, he was the Subaltern's guest, and '57 is a year that no man, Black or White, cares to speak of.' The only story actually about the Mutiny is, oddly, a macabre story for children, 'The Undertakers' in *The Second Jungle Book*. It is about three horrid scavengers of the River Sutlej, the Jackal, the Adjutant Bird, and the Mugger or crocodile. The Mugger tells of a season when rumour of rich pickings had led him to leave his own waters and make for the Ganges by Allahabad where he found the rumour true; 'the dead English came down, touching each other . . .

The three Undertakers, that 'ruffianly beast' the Adjutant, the 'mangy little Jackal' and 'the blunt-nosed Mugger of Mugger-Ghaut'.

one lay still in the slack-water and let twenty go by to take one.' Then, for a time, no bodies came down, but later, 'it was as though whole villages had walked into the water'. These wore red coats. They were not white.

The four foreign literatures that Kipling made most use of were the Indian, the French, the American, and the Roman, and three of these were foreign-language literatures. We do not know if he read Indian literature in the vernacular, but he hardly needed to, with his well-informed father to hand. However he derived his knowledge, Kipling made always admirably discreet use of Indian literary traditions, both classical and popular – the songs of Lalun in 'On the City Wall', the vernacular names for the animals of *The Jungle Books* (for Bagheera *means* a panther, Mowgli *means* a frog, and so on); he knew a great deal about Indian religions, as we can see from his almost throwaway references to different religions' practices in *Kim*, and he even knew about Indian black magic:

> A match lit up the darkness; he caught the well-known purr and fizzle of grains of incense. Then the room filled with smoke – heavy, aromatic, and stupefying. Through growing drowse he heard the names of devils – of Zulbazan, Son of Eblis, who lives in bazaars and *paraos*, making all the sudden lewd wickedness of wayside halts; of Dulham, invisible about mosques, the dweller among the slippers of the Faithful, who hinders folk from their prayers; and Musboot, Lord of lies and panic . . .

That was the old blind prostitute in *Kim*, magicking the boy – now a school-leaver, a white Sahib – against the dangers of his half year of freedom. In *Kim* there is a wealth of reference to Indian cultural, religious, and literary traditions, from the lowest to the highest. We have lost 'a half-chapter of the Lama sitting down in the blue-green shadows at the foot of a glacier, telling Kim stories out of the Jatakas' but, says Kipling sadly, though this was 'truly beautiful', it was 'otiose' and had to be removed.[5]

Not, perhaps, surprisingly, it is several times from Indian prostitutes that Kipling (or rather the Narrator, who is not, as we shall see, the same thing) gets his knowledge of Indian lore, and of these the most enchanting is Lalun of the political story 'On the City Wall' who can sing Indian traditional ballads as part of her craft.

> She played little songs on the *sitar*, and to hear her sing, 'O Peacock, cry again,' was always a fresh pleasure. She knew all the songs that have ever been sung, from the war-songs of the South, that make the old men angry with the young men and the young men angry with the State, to the love-songs of the North, where the swords whinny-whicker like angry kites in the pauses between the kisses, and the Passes fill with armed men, and the Lover is torn from his Beloved and cries, *Ai! Ai! Ai!* evermore . . .

Whether the various songs Kipling gave her are translations or pastiches I do not know, but in his earlier writing days he several times attempted stories intended to read as if directly translated from Indian speech; 'In Flood Time' from *In Black and White* is a good example, a story told to a Sahib by an old ferryman. Only an Indian could say how successful these experiments were, whether in prose or, rather more

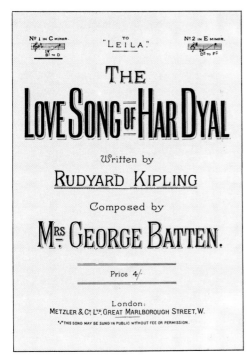

Left: Between 1892 and 1937 about 200 of Kipling's poems were set to music. This is one of the earliest, and the first of six versions of 'Mandalay', the latest in 1933.
Right: Kipling's portrait by John Collier. Though painted after his return to London, his jacket was surely made – and worn – in India. One of the most attractive pictures of Kipling in early manhood, the boy is still visible in a face that was, like his father's, always too old for its years.

rarely, in poetry. In his story 'Beyond the Pale', he presents a version of 'The Love Song of Har Dyal' (*see page 39*) as a direct translation, and so, to the European reader at least, it seems to be. But when Kipling put a poem of the same name into his collected verse, with a note that it was originally attached to this story, it was a poem in the European style that he gave there, and one only remotely connected in its matter to the original prose translation – if this is what it was:

> Alone upon the housetops to the North
> I turn and watch the lightnings in the sky –
> The glamour of thy footsteps in the North.
> *Come back to me, Beloved, or I die.*

J. MacG. Stewart in his admirable Bibliographical Catalogue of Kipling's works seems, most unusually, to have slipped up here, for he speaks of the poem *in the story* as being one of four 4-line stanzas, which it is not. However, this title, 'The Love Song of Har Dyal' was, as I heard T. S. Eliot say, the inspiration for his title, 'The Love Song of J. Alfred Prufrock'.

It was necessary for Kipling in his Indian work to master the craft of rendering a convincing foreign vernacular in English – the craft that British broadcasting attempts, and usually fails at, by use of accent rather than idiom. Most of the speech of *Kim*, for instance, is in the vernacular, though this strikes home to us only when both the vernacular and English are used in the same scene. Here is Kim 'captured' by the chaplains of his father's old regiment, talking on the one hand to them, who do not know the vernacular, and to the Lama who knows no English:

> 'Holy One, the thin fool who looks like a camel says that I am the son of a Sahib . . . it is true. I knew it since my birth . . . The fat fool is of one mind and the camel-like one of another. But that is no odds. I may spend one night here and perhaps the next. It has happened before. Then I will run away and return to thee.'
> 'But tell them that thou art my *chela*. Tell them how thou didst come to me when I was faint and bewildered. Tell them of our Search, and they will surely let thee go now.'
> 'I have already told them. They laugh, and they talk of the police.'
> 'What are you saying?' asked Mr. Bennett.
> 'Oah. He only says that if you do not let me go it will stop him in his business – his ur-gent private af-fairs.'

Indian critics say that Kipling's various uses of Indian languages are acceptable. It is rather the reader who knows only English who might complain that in some of the earliest works there is too much insertion of Indian words, but we have to remember that such Indian words would have been commonplace to the Anglo-Indians Kipling was originally writing for.

How far Kipling was proficient in speaking and understanding any Indian language we do not know. It is widely said that Kipling learned 'the vernacular' in childhood, and recovered it when he went back to India. But which vernacular?

Of Urdu, he spoke, by his own account, only 'English Urdu'. Did he speak Hindustani, of which most English knew at least a little for communicating with their servants? 'Talk Hindi,' says Kim angrily to Hurree Babu the Bengali, annoyed at being cozened in babu-English, and Hurree says, 'Now I will speak vernacular,' and switches to Hindi.

But even if Kipling did himself understand and speak Hindi, this is only one of hundreds of Indian languages and dialects, far from a universal tongue for even all of Kipling's own characters. Murray's *Guide* of 1882 indicates that the two languages most used in the Punjab and Rajputana are Punjabi and Sindi, and Kipling never claims to know either. So how far can we trust his many accounts of his talks with Indians?

The answer may well be, not very far, but another part of the answer is that it doesn't matter. It is as a creative writer that Kipling has genius, not as a more or less accurate reporter.

French literature Kipling had read since his schooldays, though, he wrote, 'French as an accomplishment was not well-seen at English schools in my time, and knowledge of it connoted leanings towards immorality.'[6] His own knowledge of

French literature was, for any Englishman, exceptional. He could not see, he said, how London literary circles 'got along with so casual a knowledge of French work', and, he added drily, 'of much English grounding that I had supposed indispensable'.[7]

Equally unusual for his time, Kipling loved American literature, especially popular American literature – the Uncle Remus stories, as everyone who has read about Stalky and the Tar-Baby will remember; *Hans Breitmann's Ballads* which he parodied as verses in the *Gazette* and whose language he used for his own Breitmann in a couple of stories; and the influence on him of Mark Twain's work, if necessarily here 'another story', must be accepted as substantial.

Greek, despite efforts to ground him in it at school, never took. Latin was another matter. The works of Horace were always dear to him. He translated Horace's ode 'Donec gratus eram tibi' into broad Devonshire while he was still at school. It ends:

> *He:* But s'posin' I threwed up Jane
> An' nivver went walkin' with she –
> An' come back to yeou again –
> How 'ud that be?

> *She:* Frye's sober. Yeou've allus done badly –
> An' yeou shifts like cut net-floats, yeou du:
> But – I'd throw that young Frye ovver gladly
> An' lovv 'ee right thru!

Much later, with his friend Charles Graves, Kipling faked translations to a supposed Fifth Book of Horace which did not then exist, though it was soon written for him by A. D. Godley, then Public Orator at Oxford. The final work, was published under the title: 'Q. HORATI FLACCI CARMINUM LIBRUM QUINTUM A RUDYARDO KIPLING ET CAROLO GRAVES ANGLICE REDDITUM ET VARIORUM NOTIS ADORNATUM AD FIDEM CODICUM MSS. EDIDIT ALUREDUS D. GODLEY OXONII APUD BASILIUM BLACKWELL MDCCCCXX.'

This book tries to show something of what went into the deep well from Kipling's travels – or rather, what was available for use, for it must always remain mysterious and extraordinary to find that what 'took' and what did not, what sank to the bottom of the well, and what, more or less transformed, surged up on to the page. Sometimes stories told to Kipling by other people were dropped in. He several times intimates that he is retelling a story given him by someone else and this may well be true, at least as far as the germ of it goes, for he was not averse from other people's suggestions, provided of course, that the people were the right people and the suggestions chimed. It was, for instance, Kipling's cousin, Ambrose (Ambo) Poynter, who came to Kipling's Sussex home, Bateman's, and said, 'Write a yarn about Roman times here,' and then suggested the name Parnesius for the Centurion who should tell the tale.[8] And from Kipling's earliest writing days in India, he was avid for the specialized knowledge that men from other crafts could give him:

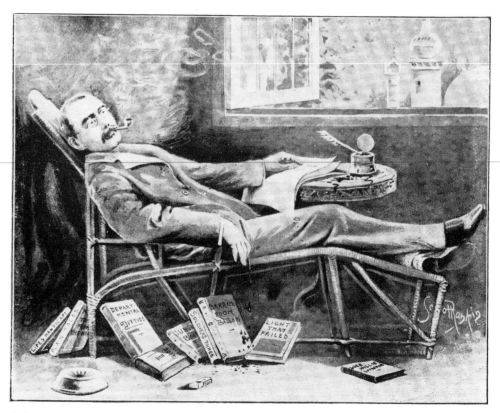

In June 1897 Kipling's story for boys, 'Winning the Victoria Cross', was published in the Windsor Magazine, *prefaced by this cartoon of a ruminant Kipling by Scott Rankin.*

– In that Club [the Punjab Club at Lahore] and elsewhere, I met none except picked men at their definite work – Civilians, Army, Education, Canals, Forestry, Engineering, Irrigation, Railways, Doctors, and Lawyers – examples of each branch and each talking his own shop. It follows then that that 'show of technical knowledge', for which I was blamed later came to me from the horse's mouth, even to boredom.[9] ['Civilians' here, means men of the Indian Civil Service.]

So much for some, certainly only a small part, of the input. Of the process of maceration, Kipling no more than any other writer, can tell us anything worth knowing, though he has some interesting things to say about abortive attempts to bring the material out too soon. The Parnesius suggestion from Ambo Poynter was in principle accepted, but the right stuff was a long time coming out. A story about a Baltic pirate passing in the fog 'the Roman fleet abandoning Britain to her doom' might have served, Kipling says, as a 'pipe-opener' (that disposable beginning known to most writers, whose purpose is simply to get things moving), but it didn't work. A Daniel Defoe story was tried and thrown away, and a Dr Johnson story too.

Then he stopped trying and 'walked the other way' and 'the whole thing set and linked itself'.[10] Similarly with the not very good South African story 'The Captive', which would not come until Kipling's Daemon, his inspiration, told him to 'Paint the background first, once for all, as hard as a public-house sign –';[11] and the finally excellent medieval story, 'The Eye of Allah' which foundered until the Daemon said, 'Treat it as an illuminated manuscript.'[12] This short-sighted man was always to be profoundly responsive to visual stimuli.

Comes the moment when the ripe pear drops, when, as Kipling once put it, he 'began to hatch'. As a journalist, and for the purposes of journalism, he knew, as every journalist must, how to manage the whole process of input, maceration, and hatching so as to fit the time and space available. With more creative – and non-deadlined – work, the process is never so simple, and the hatching often the hardest of all. Frequently for Kipling, and from boyhood onwards, this moment was at dawn when, often, a little wind gets up and dies away again. He knew this moment first when he was twelve years old, and it recurs again and again in his work. He used it tellingly as an image to stand for the Renaissance, one of the greatest creative moments in man's history:

> At two o'clock in the morning, if you open your window and listen,
> You will hear the feet of the Wind that is going to call the sun.
> And the trees in the shadow rustle and the trees in the moonlight glisten,
> And though it is deep, dark night, you feel that the night is done.
>
> So do the cows in the field. They graze for an hour and lie down,
> Dozing or chewing the cud; or a bird in the ivy wakes,
> Chirrups one note and is still, and the restless Wind strays on,
> Fidgeting far down the road, till softly, the darkness breaks . . .
>
> So when the world is asleep, and there seems no hope of her waking
> Out of some long, bad dream that makes her mutter and moan,
> Suddenly, all men arise to the noise of fetters breaking,
> And every one smiles at his neighbour and tells him his soul is his own!
>
> from 'The Dawn Wind – The Fifteenth Century'

The business, more or less laborious, of getting it down on paper comes next, and it is now that all the paraphernalia may come into use: the Waverley nibs, the off-white paper, the pen-wipers. Yet sometimes the work is not laborious at all, and these, as Kipling knew, are times to make every writer rejoice – and, if the writer is wise, not only to rejoice but to beware.

This is when inspiration takes over, when the invention seems to 'come of itself', as Kipling once put it, and the writing hand is too slow for the speed of creation;[13] 'the pen took charge and I watched it write,' he reported of the Mowgli stories. Kipling personified the sensation of such moments as his Daemon, and he valued his Daemon's presence as the *sine qua non* of creation. 'When your Daemon is in charge,' he wrote, 'do not try to think consciously. Drift, wait, and obey.'[14]

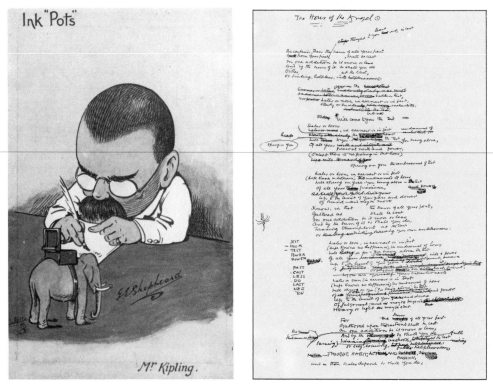

Left: A likeable cartoon of 'That little black demon of a Kipling', as Henry James described him in a letter of 1891, to Robert Louis Stevenson in Samoa.
Right: The Higher Editing: When 'The Hour of the Angel' finally appeared in Land and Sea Tales *in 1923, it was fourteen lines long, with a last line 'And none can change us, though they die to save!' not yet in the rough.*

For Kipling knew, as every true craftsman must know, that without that 'divine afflatus', no superb work will be done. He knew too, and not all creators know this, that work done under this influence is not necessarily good. The last stage in the creative process is, or ought to be judgment.

Kipling when dissatisfied was always prepared to discard. (His poem 'Recessional' went into the waste-paper basket, and was retrieved by a visiting American friend.) He tried to follow advice his father gave him at the start of his career, which was never to 'write short', always to write more than he needed and then cut.

Once the journalist became the creative writer with time in hand, this part of the process became a rite, a ritual, which Kipling called 'the Higher Editing'. There must be Indian ink, and ground for the purpose, not out of a bottle. There must be a brush. The finished work is read, and superfluities immediately perceived are brushed out. The work is laid aside. Some time later it is reread and shortened again. Next time, it is picked up, it is privately read aloud, and reveals whether it needs further brushwork or not. The shorter the story, the more brushwork needed, the longer the story, the less brushwork, the longer lie-by. 'I have had tales by me for three or five years, which shortened themselves almost yearly.'[15]

It has to be said that a great deal of poor work did, none the less, slip through the Higher Editing. Whether the Daemon had failed in the writing or in guiding the editing judgment, it is certain that much was accepted as satisfactory, in both verse and prose, which is embarrassing and unworthy. To detail 'the worst of Kipling' would be a macabre exercise, but there is no denying that much of it, and, in particular, the worst stylistic tricks, can get in the way of fully appreciative reading. Every reader will pick his own bugbears. Among mine are the coy modes of address – 'Best Beloved' in the *Just So Stories*, 'you from the other side of the county' in 'They'; the would-be childish language, like 'satiable for insatiable, 'sclusively for exclusively; the lazy use of archaisms, like 'aught' and 'anon' in the poem quoted on page 6; above all, the terrible knowingness; for instance, in 'The Finest Story in the World', when the Narrator accepts the bank-clerk's description of the wave topping the bulwark because he had heard the same thing from another man whose ship had gone down and 'I had travelled ten thousand weary miles to meet him and take his knowledge at second hand.' In few writers – only Dickens comes to mind – is the gap between best and worst so wide. It is as if quite different men were at work; and so, in a sense, they were.

The account I have given so far of Kipling the craftsman is mostly his own, and mostly it rings true. But to try to understand anything about Kipling, we have to remember that Kipling had more than two sides to his head. It is not one Kipling we have to understand, not even just two, but at least three, and one of them, the one that seems the most accessible, is as often as not thrown out as a deliberate smokescreen.

The first Kipling is simply a shorthand name for the work. 'Do you like Kipling?' we might say, or 'Hardy?' or 'Browning?', meaning, in each case, the corpus of work, unrelated to the writer. The third Kipling is the 'real' person, in so far as real people can ever be perceived, which in Kipling's case is, as yet, hardly at all. The second Kipling, the one we must be wary of, is the one that Kipling himself presents to us.

This smokescreen Kipling personality is the Narrator, or, as he calls himself in an early story, 'The House of Suddhoo', the chorus. In addition to the four principal characters, he tells us, 'there is Me of course; but I am only the chorus that comes in at the end to explain things' – though in fact in this story and in most written to this general formula, he is there all the way through.

Many writers have used this device of inventing a personality to whom the story is told or who plays a minor but necessary part in its development, a sort of godling from the machine, and one who usually colours the story with what appears to be his own outlook and attitude. But if we take this invented creature as identical with its inventor, we are probably mistaken. Chaucer among the Canterbury pilgrims presents himself as a bumbling fool and an inept poet; whereas we know from his work that he was a magnificent poet, and from his life that he was probably nearer to Le Carré's George Smiley than a fool. George Eliot's *persona* was that of a saint, the reality nearer to a whited sepulchre. Sometimes the real Kipling may have been identical with his defensive invention, more often, more probably, he was not.

We, however, have to take account of this smokescreen personality, this chorus, this Narrator – I shall call him the last – because he is often obtrusive in the work; because it is he, not the real Kipling, who wrote about Kipling's travels for publication; and because it was he who, in the last year of Kipling's life, wrote *Something of Myself*, the deliberately composed, evasive, and often forgetfully inaccurate autobiography, which told – or purported to tell – us, the public, as much about himself as he ever wished us to know.

So what was he like, this Narrator, who began his literary life from the moment Kipling started his newspaper work? He was (though in reality only sixteen when Kipling first used him), a man of the world, a man whom other men liked to talk with in clubs, a man to trust and depend on; as the Major in the early story 'Thrown Away' depended on the Narrator to help pass off a suicide as a noble death, as the family of Mr McLeod the Jewish furrier in a later story, 'The House Surgeon', depended on the Narrator to free their home from a brooding presence. He is a man of fine feelings; many Narrators can easily make their readers feel of coarser clay, though Kipling cannot always bring this off. We can feel with him the awfulness of the politician in the Stalky story, 'The Flag of their Country' when he unfurls a Union Jack and waves it at the schoolboys; but *we* feel as embarrassed as the schoolboys are by the 'jelly-bellied flag-flapper' when we read the Narrator's explanation of *their* embarrassment that 'the reserve of a boy is tenfold deeper than the reserve of a maid, she being made for one end only by blind Nature, but man for several'.

The Narrator is much given to practical jokes. He is very knowing, is the Narrator, and with a kind of knowingness that many critics found offensive from the start, and not, as he himself suggested, because they suspected that he didn't really know, but because he was so often such a show-off when he did. In, for instance, his early story 'The Ship That Found Herself', when separate parts of a new ship talk their way across the Atlantic, we can't but feel the intention is rather to show off the Narrator's knowledge of shipbuilding than to tell a moral tale about the team spirit. I do not like Kipling the Narrator. Fortunately, in all Kipling's best work, he is absent or decently unobtrusive.

It is proper and decorous to close this chapter on Kipling's craftsmanship by indicating two examples of his craft *about* his craft, a story and a poem, when he was writing at his best. Both are to do with Shakespeare.

The story is called 'Proofs of Holy Writ', one of Kipling's excellently ambiguous titles. It was first published in 1934, but is not yet in a collected edition in England. It is a story of Shakespeare retired, sitting at his ease in the garden of New Place, his fine house in Stratford-upon-Avon, and with him his friend, the poet and dramatist

Ben Jonson, come down from London to visit him. A messenger arrives from Oxford, bringing to Shakespeare a bundle of book proofs for his comments and revisions. Ben Jonson discovers to his horror that his friend of 'small Latin and less Greek' has been called upon to help with the Authorized Version of the Bible.

Eagerly Jonson, that overbearing Boanerges,* seeks to improve his less well-educated friend's simple approach to the proofs. Brilliantly, Kipling shows the quality of each man's handling of the Latin text, the courteous deftness with which Shakespeare picks Jonson's brain for the Latinity, then goes his own way. The passages that result are from Isaiah, Chapter 60.

After reading 'Proofs of Holy Writ', one can hardly *not* believe that Shakespeare was called in to advise on the Authorized Version of our Bible.

The poem on the craft of creation, one of the best poems that Kipling wrote, first appeared in 1919, in the verse collection *The Years Between*. It is called 'The Craftsman'.

> Once, after long-drawn revel at The Mermaid,
> He to the overbearing Boanerges
> Jonson, uttered (if half of it were liquor,
>   Blessed be the vintage!)
>
> Saying how, at an alehouse under Cotswold,
> He had made sure of his very Cleopatra
> Drunk with enormous, salvation-contemning
>   Love for a tinker.
>
> How, while he hid from Sir Thomas's keepers,
> Crouched in a ditch and drenched by the midnight
> Dews, he had listened to gypsy Juliet
>   Rail at the dawning.
>
> How at Bankside, a boy drowning kittens
> Winced at the business; whereupon his sister –
> Lady Macbeth aged seven – thrust 'em under,
>   Sombrely scornful.
>
> How on a Sabbath, hushed and compassionate –
> She being known since her birth to the townsfolk –
> Stratford dredged and delivered from Avon
>   Dripping Ophelia.
>
> So, with a thin third finger marrying
> Drop to wine-drop domed on the table,
> Shakespeare opened his heart till the sunrise
>   Entered to hear him . . .

*The name means 'sons of Thunder' and refers to James and John, the sons of Zebedee (Luke 9:54) who wanted to call down fire from heaven on the disbelieving Samaritans.

CHAPTER FOUR

A LONG WAY
EAST OF SUEZ

Years when I raked the Ports wi' pride to fill my cup o' wrong –
Judge not, O Lord, my steps aside at Gay Street in Hong Kong! . . .

from 'McAndrew's Hymn'

N 9 March 1889, with Aleck and Ted Hill, Kipling left Calcutta on the SS *Madura*, known in Calcutta as the Mutton-Mail because it took sheep and the mail to Rangoon. There Kipling and the Hills trans-shipped to the SS *Africa*, and, at Singapore, to the *Nawab*. Kipling reported this journey in regular 'Letters' to the *Pioneer* in which Aleck Hill appeared as 'the Professor' and Ted Hill not at all. Most of the despatches were marred by the terrible jocularity that so often afflicted Kipling when writing in his own person: as witness the contrast between the two literary results of the steamer's unscheduled stop at Moulmein, the second largest city in Burma, which since 1885 had been annexed to British India.

First, from the account Kipling sent back to the *Pioneer*:

– a sleepy town, just one house thick . . . inhabited by slow, solemn elephants, building stockades for their own diversion. There was a strong scent of freshly sawn teak in the air . . . When the elephants had got an appetite for luncheon they loafed off in couples to their club, and did not take the trouble to give us greeting and the latest mail papers; at which we were much disappointed, but took heart when we saw upon a hill a large white pagoda . . . I should better remember what that pagoda was like had I not fallen deeply and irrevocably in love with a Burmese girl at the foot of the first flight of steps . . . Far above my head there was a faint tinkle, as of golden bells, and a talking of the breezes in the tops of the toddy-palms – *from From Sea to Sea*

And from the poem he wrote in 1890:

By the old Moulmein Pagoda, lookin' lazy at the sea,
There's a Burma girl a-settin', and I know she thinks o' me;
For the wind is in the palm-trees, and the temple-bells they say:
'Come you back, you British soldier; come you back to Mandalay!'
    Come you back to Mandalay,
    Where the old Flotilla lay:
    Can't you 'ear their paddles chunkin' from Rangoon to Mandalay?

A Burma Girl – 'When all our troops are back from Burma there will be a proverb in their mouths, "As thrifty as a Burmese wife", and pretty. English ladies will wonder what in the world it means.' ('Georgie Porgie')

On the road to Mandalay,
Where the flyin'-fishes play,
An' the dawn comes up like thunder outer China 'crost the Bay!

'Er petticoat was yaller an' 'er little cap was green,
An' 'er name was Supi-yaw-lat – jes' the same as Theebaw's Queen, . . .

With 'er arm upon my shoulder an' 'er cheek agin my cheek
We useter watch the steamers an' the *hathis* pilin' teak.
Elephants a-pilin' teak
In the sludgy, squdgy creek
Where the silence 'ung that 'eavy you was 'arf afraid to speak!
On the road to Mandalay . . .

But that's all shove be'ind me – long ago an' fur away.
An' there ain't no 'buses runnin' from the Bank to Mandalay;
An' I'm learnin' 'ere in London what the ten-year soldier tells:
'If you've 'eard the East a-callin', you won't never 'eed naught else.'
No! you won't 'eed nothin' else
But them spicy garlic smells,
An' the sunshine an' the palm-trees an' the tinkly temple-bells;
On the road to Mandalay . . .   from 'Mandalay'

It was on this journey that Kipling was afflicted with a permanently influential kind of culture-shock. He discovered fear and hatred of any peoples who might assail his almost unthinking belief that the world looked up to the invincible British Empire. He already had an automatic hatred of the threatening Russians – most people of his kind in India did. He dealt with Indian nationalism by believing that Indians lacked all the positive qualities that could enable them to govern their own country well. He was soon to hate Americans, though always ambivalently. Now – with one puzzled reservation – he had to hate the Chinese.

He first met Chinese in large numbers in Penang, and he was disturbed: 'They were the first army-corps on the march of the Mongol.' At Singapore, a sunburned man spoke of the need for a million coolies in North Borneo, and Kipling generously offered Indians. But the man from North Borneo was contemptuous. 'Your men are no good . . . We must have Chinese coolies.'[1]

By the time that Kipling arrived in Hong Kong, he had reached his painful conclusion.

> If we had control over as many Chinamen as we have natives of India, and had given them one tithe of the cosseting, the painful pushing forward, and studious, even nervous regard of their interests and aspirations that we have given to India, we should long ago have been expelled from, or have reaped the reward of, the richest land on the face of the earth.[2]

'You think,' he wrote to the *Pioneer,* '. . . that you are helping forward England's mission in the East. 'Tis a pretty delusion, and I am sorry to destroy it, but you have conquered the wrong country. Let us annex China.'

The reservation to Kipling's wholesale hatred of the Chinese (and Lockwood's son could not but make it) was the exquisite taste and quality of their craftsmanship. After visiting Canton and Hong Kong, they must, he felt, have a soul, and in hideous pidgin he asked the shopkeeper, 'Have you got one piecee soul – allee same spilit? No savvy?'[3] The shopkeeper did not savvy.

There is no doubt that Kipling was really frightened by the Chinese potential, and even allowing something for would-be humour, something for his intended readership, his attitude to the Chinese is beastly. On an excursion to Canton, looking at an exquisitely embroidered petticoat, he said to the Professor,

> 'Now I understand why the civilised European of Irish extraction kills the Chinaman in America. It is justifiable to kill him. It would be quite right to wipe the city of Canton off the face of the earth, and to exterminate all the people who ran away from the shelling. The Chinaman ought not to count . . . because they are unlike any people I ever met before. Look at their faces. They despise us, and they aren't a bit afraid of us either . . . The time is coming when there will be no European gentlemen – nothing but yellow people with black hearts.'
> from From Sea to Sea

In Hong Kong, Kipling and the Professor went brothel-crawling 'from a genuine desire to see what they call life with a Capital Hell'. They finally fetched up at a

'Hong Kong – with five million tons of coal, five miles of shipping, docks, wharves . . . forty million pounds of trade, and the nicest picnic-parties that you ever did see.' (From Sea to Sea, *let. 9*)

house Kipling calls Corinthian Kate's, where a girl with the fear of death on her took Kipling for a doctor, and told him nightmares and lies until dawn.

> 'I say, Doctor, did you ever know Cora Pearl?'
> 'Knew *of* her.' I wondered whether she was going to walk round the room to all eternity with her eyes glaring at the ceiling and her hands twisting and untwisting one within the other.
> 'Well,' she began in an impressive whisper, 'it was young Duval shot himself on her mat, and made a bloody mess there. I mean real bloody. You don't carry a pistol, Doctor? Savile did. You didn't know Savile. He was my husband in the States. But I'm English, pure English. That's what I am. Let's have a bottle of wine . . .' and on and on till she fell asleep, her mouth twitching, her body shivering. 'I had fancied that the house had nothing sadder to show me than her face. Here was I wrong.' At dawn Corinthian Kate woke up reeling drunk with her 'companion', swore 'in a thick, sodden voice such as I have never yet heard a man swear . . . The companion collapsed shivering on one of the couches, and Kate swayed to and fro and cursed God and man and earth and heaven with puffed lips. If Alma-Tadema could have painted her, – an arrangement in white, black hair, flashing eyes, and bare feet, – we should have seen the true likeness of the Eternal Priestess of Humanity.'

These Hong Kong horrors are Kipling's best brothel reportages. They are to be found in Letter VIII of *From Sea to Sea*.

On the P & O steamer *Ancona*, Kipling and the Hills left the disturbing Chinese, and, after a seasick voyage, they reached Japan, where the natives existed only to delight the Western tourist and there need be no fears for the Empire.

> The rickshaw shot me into the *Mikado*, First Act. I lay back on the velvet cushions and grinned luxuriously at Pitti-Sing, with her sash, and three giant hair-pins in her blue-black hair, and three-inch clogs on her feet . . . her laugh, the laugh of a lady, was my welcome to Japan. Can the people help laughing? I think not. You see, they have such thousands of children in their streets that the elders must perforce be young lest the

babes should grieve. Nagasaki is inhabited entirely by children ... A four-foot child walks with a three-foot child who is holding the hand of a two-foot child, who carries on her back a one-foot child who – but you will not believe me if I say that the scale runs down to six-inch little Jap dolls such as they used to sell in the Burlington Arcade.

from From Sea to Sea

Kipling was enraptured by this 'land of Little Children, where the Babies are the Kings', as he called it, enraptured by its people and its food, its architecture and its architects. The only visual flaw (as, again, Lockwood's son could not but perceive) was his own presence there:

'You must take off your boots,' said Y-Tokei. I assure you there is no dignity in sitting on the steps of a tea-house and struggling with muddy boots ... Take at least one pair of beautiful socks with you when you come this way. Get them of embroidered *sambhur* skin, of silk, if you like, but do not stand, as I did, in cheap striped brown things with a darn at the heel, and try to talk to a tea-girl.

from From Sea to Sea

Below: Kipling does not seem to have been aware of the tea-ceremony as such, but he noticed with surprise that though the tea-house system of the Japanese filled him with pleasure, this was 'a pleasure that I could not fully comprehend'. (From Sea to Sea, let. 14)

Opposite: 'We ... are going to Kobé by way of the Inland Sea ... Messrs. Cook and Son charge about one hundred rupees extra for the run ... The tourists say "Oh my!" at thirty-second intervals.' (From Sea to Sea, let. 12)

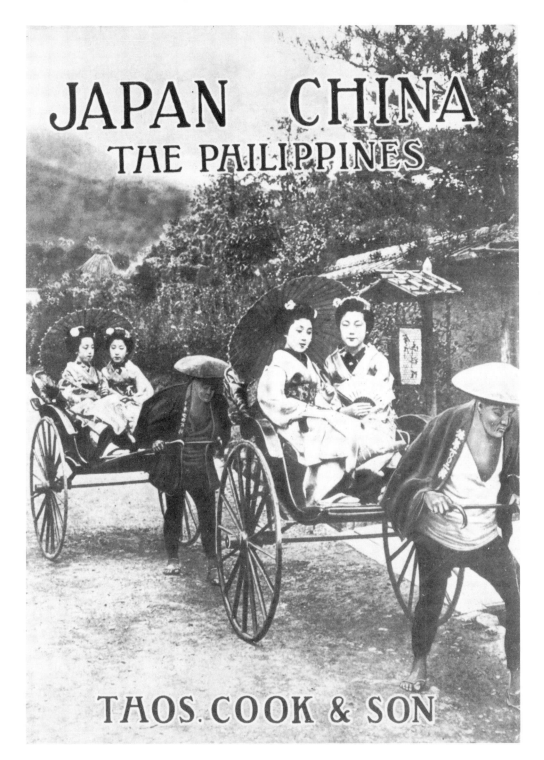

The food however, was beautiful – 'a red lacquered bowlful of fish boiled in brine, and sea-anemones . . . A paper-napkin tied with gold thread enclosed our chopsticks; and in a little flat saucer lay a smoked crayfish'.[4] The temples of Nikko were beautiful as even Kipling's facetious description makes plain; but he left them early to return to Tokyo and study the modern side of Japan: 'this place annoys me because I do not understand it.'[5]

The Japanese Army restored his good humour; one company he saw on parade even reminded him of our own Gurkhas:

> It was an unChristian thought, but I would have given a good deal to see that company being blooded on an equal number of Our native infantry – just to know how they would work. If they have pluck, and there is not much in their past record to show that they have not, they ought to be first-class enemies. Under British officers . . . they should be as good as any troops recruited east of Suez.
> from *From Sea to Sea*

But Japan is not our enemy or likely to be. Certainly, her people understand beauty as we do not, but –

> Mercifully she has been denied the last touch of firmness in her character which would enable her to play with the whole round world. We possess that – We, the nation of the glass flower-shade, the pink worsted mat, the red and green china puppy dog, and the poisonous Brussels carpet. It is our compensation.
> from *From Sea to Sea*

Yet Japan and the Japanese were visibly and rapidly changing. 'Civilisation was eating into them', and Kipling prophesied that it would bankrupt them, both financially and aesthetically.

Four years later he came back to Japan on another round-the-world trip, this time from west to east, and on his honeymoon. In Yokohama he went to the bank one morning to draw some money, and the Manager urged him to take still more. Well, may be, said Kipling, he'd come back that afternoon and do so, but by the afternoon the parent bank in America had gone bust, and the young Kiplings, only three months married and with a child on the way, were ruined. There was nothing for it, but to beg Thomas Cook for a refund on their tickets, and take a boat back to America.

CHAPTER FIVE

KIPLING IN EUROPE

Yes, I have sighed for London Town,
  And I have got it now:
And half of it is fog and filth,
  And half of it is row.

from *'In Partibus'*

F course Europe – Belait – was Home to all Anglo-Indians, though it was a long time before Rudyard Kipling was at home there. London he had first known when he came for holidays from the House of Desolation at Southsea to The Grange, the Burne-Joneses' house in Fulham. The openwork iron bell-pull on their gate let him in to 'all felicity'; eventually he begged it for his own house 'in the hope that other children might also feel happy when they rang it'.[1]

When at last his mother came back and released him from Southsea for ever, she took lodgings for some weeks in the Brompton Road and gave the children season tickets for the South Kensington Museum. There Ruddy revelled in the treasures and became convinced that 'books and pictures were among the most important affairs in the world',[2] a conviction which must have been reinforced by his sojourns with the Burne-Joneses and their company, remembering the day when Uncle Topsy – William Morris – had creaked to and fro on the nursery rocking-horse while he intoned the Saga of Burnt Njal; by the literary, artistic ladies near Addison Road to whom Alice confided Ruddy when she had to go back to India; and by his Headmaster and his 'aesthetic' friend Beresford/M'Turk.

So when Kipling went to India, he certainly regarded himself (as Carrington says) as a progressive, a rebel, a liberal, aesthetic, decadent pessimist. (Surely this was part of the reason why they did not take to him in the Club at Lahore.) He probably did not realize, when he first came back, how much London literary society had changed or how much India and his world-wide journey had changed him. His two London years, from 1889 to 1891, were confused and unhappy.

His amatory life at that time was both serious and wavering, as Chapter Six will show. And in the literary capital of the world he got off on the wrong foot, which was to influence his reputation for the rest of his life, and beyond it.

From the Railway Books in particular, a certain *réclame* had preceded Kipling from India. A few people – it was soon to be many more – were aware of *Plain Tales* and *Departmental Ditties*. English editions of these quickly appeared, and Rudyard readily wrote new poems for any editor who wanted them. Almost every recent poem in *Barrack-Room Ballads* of 1892 had been published already in an English magazine, and many in American magazines too.

This new work that Kipling was producing so prolifically struck chords of patriotic pride which had not been twanged for a very long time – but not among the cream of the literary profession. It was to be Kipling's misfortune that his work was of immediate appeal to the middle-brow literary world and accessible to the popular reading public. It was the literati who did not know what to make of it, and disliked it.

Certainly Kipling would never have admitted to wanting praise from Oscar Wilde who had said that:

> As one turns over the pages of his *Plain Tales from the Hills*, one feels as if one were seated under a palm tree reading life by superb flashes of vulgarity. From the point of view of literature Mr. Kipling is a man of talent who drops his aspirates. From the point of view of life he is a reporter who knows vulgarity better than anyone has ever known it . . . our best authority on the second-rate.[3]

India had turned Kipling against fashionable decadence. Already in 1887 he had parodied poor Ernest Dowson in the *Gazette*. How many of his readers would have known that 'Blue Roses' was a skit, or, indeed, what people he was savaging in the verses he sent the *Gazette* a few weeks after his arrival in London?

mr Rudyard Kipling

But I consort with long-haired things
   In velvet collar-rolls,
Who talk about the Aims of Art,
   And 'theories' and 'goals',
And moo and coo with womenfolk
   About their blessed souls . . .

Max Beerbohm later devoted a share of his small but enchanting talent to the destruction of Kipling. Kipling wisely did not answer back. But he cared. He could not but have known that the editors and critics who accepted him so enthusiastically – W. E. Henley, Rider Haggard, Herbert Stephen – were, in literary terms, second-rank.

On 14 May, 1898, The School Budget of Horsmonden School, Kent, printed Kipling's humorous refusal to contribute. The next number, of 28 May, contained this cartoon by Max Beerbohm.

That Kipling was poor in London turned out to be enriching. Most of his savings had gone on his travels and on the oriental knick-knacks with which he adorned his lodgings in Villiers Street, just behind Charing Cross.

> My rooms were above an establishment of Harris the Sausage King who, for tuppence, gave as much sausage and mash as would carry one from breakfast to dinner when one dined with nice people who did not eat sausage for a living . . . and fourpence, which included a pewter of beer or porter, was the price of admission to Gatti's.[4]

For, to his great good fortune, Gatti's famous music hall was opposite Embankment Chambers where he lodged. From his window he could watch the artistes arriving in cabs from their latest evening engagement, dashing off in cabs to the next one. 'The smoke, the roar, and the good fellowship of relaxed humanity at Gatti's were, Kipling said, powerfully influential on the *Barrack-Room Ballads*. He even wrote one song himself which was accepted for the Hall. The chorus ran:

> . . . don't try for things that are out of your reach,
> And that's what the Girl told the Soldier.
> Soldier! Soldier!
> An' that's what the Girl told the Soldier.

One needs the tune – but then, we need the tunes to a great many of Kipling's verses. Some, no doubt, would come from the Halls, some from the Methodist hymnal, some from the nursery. Certainly it is not only Kipling's not very fetching music-hall ditty but many of the *Barrack-Room Ballads*, and other poems too, that would be richer if we could know which were the tunes that were ringing in Kipling's ears as he wrote them.

One must always look at Kipling's full titles. *Barrack-Room Ballads and Other Verses* was first published in London in March 1892, and the section called 'Barrack-Room Ballads' took up only about a third of the book. Most of Kipling's best soldier poems are here. Of those already mentioned in this book, *Barrack-Room Ballads* included 'Danny Deever', 'Tommy', 'Gunga Din', 'Loot', and several more. In the rest of the book are many good verses and several mediocre ones, as in all Kipling's collections of verses or stories: among those mentioned here are 'The Ballad of East and West' and 'The English Flag'. Lord Birkenhead says of the *Barrack-Room Ballads* as they originally appeared in W. E. Henley's *Scots Observer*, that they fell upon a 'shocked but enraptured public'. The adjectives are well chosen, but probably one should take each as applying to a different public, the enraptured popular taste which found in Kipling an entirely acceptable poet, but the serious poetry-reading public shocked by this entirely new combination of what was felt to be simultaneously quality and vulgarity. The shock has persisted, and from it there has not yet emerged a satisfactory serious critique for Kipling's verse.

In prose, Kipling was writing superbly. The stories of *Life's Handicap* of 1891 and of *Many Inventions* of 1893 had almost all appeared in both English and American periodicals before being collected into these books. Among them were some of his finest stories about India – the droll 'Namgay Doola', the tragic 'Without Benefit of Clergy', the horror story 'At the End of the Passage' in the earlier volume, and in the later, 'In the Rukh', which was the Mowgli story that preceded *The Jungle Books*; and '"Love-o'-Women"'. There also appeared in *Many Inventions*, as in subsequent collections, a very few stories based on London, though London was never to be a major source of inspiration to Kipling. There was the farce, '"Brugglesmith"' of 1891, in which the humiliated Narrator trundles a drunk, tied to a hand-cart, across London. More interesting is 'The Record of Bedalia Heronsfoot', written in 1890, one of the London slum stories fashionable at the period (young John Buchan wrote a couple for the *Yellow Book*!) but marred by the sentimentality under the effectively coarse realism.

He was delighted to be asked to join the Savile Club, and cannot have been displeased to receive an extraordinary tribute in *The Times*, which on 25 March 1890 gave a full leading article to his work. This referred to his stories about both Simla and 'the station', and about 'that most unfortunate result of our settlement in India, the Eurasian', called him 'the discoverer, as far as India is concerned, of "Tommy Atkins" as a hero of popular romance', but regretted that his style was not yet as polished as that of Guy de Maupassant. This was accolade indeed! Invitations to dinner poured in, but his social manner was still ungracious and he treated too many of his would-be hosts with scant courtesy. Moreover, on the financial side, despite his extraordinary success, not all was cakes and ale. He had tried to market his own work but made bad bargains, until Sir Walter Besant introduced him to A. P. Watt, who doubled his income in three months and whose firm remained his literary agents for the rest of his life.

But no agent could then protect an author from barefaced pirating in the United States where works were reprinted with no payment of copyright fees. Kipling's public fury with the American firm Harper's was not soothed by a letter in the *Athenaeum* from the novelists Walter Besant, Thomas Hardy, and Walter Black, defending Harper's. Kipling exploded in 'The Rhyme of the Three Captains', a swashbuckling diatribe of a poem, also published in the *Athenaeum*, in which the offending authors, identified by pun – 'the bezant is hard, ay, and black' – were sending whimpering flags of surrender to the pirate fleet, with Kipling as the fearless skipper of a lone, brave privateer.

The culmination of Kipling's London miseries was the poor reception given in 1891 to his first novel, *The Light that Failed*, published in New York with a happy ending and in London with a sad one. Both were ready by November 1890, and it is said that Kipling's final choice of the sad ending was due to his old love, Flo Garrard, failing to make a hoped-for response to the happy one.

Kipling believed that if literary London had known more of French literature his novel's reception would have been warmer, and he was probably right. The novel's themes, a man's obsession for a woman unsuited to him, the right weight to be given to art, good and bad, in men and women's lives, were themes more common in

French than in English novels. Literary London had taken its current fashion of languid decadence from a limited range of French writers, of whom Baudelaire, Verlaine, and Rimbaud, were prepotent. The harsher realism typified by, say, Zola, when they recognized it in Kipling, they tended to dismiss with a glancing reference to Pierre Loti, though Maupassant would have been more to the point, or, more classically, Balzac.

But the French literati did recognize Kipling's genius, and have always rated *The Light that Failed* and much of the other work more highly than the English did. And when, some years later, André Maurois translated 'If', it was not to mock at it but to round out his affectionate sketches of the typically English officer in his book *Les Silences du Colonel Bramble*:

> Si tu peux rencontrer Triomphe après Défaite
> Et recevoir ces deux menteurs d'un même front,
> Si tu peux conserver ton courage et ta tête
>   Quand tous les autres les perdront,
> Alors les Rois, les Dieux, la Chance et la Victoire,
> Seront à tout jamais tes esclaves soumis,
> Et, ce qui vaut mieux que les Rois et la Gloire,
>   Tu seras un homme, mon fils.

The respect of the French was gratifying to Kipling, for he had loved their country since boyhood. When he was twelve, Lockwood had been sent from India to take charge of the Indian exhibits in the 1878 Paris Exhibition and had taken young Rudyard to Paris with him. There he saw to it that Rudyard learned to speak and read French, and then let him roam the city freely. This experience was, Kipling said later, an education in itself, and set his life-long love for France. For myself, he wrote:

> I hold it in truth with him who sung
> Unpublished melodies,
> Who wakes in Paris, being young,
> O' summer, wakes in Paradise.

To this poor little verse, Kipling gives no provenance.

At the start of the disappointing London years, Kipling took himself off to France again to see the 1889 Exhibition in Paris. Presumably it was then that he also saw some village which served for Vitry-sur-Marne of the painting school in *The Light that Failed*. In Paris, he stayed 'at a small hotel in the Batignolles, dominated by a fat elderly landlady who brought me unequalled *café au lait* in big bowls'.[5] Years later, visiting war-torn France in 1915, this landlady came back to his mind as a symbol of indomitable France, a precursor of the Mother Courage of Brecht who so much admired Kipling's work:

> I saw descendants of my old landlady of the Batignolles – slippered, untidy, voluble –
> dealing out bowls of soup to the *poilus*, or driving cows in ploughs not too far behind the

Lockwood Kipling's success with the Pavilion of the Prince of Wales's Indian collection at the Paris Exhibition of 1878 (shown here) led to his supervising the decoration of the Durbar Room at Osborne for Queen Victoria.

shells. That is why I desire a colossal statue on one of the Seine bridges to that enduring woman who also stood fast and said: *'Faut pas s'en faire'*.   from *Souvenirs of France*

After that war, Kipling came to know France well: 'the brick bulk of Albi Cathedral seen against the moon', and the enrichment of light that the weather's etching had added to the glass of Chartres; the remote Canigou mountain in the eastern Pyrenees, and Le Levandou when it was still an unexploited fishing village. Kipling had been devoted to motor-cars ever since motor-cars first appeared on the roads, had owned them from his first steam-driven 'Locomobile' of 1900 to the enormous Rolls-Royce still standing in the garage at his Sussex home. He was already touring France by motor, when motor-cars, of the huge horse-power of those days, had to be lowered into, and hoisted out of, the holds of the Channel ferries by crane.

> Once again the Steamer at Calais – the tackles
> Easing the car-trays on to the quay. Release her!
> Sign – refill, and let me away with my horses.
> (Seventy Thundering Horses!)
> Slow through the traffic, my horses! it is enough – it is France!

Whether the throat-closing brick-fields by Lille, or her pavés
Endlessly ending in rain between beet and tobacco;
Or that wind we shave by – the brutal North-Easter,
Rasping the newly dunged Somme.
(Into your collars, my horses!) It is enough – it is France . . .

Whether the broken, honey-hued, honey-combed limestone,
Cream under white-hot sun; the rosemary bee-bloom
Sleepily noisy at noon and, somewhere to Southward,
Sleepily noisy, the Sea.
(Yes, it is warm here, my horses!) It is enough – it is France! . . .

from 'Song of Seventy Horses'

Kipling never learned to drive, was always chauffeur-driven, though the presence of the chauffeur is usually concealed, as it is in 'They'. But it is 'my Mr. Leggatt', the chauffeur who does the driving in the enchanting story of 1924, 'The Bull that Thought', which opens with a speed trial along RN113, a stretch of arrow-straight road in Provence, from Salon to St Martin-de-Crau, '. . . a road so mathematically straight, so barometrically level, that it ranks amongst the world's measured miles . . . thirty kilometres as near as might be; and twenty-two of them without even a level-crossing.'

This story of Apis, the wicked witty fighting bull from the Camargue, is one of the very best of Kipling's animal stories, Apis remaining always just within the mental capacity of a fighting bull; though some critics have seen deeper meanings. The only other Provençal story, 'The Miracle of St. Jubanus' of 1930, is one of these in which someone's humiliation sends everyone else into hoots of healthy laughter.

Other than France, nothing in modern Europe roused Kipling's Daemon, not even Italy, where he visited the Dufferins in 1890, on a trip he hoped would avert the impending breakdown to which the strains of his London life were bringing him. Yet two lines from a poem he wrote in 1911 are an evocative recall of the Italian Mediterranean. The Roman centurion who wants to stay in Britain is tracing his comrades' journey home:

You'll take the old Aurelian Road through shore-descending pines
Where, blue as any peacock's neck, the Tyrrhene Ocean shines . . .

from 'The Roman Centurion's Song'

Seemingly, Kipling preferred Italy distilled through other men's work: through Horace, through Dante, and through Robert Browning whom he so often echoed.

But in one respect Europe as a whole fired Kipling, and this, though he was no Christian believer himself, was Europe as Christendom. There is that excellent thirteenth-century story 'The Eye of Allah' of 1926, set in a cosmopolitan English monastery, whose Abbot is entertaining guests: the physician, Roger of Salerno, Roger Bacon from Oxford, and his own wayward artist-monk John of Burgos, just

F. Matania, who illustrated 'The Eye of Allah' for the Strand *magazine in September 1926, was perhaps the best magazine artist of his period, specializing, after the war, in the richly historical.*

back from Spain with a red cornelian necklace for the Abbot's poor sick lady, raw colours to grind for the Sub-Cantor who colours in the manuscripts, and for himself a glass of 'art optic' from the clever Moors which has enabled him to see in a drop of water his models for the devils that entered the Gadarene Swine, for his illuminated manuscript of St Luke's Gospel:

> Some devils were mere lumps, with lobes and protuberances – a hint of a fiend's face peering through jelly-like walls. And there was a family of impatient, globular devillings who had burst open the belly of their smirking parent, and were revolving desperately toward their prey. Others patterned themselves into rods, chains, and ladders, single or conjoined, round the throat and jaws of a shrieking sow, from whose ear emerged the lashing, glassy tail of a devil that had made good his refuge.

The watchers were enthralled. They were men of a quality to perceive the service that this invention could offer not only to art but to medicine, to what was not yet called science. But what the Abbot, wise in his own time, knew was that the hour had not yet come. 'In the eyes of Mother Church, we have seen more than is permitted to man . . . You can hear the faggots crackle!' The ending is harsh but, for the thirteenth century, the right one.

Kipling wrote other stories and poems on medieval Christendom, all good, and even one poem, supposedly by Chaucer as it might have been copied out by a scribe from Antwerp:

> Noontide repayeth never morning-bliss –
>   Sith noon to morn is incomparable;
> And, so it be our dawning goth amiss,
>   None other after-hour serveth well,
> Ah Jesu-Moder, pitie my oe paine –
>   Daiespringe mishandeelt cometh nat agayne!

from 'Dayspring Mishandled'

This version, all but the last two lines 'modernized', reads aloud impeccably in Chaucerian English, but it has one oddity: its key-word, 'dayspring' was used by Chaucer's contemporary, John Gower, but not by Chaucer himself.

Two important Christian stories were set at an earlier date. One, 'The Church that was at Antioch' of 1929, is about the Apostles Peter and Paul, and the young Roman police officer, killed while trying to protect the troublesome Christians who are determined to hold, as you could say, their demos: for Kipling, the Roman and the British Empires reflected each other. The other, 'The Manner of Men' of 1930, is about Paul's journey to Rome and the Malta shipwreck, told by the young Spanish captain of the ship.

In his last years, Kipling was fascinated by St Paul. Perhaps he saw the duty of being all things to all men that revelation had laid upon St Paul reflected in the subservience that the artist must endure when his Daemon takes hold of him. Something of this kind he expressed in 'At His Execution' of 1932, one of his better poems, one of his most European:

> I am made all things to all men –
>   In City or Wilderness
>   Praising the crafts they profess
> That some may be drawn by the Lord –
> By any means to my Lord! . . .
>
> I was made all things to all men,
> But now my course is done –
> And now is my reward . . .
> Ah, Christ, when I stand at Thy Throne
> With those I have drawn to the Lord,
> Restore me my self again!

CHAPTER SIX

LE PAYS DE TENDRE: I
MEN AND WOMEN

For a man he must go with a woman, which women don't understand –
Or the sort that say they can see it they aren't the marrying brand . . .

from 'The "Mary Gloster"'

O our post-Freudian age, it must appear surprising that
Rudyard Kipling did not blame someone and probably his
mother for his desertion at Southsea. Apparently he did not,
but rather adored his mother for taking him away from that House
of Desolation and making him happy again. From that time until
his marriage, the Family Square of the Pater, the Mother, Trix,
and Ruddy (the meaning of Square here included the Freemasonry
sense of 'being on the Square', belonging to the Craft) was to provide Ruddy with
his bulwark and, in distress, his comfort as well as constructive literary criticism
and often the very material his art, at that moment, needed.

Not only his own immediate family but his larger group of aunts and uncles and
cousins were reliable friends and supports to Ruddy. Rudyard's favourite aunt was
Georgie Burne-Jones; and her children, Philip and Margaret (or 'Wop') were his
best-loved cousins until Margaret married J. W. Mackail, a classicist of liberal and,
to Rudyard, unsympathetic views. When Rudyard came back to London, Philip
Burne-Jones and Ambo Poynter were to be for a time his best friends in his own
generation, though among the cousins it was to be Stanley Baldwin who eventually
came closest to him; but in the last years of his life. Rudyard found even Stanley's
views too liberal to stomach, and nearer, he would mutter gloomily, to Socialism
than to true Conservatism.

It was in the Burne-Jones home in Fulham, on holiday from Southsea, that the
child Ruddy found a love that would stay with him all his life when, in the evenings,
he and his cousins would 'hang over the stairs and listen to the loveliest sound in the
world – deep-voiced men laughing together over dinner'.[1]

A love for the company of men (hopefully deep-voiced), in a congenial environ-
ment was one that always remained with Kipling. The Punjab Club at Lahore, the
'little Savile', as he called it, the smoking-rooms of liners, the Masonic Lodges, and
the several other clubs he eventually belonged to, including, from 1897 and
surprisingly early, the Athenaeum: all such gatherings had to be, mostly still have

Edward Burne-Jones's painting of his wife and children. Philip was a painter of limited quality; he never married, and died in 1926. Margaret, lovely and witty, was the mother of the writers Angela Thirkell and Denis Mackail.

to be, composed exclusively of men. Once only, Kipling met a woman whom he tried to treat as if she were a man. This was Mary Kingsley, the African explorer, 'the bravest woman in all my knowledge', he said of her, though he could not have known this when he first met her, for she was then tied to her ailing parents and had not been to Africa. This, according to the memory of his old age, had been at tea with the 'Dear Ladies' around 1890. They had walked towards their homes together, talking 'of West African cannibals and the like. At last, the world forgetting, I said: "Come up to my rooms and we'll talk it out there." She agreed, as a man would, then suddenly remembering said: "Oh, I forgot I was a woman. 'Fraid I mustn't."[2]

When Rudyard was a young man, non-sexual friendships with women, conducted as freely as friendships with men, were almost impossible. The relationships a man like Rudyard could have with women began with reverence, such as a man owed his mother. In the sexual field there could be covert sexual relationships, flirtations, serious approaches to marriage, and infatuations.

Kipling came early to the last, as he did to most manifestations of maturity. Already at the age of twelve when he first went to Westward Ho! he had the makings of a moustache, and by his last term he was so hairy that he was ordered to buy and use a razor. The development of facial and, presumably, body hair in boys is usually taken as a sign of sexual ripening, and in Rudyard's case it probably was.

His first love would seem to have been for Florence – Flo – Garrard, and infatuation is a right word for it. Rudyard met and fell for Flo when he was only fourteen-and-a-half. He had gone down to Mrs Holloway's at Southsea to fetch Trix away for the holidays: strange that he could go there, strange that Trix was still there, three years after her brother's reported agonies in that House of Desolation. In 1880 Flo Garrard was boarding there, another child whose parents were abroad. Carrington, the first biographer to speak of Flo, describes her:

> She was a little older than Rudyard, a straight slender girl with a beautiful ivory-pale face and a cloud of dark hair, but badly brought up in continental hotels and very ill-educated. With a shrewd sophisticated manner, she was self-centred and elusive, lacking in sympathy and affection.[3]

Where and how Flo and Rudyard would meet is not now known, or how far she was known to his family. Before he went off to India in 1882, he had persuaded her to agree to something he thought of as an engagement, but the fact that some of his earliest Indian stories are about young men who arrive in India with secret attachments back Home to hamper their Indian commitments, need not be taken as closely relevant to Flo. In the summer of 1884, Flo wrote to Rudyard, breaking the engagement, such as it was.

Five years later in London Rudyard met Flo again, and, it appears, most distressfully for him. Flo had been training at the Slade School of Art, and is generally believed to have been the model for Maisie in Kipling's novel *The Light that Failed* of 1890, the selfish, heartless girl who put her art, which was not very good, before the love of the devoted hero; though most readers of the novel are more intrigued by the nameless, shadowy, red-haired girl who loved the hero truly.

Rudyard would seem in his own mind to have cast Flo in the role of his Manon Lescaut. Prévost's novel about the heartless girl turned courtesan who dies, disgraced and desolate, in the arms of her faithful first lover, had worked on Rudyard since he was caught by a picture of Manon's death which he saw in Paris when he was twelve; and he himself said that *The Light that Failed* was 'a sort of inverted, metagrobolised phantasmagoria based on *Manon*'.

Lockwood's plaque of young Dick and Maisie with goat and pistol for the Outward Bound edition of The Light that Failed. *Maisie's original, Flo Garrard, had kept a goat at Auntie Rosa's.*

Martin Fido, in his book on Kipling, intimates that Kipling met Flo in 1900; according to Lord Birkenhead, Mrs Fleming – Trix – told him that Rudyard had said to her in 1902 that Flo had died three months earlier of 'neglected lungs'. What, if any, continuing relationship there had been must remain, for the time being, one of the many shadowy patches.

But though Flo Garrard had cut deep before Rudyard went to India, she had not held him back from other amatory forays during the Indian years. Flirtation was a way of life there, and Kipling flirted, and especially in the Hill-stations during his hot-weather leaves. Adultery was a way of life there too, as many of Kipling's Indian stories make cynically plain, but there is no reason to suppose that he himself indulged in it. When he did become seriously fascinated by a married woman, the

American Ted Hill at Allahabad, this may well have been because she had the kind of boyishness that was later to attract him in Mary Kingsley. The 'tomboy type' appealed strongly to many men at that time, perhaps because unthreatening and the antithesis of the woman whom Kipling in 1897 was to call 'The Vampire' – whence our word '*vamp*':

> A fool there was and he made his prayer
> (Even as you and I!)
> To a rag and a bone and a hank of hair
> (We called her the woman who did not care)
> But the fool he called her his lady fair –
> (Even as you and I!) . . .

> from 'The Vampire'

Kipling's friendship with Ted Hill was, however, equally with her husband.

In India, young Kipling's sexual needs had not gone unfulfilled. He could not put aside his higher flights in writing, he wrote to his friend Kay Robinson in Allahabad, 'any more than I/you can put aside the occasional woman which is good for health and the softening of ferocious manners'.[4] There may have been some boyish boastfulness there, but the ease with which Kipling writes about available Indian women suggests knowledge, not yearning. These women were the intelligent and attractive Indian prostitutes of whom he wrote with so much more grace than he did of Englishwomen. The loveliest of these fictional girls was certainly Lalun of the story 'On the City Wall' who had been variously compared:

> . . . to the Moon, the Dil Sagar Lake, a spotted quail, a gazelle, the Sun on the Desert of Kutch, the Dawn, the Stars, and the young bamboo. These comparisons imply that she is beautiful exceedingly according to the native standards, which are practically the same as those of the West.

Then there were Janoo and Azizun, two Kashmiri 'Ladies of the City', sensible girls who lived 'In the House of Suddhoo' (the story's title) and called in the Narrator to pronounce on some questionable magic; 'Azizun', we are told, 'has since married a medical student from the North-West and has settled down to a most respectable life'. Such girls as these were several cuts above the bazaar prostitutes who, to Kipling's loudly expressed distress, spread venereal disease so disastrously among the British soldiers. 'The most ancient profession in the world', as he called it, he saw in its higher reaches as stocked by decent honourable girls, fulfilling a necessary function. He had not perceived that to sustain this attitude, the girls of this trade needed, for him, to be Indians.

If Kipling's own account is to be trusted, the first prostitute he met who was not an Indian woman was the soldier's widow of the red-light district in Calcutta.

> She is a rather pretty, slightly-made Eurasian, and whatever shame she may have owned she has long since cast behind her. A shapeless Burmo-native trot . . . calls Mrs D–

Two pretty girls of what Kipling called 'the Ancient Profession', and of such status that they might well 'with braided hair, await the Maharajah's coming'. (Naulahka)

'Mem-Sahib'. The word jars unspeakably. Her life is a matter between herself and her Maker, but in that she – the widow of a soldier of the Queen – has stooped to this common foulness in the face of the city, she has offended against the white race.

It was almost incidental to this iniquity that Mrs D— had been accused of murdering her husband by poisoning his drinking water.

'And – ah – *did* you?'
''Twasn't proved,' says Mrs D— with a laugh, a pleasant lady-like laugh.

Kipling had written that account for the *Pioneer* in 1888. In 1893, he published his superb story, '"Love-o'-Women"'. It is about a gentleman-ranker who has locomotor ataxy – and, the doctor says to Mulvaney, who recounts it to the Narrator, 'ut comes from bein' called Love-o'-Women'. The regiment returns from its latest engagement on the Frontier to Peshawar, Love-o'-Women carried in a dooli, a litter, for he can no longer walk. On the way into town they come to a little house: 'Faith, at long eye-range it did not take me a wink to see fwhat kind av house ut was.' The woman who had ridden out to meet the regiment was standing on the verandah. And Love-o'-Women, whom they had said would never walk again, swung himself out of the dooli and on to his feet, and walked up to her:

> The woman stud in the verandah. She'd been a beauty too, though her eyes was sunk in her head, an' she looked Love-o'-Women up and down terrible. 'An',' she sez, kicking back the tail av her habit, – 'An',' she sez, 'fwhat are you doin' *here*, married man? . . . Fwhat do you do here?' she sez, an' her voice wint up. 'Twas like bells tollin' before. 'Time was whin you were quick enough wid your words – you that talked me down to hell. Are ye dumb now?' An' Love-o'-Women got his tongue, an' sez simple, like a little child, 'May I come in?' he sez.
>
> 'The house is open day an' night,' she sez, wid a laugh . . . 'An' now?' she sez, lookin' at him; an' the red paint stud alone on the white av her face like a bull's eye on a target.
>
> He lifted up his eyes, slow an' very slow, an' he looked at her long an' very long, an' he tuk his spache betune his teeth with a wrench that shuk him.
>
> 'I'm dyin', Aigypt – dyin',' he sez. Ay, those were his words, for I remimber the name he called her. He was turnin' the death-colour, but his eyes niver rowled. They were set – set on her. Widout word or warnin' she opened her arms full stretch, an' 'Here!' she sez. (Oh, fwhat a golden mericle av a voice ut was!) 'Die here!' she sez; an' Love-o'-Women dhropped forward, an' she hild him up, for she was a fine big woman.
>
> I had no time to turn, bekaze that minut I heard the sowl quit him – tore out in the death-rattle – an' she laid him back in a long chair, an' she sez to me, 'Misther soldier,' she sez, 'will ye not wait an' talk to wan av the girls? This sun's too much for him.'

The story is imperfectly constructed. There is too much and too various matter in it before it comes to its climax in the verandah of the brothel, but that climax is so excellent that we soon forget the load of preliminary detail it is dragging behind it. To use a narrator – in this case, the secondary narrator, Mulvaney – to tell a story that entails repeating words he could have only imperfectly understood is a trick that can easily lose credibility. Kipling carries it off perfectly here, as he did many years later in 'A Madonna of the Trenches' (*see pages 96-7*). More, in '"Love-o'-Women"' Kipling's art has come to terms with the fact that white women may choose – or need – to become prostitutes. His view of the trade is no longer that of the brash young man who can use the skilled Indian women with no qualms on his side and the assumption of none on theirs.

That art was always more responsive to the gutter than to the stars and when it came to writing about innocent love, Kipling's pen was uncertain. His model story of innocence, so far as young men are concerned, is 'The Brushwood Boy' of 1895. Cottar, its hero, is clean-living and clean-thinking to the point of puerility. (All that is odd about him is the dreaming in which, from boyhood, he meets the girl who is to be his mate.) In India he runs after no woman, 'white *or* black', as the Major comments. His men are 'united in adoring' him. In action, he wins the DSO and his captaincy.

When he goes home on leave, he is marked down on the P & O boat by a woman who was clearly not quite-quite, for her name is Mrs Zuleika, an unEnglish name, a

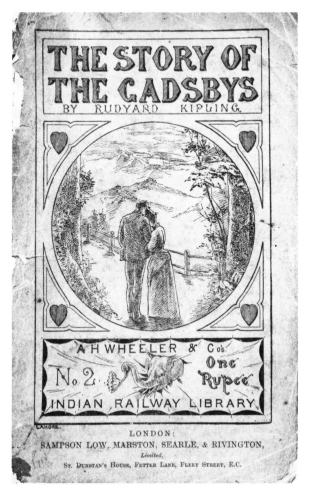

The Story of the Gadsbys (see page 94) *ends with a cynical poem called 'The Winners', whose moral is that 'Down to Gehenna or up to the Throne,/He travels the fastest who travels alone.'*

name redolent of Eastern wiles, perhaps even Eastern blood. (Kipling's naming is often meaningful and should never be taken for granted.) But Georgie Cottar simply doesn't know what Mrs Zuleika is after. When she speaks of his marrying some nice girl, he says, 'but there's heaps of time for marryin', an' all that sort of thing; ain't there?' So home he goes to the little country estate, where, like his soldiers, the servants, indoor and outdoor, all adore him. At last he climbs up to his old night nursery at bedtime. 'Then who should come to tuck him up for the night but the mother? And she sat down on the bed, and they talked for a long hour, as mother and son should, if there is to be any future for our Empire . . . so she blessed him and she kissed him on the mouth, which is not always a mother's property.'

On innocent young English girls in love, Kipling tends to hold back, and usually to keep a sting for the tail. In 'False Dawn', for instance he describes a girl who has just been proposed to by the man she loves:

> I saw that look on her face which only comes once or twice in a lifetime – when a woman is perfectly happy and the air is full of trumpets and gorgeously-coloured fire, and the Earth turns into cloud because she loves and is loved.

But – and this is characteristic of Kipling's better writing about love in the middle classes – the glory must be wiped off the girl's face. In the dark confusion of the sandstorm that had enveloped the picnic party, the man had proposed to the wrong sister.

Kipling made another young English innocent in *The Story of the Gadsbys* of 1891, a long-short story of eight episodes told in dialogue, and not a nice story at all. Captain Gadsby is having an affair with Mrs Herriott and considering another one with Mrs Threegan. But he notices Mrs Threegan's daughter, Minnie, proposes to her, and at a dinner-party, where no public scene can be made, tells Mrs Herriott that it's all off. Marriage, and the hostages given to fortune, force on him a loss of the nerve essential to soldiering, 'I'm talking like a cur, I know; but I tell you that, for the past three months I've felt every hoof of the squadron in the small of my back every time that I've led.'

So Gadsby prepares to sell out and go home to wide estates and an eventual peerage, knowing that his friend will judge him a coward and that his wife 'will think a little bit the worse of him for the rest of her days'.

This *conte* or playlet is less than Kipling's best, but it offers an interesting sidelight on late-Victorian marriage customs, confirmed by some similar evidence from other authors. Minnie and Pip Gadsby have been married for a little while when she finds him one day in the stables examining Army saddles, his shirt sleeves rolled up, and she notices a scar on his arm: 'I've never seen it before. It runs all up the arm. What is it?' The inference must be that love-making between this married couple takes place in the dark, or clad, or both.

*   *   *

Apart from the traumatic meeting with Flo, nothing is known of Kipling's sex-life between his return to England in 1889 and his departure in 1891. His love-life in London was a mess. He had returned to England more or less engaged to Mrs Hill's younger sister, Caroline Taylor, but the engagement, such as it was, wilted and died – perhaps for religious reasons, perhaps because Rudyard had met Flo again? – and after Professor Hill's premature death in 1890 he made no amatory moves towards the widow. Moreover, after 1890 Caroline Balestier, a new challenge, had come determinedly upon the scene. But for the moment family affections and male friendships still held.

Rudyard's parents had Home leave from the early summer of 1890 until the late summer of 1891. His constant affection for good men friends, too, found abundant

Carrie

Left: The magnetic Wolcott Balestier who in 1888 set up his office in Dean's Yard, Westminster, and charmed literary London. His friends included Meredith, Hardy, Whistler, Gosse, and Henry James. Right: A 'carte-de-visite' photograph of Caroline Balestier, the elder of Wolcott's sisters and three years older than Rudyard; 'poor little concentrated Carrie', Henry James wrote of her to his brother William after Wolcott's funeral.

new outlets in the many friends he made in literary life, among them notably W. E. Henley, poet, man of letters, Editor of the *Scots Observer*, and Rider Haggard about whose work, with Kipling's, the litterateur J. K. Stephen wrote, in 1891, some wicked verses – which Kipling enjoyed. When, Stephen asked, would come the day

> When there stands a muzzled stripling,
> Mute, beside a muzzled bore:
> When the Rudyards cease from kipling
> And the Haggards ride no more?

One friendship Kipling made at that time fundamentally changed his life. This was with Wolcott Balestier, a young American who had come to London in 1888 as agent for a New York publisher, Lovell & Co. Introduced by the writer Edmund Gosse, the two young men found each other kindred spirits, and decided to write in harness an Anglo-American novel about India. They called it *The Naulahka, a Novel of East and West*. 'Naulakha' is the Hindi word for 900,000 rupees and is, incidentally, the name of a white marble pavilion in Lahore reputedly costing this sum; Naulakha is said to have been mis-spelt in the novel's title, but as the contemporary Murray's *Guide* comments, 'The spelling of Indian names is in a state of confusion. There are only three towns in India with a fixed spelling – Bombay, Calcutta, and Madras.'

It has been suggested that before Kipling left for the Antipodes, he had reached an understanding with Wolcott's sister Caroline. It is said too that when Alice Kipling first met Carrie in London, in 1890, she had commented, 'That woman is going to marry our Ruddy.' Some friends had thought that Rudyard might be looking to the younger, prettier Balestier girl, Josephine. But when, in late December 1891, he heard in Lahore that Wolcott had died in Dresden from typhoid fever, he dashed home, and on 18 January 1892, a week after his arrival in London, he married Carrie Balestier at All Souls', Langham Place. This was in the middle of a flu epidemic. Carrie's mother and sister were ill, and so were many of Rudyard's family and friends. His cousin, Ambo Poynter, gave away the bride, who was dressed in plain brown wool; Henry James, who at Carrie's call had gone to Dresden to succour the bereaved family, was best man; and William Heinemann was there and Edmund Gosse with his wife and son. That was all.

No one seems ever to have liked Carrie very much. Certainly Alice never did. Lockwood's view of Carrie was that she was 'a good man spoiled', and Henry James, who thought her capable but deplored the match, spoke of the 'almost manly nature of her emotion'. She looked after Rudyard, both his physical health and his financial affairs, with what even the loyal Carrington describes as 'an irksome particularity'. 'The marriage,' Carrington goes on, 'perhaps was more satisfactory on her side than on his.'[5] It was indeed a far cry from the witty vivacity of Rudyard's mother and the sensitive charm of his aunts, from that Belle Dame Sans Merci, Flo Garrard, lovely Lalun and her kind, the smart sophistication of the Simla salons, the tomboyish charm of Ted Hill and the fresh American friendliness of her sister, to this plain, heavy, parsimonious woman with no ounce of glamour, no response to romance, and none of the constructive capacity for literary criticism that Kipling's mother, as well as his father, had so valuably given him. It is said that Kipling believed this marriage to be Wolcott's deathbed wish.

We can hardly be surprised that Kipling wrote no more witty, cynical stories about middle-class adultery. For the most part, his heart's affections seem concentrated now on children and on animals. But there are still two aspects of his art that are worth mention in an adult context.

First, there are strange stories of adult infatuations, of which two stand out. One is the mysterious and incomprehensible 'Mrs. Bathurst'. Here Vickery, a warrant-officer in the Navy, a married man with a child and 'within eighteen months of his pension', has visited a cinematograph in Cape Town. There he saw a film of the Western Mail coming into Paddington and among the alighting passengers Mrs. Bathurst whom he had met in Auckland where she kept a small hotel. We are told that Vickery, or Click, as he was called, for his ill-fitting dentures, went to every showing of the film; we know he was sent up-country and then, it seems, deserted. And we know that two charred bodies were found by the railway line up beyond Bulawayo, and that one of the bodies had Vickery's false teeth. Guesses galore have been made as to Kipling's intended meaning. None is satisfactory.

In Kipling's second important story on this theme of infatuation, 'A Madonna of the Trenches' of 1924, we cannot, once again, be sure what he meant his readers to infer, but better, more disciplined construction leaves the reader's final dubiety within the limits acceptable to good story-telling. This is a wartime story. An hysterical young soldier on leave stumbles into the Masonic Lodge in London, and brokenly tells how the Sergeant, whom he'd known all his life, met his dead Auntie Bella Armine – 'Ma's younger sister, an' she nearer fifty than forty' – by the trench whose floor is frozen corpses which creak when you walk on them. What did it advantage him, the Sergeant had said, to have fought 'beasts of officers' (that is 'beasts at Ephesus' from the Burial Service) if the dead didn't rise? 'Come in, my dear,' the Sergeant had said to the wraith, and the soldier had seen them go together into the dugout, and the door wedged shut, with the coke braziers burning inside.

The second aspect that no reader of Kipling can fail to notice is the extent to which there appear in the corpus the beating of white boys and men, and, still more, the tying up and torturing. When the Woman beat the fictional child, in 'Baa, Baa, Black Sheep', he was appalled. '"But – I'm – I'm not an animal!" said Punch.' But in Kipling's recollections of Westward Ho! beating had become meritorious. We find both beatings and torture in *Stalky & Co.*, the latter in the story 'The Moral Reformers', where the bullying boys are themselves tied up and bullied, the former most aggressively in 'A Little Prep', where the Headmaster sets out to cane the whole school. Lord Baldwin denies this ever happened: and Janet Adam Smith, in John Gross's symposium on Kipling, remarks that: 'The mild Cormell Price used the cane sparingly, while the fictional Head is a tremendous swisher and thwacker.'[6] Already in 'The Bronckhurst Divorce Case' of 1888 we find Strickland, who nosed out the false evidence, dropping 'a gut trainer's whip' for the wronged man Biel to pick up, and cut the cad Bronckhurst 'into ribbons'; and in 'A Friend's Friend', another story from *Plain Tales*, the man who disgraced his host by getting drunk at a party is tied up and spattered with gelatine and meringue cream, humiliation of a kind far from uncommon in Kipling's work. Some people have attributed such episodes to a streak of cruelty in Kipling.

This was probably not the explanation. Whatever aberrant sexual needs Kipling may have had, he was fundamentally a loving and enthusiastic man, and he had many loves important to his life and work – for his extended family and the friends who lasted him for his or their lives long; for children and for animals; for houses and motor-cars; for soldiers and sailors; for the Empire, and for travelling, so long as this could be done in reasonable safety and comfort. All these loves were part of the fabric of his life and of the matter of his works.

97

CHAPTER SEVEN

FROM AUSTRALASIA TO SOUTH AMERICA

> . . . the shouting seas drive by,
> And the engines stamp and ring, and the wet bows reel and swing,
> And the Southern Cross rides high! . . .

from 'The Long Trail'

UDYARD Kipling in 1891 first crossed the Line. He left South-
ampton on 22 August in the Union Castle boat SS *Mexican*, on a
journey that was to take him to Madeira, to the Cape, and then
on to Australia and New Zealand. The breakdown that London
life had threatened him with had been postponed by the Italian
trip of 1890, and again by the always healing presence of his
parents who had come to England on eighteen months' leave
from the spring of that year. In the late spring of 1891, Kipling took a short,
would-be incognito trip to New York with his uncle Fred Macdonald to see Fred's
brother Harry. Probably they had known that Harry was ill. He died while they
were still on their way. Fred stayed on in New York to help settle Harry's affairs,
and Rudyard, who was being recognized and pestered by reporters, went back to
England.

He was working on *The Naulahka* then with Wolcott Balestier, and July was
spent in the Isle of Wight with the Balestier family. Whether he was seriously
wooing Caroline Balestier or she him, he obviously felt a desperate need to get far
away from England and its intolerable pressures. So in August off he went.

For the early autumn he lingered at the Cape, already relaxed and restored, and
open to the influences of the new materials he must now amass to replace the Indian
experience. Then on 25 September he set off again, this time in the Shaw-Saville
steamer, the SS *Doric*, nearly empty this trip, for Australia. The boat took the
so-called Great Circle route to the southward to take advantage of the westerly
winds that roared in the 'forties, and a vile journey it was. Kipling recalled it
through McAndrew, his Chief Engineer:

> We'll tak' one stretch – three weeks an' odd by ony road ye steer –
> Fra' Cape Town east to Wellington – ye need an engineer.
> Fail there – ye've time to weld your shaft – ay, eat it ere ye're spoke;
> Or make Kerguelen under sail – three jiggers burned wi' smoke!

A contemporary photograph of Sydney quayside. 'Greeting! My birth-stain have I turned to good;/Forcing strong wills perverse to steadfastness . . . And at my feet Success!' Kipling's tribute to Sydney in 'The Song of the Cities'.

An' home again – the Rio run: it's no child's play to go
Steamin' to bell for fourteen days o' snow an' floe an' blow.
The bergs like kelpies overside that girn an' turn an' shift
Whaur, grindin' like the Mills o' God, goes by the big South drift.
(Hail, Snow and Ice that praise the Lord. I've met them at their work,
An' wished we had anither route or they anither kirk.) . . .

from 'McAndrew's Hymn'

At last the *Doric* reached Hobart in Tasmania, and set off again for Wellington, with, according to his biographers, Kipling still on board; in *Something of Myself*, he says that he landed in Melbourne and went to Sydney before leaving for Hobart and New Zealand, but, as often in that late autobiography, his memory apparently played him false. The *Doric*, was, he says, escorted into Wellington harbour by the white shark known as Pelorus Jack.

What has hitherto been the almost total confusion of Kipling's journey to the Antipodes was cleared up in 1963 by the Rev. J. B. Primrose[1] from the time that

99

Melbourne where Kipling found himself, 'in a new land with new smells and among people who insisted a little too much that they also were new'. (Something of Myself)

Kipling left England not, as had been supposed, on the SS *Moor* and not from London Docks. In New Zealand, by Mr Primrose's well-documented account, Kipling went from Wellington to Auckland ('soft and lovely') by way of the thermal districts, and at Auckland took the 423-ton *Mahinapua* to New Plymouth, thence by train back to Wellington. He left on 2 November on the SS *Talune* (2,087 tons) which crossed the Tasman Sea to and from New Zealand to Australia until 1924.

The *Talune* called at Lyttleton, where Kipling had time to visit Christchurch and a former Latin master at Westward Ho!, now a professor; at Port Chalmers, with a visit by Kipling to Dunedin; and Bluff, where Kipling might have landed and gone to Invercargill. Then on 6 November the *Talune* took off for Australia and landed Kipling in Melbourne in time for the Melbourne Cup, which he was offered, but refused, the honour of reporting. There was barely time for him to do more in Australia than take the train to Sydney before 14 November when he must take the SS *Valetta* for Colombo in Ceylon.

There is no explaining the fact that New Zealand, which Kipling liked well, evoked hardly any creative writing. The anonymously published New Zealand story claimed for him, 'One Lady at Wairakei', is almost certainly a fake, poor in quality beyond Kipling's worst and not written in his vocabulary. New Zealand came in, of course, for her fair share in those intermittent long poems that rounded up the Empire, and New Zealand's best part in those is probably her verse in 'The Flowers' of 1896, though the repetition of 'myrtle' is weak:

> Buy my English posies!
>   Here's your choice unsold!
> Buy a blood-red myrtle-bloom,
>   Buy the kowhai's gold
> Flung for gift on Taupo's face,
>   Sign that spring is come –
> Buy my clinging myrtle
>   And I'll give you back your home!
> Broom behind the windy town, pollen of the pine –
> Bell-bird in the leafy deep where the *ratas* twine –
> Fern above the saddle-bow, flax upon the plain –
> Take the flower and turn the hour, and kiss your love again!

But – glancingly, allusively – something more came from New Zealand than the pleasant conventional tributes. Some years later, a memory trace awakened a story which certain critics have called Kipling's greatest, though none can assert he perfectly understands Kipling's intention:

> All I carried away from the magic town of Auckland was the face and voice of a woman who sold me beer at a little hotel there. They stayed at the back of my head till ten years later when, in a local train in the Cape Town suburbs, I heard a petty officer from Simons Town telling a companion about a woman in New Zealand who 'never scrupled to help a lame duck or put her foot on a scorpion'. Then – precisely as the removal of the key-log in a timber-jam starts the whole pile – those words gave me the key to the face and voice at Auckland, and a tale called 'Mrs. Bathurst' slid into my mind, smoothly and orderly as floating timber on a bank high river.[2]

New Zealand may have offered more still. As we shall see in Chapter Twelve, as is, indeed, a well-known fact about Kipling's work, such small workaday steamers as the 'bucking Bilbao tramp' of his poem 'The Long Trail' appear so often in his verse and prose and usually, it seems with such intimate knowledge of their workings and behaviour, especially in bad weather that it is hard to believe that all this is sheer invention, helped out, perhaps, by visits in ports. But in all Kipling's journeys there is no record of his ever having travelled on such boats – unless he is drawing on his experiences in the little SS *Mahinapua* from Auckland to New Plymouth, a passage said to be usually a rough one, and in the SS *Talune*. The small and rickety coast-wise craft in which he said, in *Something of Myself*, he had travelled from Sydney to Wellington may have been a confused memory of the *Mahinapua*; and clearly the *Talune* was what he speaks of as 'another small steamer' in which he sailed, he said, from Invercargill to Australia by way of the South Atlantic, with General Booth on board.

> We stood out and at once took the South Atlantic. For the better part of a week we were swept from end to end, our poop was split, and a foot or two of water smashed through the tiny saloon. I remember no set meals. The General's cabin was near mine, and in the intervals between crashes overhead and cataracts down below, he sounded like a wounded elephant.[3]

The South Atlantic we should probably accept as one of those unverified inaccuracies that Lockwood Kipling warned his son against; it is, none the less, a very long way from the Tasman Sea, which must be what Kipling intended. It is perfectly possible that he made not one but two journeys with General Booth, who had been in New Zealand at the time, and that he was a fellow passenger on this boat as well as on the SS *Valetta (see page 23)*. And, for lack of other candidates, it would seem to have probably been the *Mahinapua* and the *Talune* that gave Kipling his experience of little rough steamers in heavy seas.

In his own person Australia appealed to Kipling less than New Zealand had done. He found Sydney 'populated by leisured multitudes all in their shirt-sleeves and all picnicking all the day. They volunteered that they were new and young, but would do wonderful things some day –', and because he was writing after the Boer War and the Great War, he ended 'which promise they more than kept.'[4] But though Kipling himself responded so coolly to Australia, his Daemon found it exciting, and one story that the Daemon gave him needs to be recited in an Australian voice with the incantatory rhythm implied by its title, 'The Sing-Song of Old Man Kangaroo'. This is the story of the 'Different Animal' called Kangaroo, with four short legs and inordinate pride, who demanded of the Big God Ngong that he be made different from all other animals by four o'clock that afternoon. So Big God Ngong called up Yellow-Dog Dingo, and ordered him to chase kangaroo:

> He ran through the desert; he ran through the mountains; he ran through the salt-pans; he ran through the reed-beds; he ran through the blue gums; he ran through the spinifex; he ran till his front legs ached.
> He had to!
> Still ran Dingo – Yellow-Dog Dingo – always hungry, grinning like a rat-trap, never getting nearer, never getting farther – ran after Kangaroo.
> He had to!
> Still ran Kangaroo – Old Man Kangaroo. He ran through the ti-trees; he ran through the mulga; he ran through the long grass; he ran through the short grass; he ran through the Tropics of Capricorn and Cancer; he ran . . . to the Wollgong River . . . so he stood on his legs and hopped.
> He had to!
> He hopped through the Flinders; he hopped through the Cinders; he hopped through the deserts in the middle of Australia. He hopped like a Kangaroo. . . .

> from the *Just So Stories*

102

It is clear even from that sing-song that Kipling was awed by the immensity of Australia, though he saw little of it. Unexplored country was somewhere he never went to or wanted to go to, but, as so often, he can convince us that this is what it *must* have felt like, to cross known frontiers, and push on, and on:

> 'There's no sense in going further – it's the edge of cultivation,'
> So they said, and I believed it – broke my land and sowed my crop –
> Built my barns and strung my fences in the little border station
> Tucked away below the foothills where the trails run out and stop:
>
> Till a voice, as bad as Conscience, rang interminable changes
> On one everlasting Whisper day and night repeated – so:
> 'Something hidden. Go and find it. Go and look behind the Ranges –
> 'Something lost behind the Ranges. Lost and waiting for you. Go!'...

'The Explorer' is a long poem, and a good one, and, like almost everything else quoted here, it should be read in full. It was written in 1898, before the Boer War, to which the Australian contribution reawakened Kipling's interest in Australians. A tolerable story, 'A Sahib's War', told to the Narrator by a Sikh, shows the Australians through Indian eyes. The Indians called them the Durro Muts ('Do not be afraid') because they were always saying 'No fear', and they respected the Durro Muts as greater horse-thieves than even the Pathans. 'The *Durro Muts* cannot walk on their feet at all... "No fee-ah," say the *Durro Muts*.'

This story must have given Kipling particular gratification in that it showed different members of the British Empire fighting together for the British cause in South Africa.

The best that Kipling wrote about the Australians in South Africa, and one of his better poems, calls again for an Australian voice, if only in the mental ear ('wattle' is a mimosa-type acacia):

> And I smelt wattle by Lichtenberg –
>   Riding in, in the rain!
>
> It was all Australia to me –
>   All I had found or missed:
> Every face I was crazy to see,
>   And every woman I'd kissed:
> All that I shouldn't ha' done, God knows!
>   (As He knows I'll do it again),
> That smell of the wattle round Lichtenberg,
>   Riding in, in the rain!...
>
> from 'Lichtenberg'

The war in Europe produced its Australian story, 'A Friend of the Family'. It is one of several told to the Narrator in a Masonic Lodge in London, this one about a Queensland drover, a man who was of necessity of a quite exceptionally solitary

103

·ROBERT·LOVIS·STEVENSON·

Kipling was devoted to Stevenson's work, especially to The Wrong Box. *Stevenson reserved judgment on Kipling. 'He alarms me by his copiousness and haste,' he wrote to Henry James in 1890.*

nature, invisible save when he wanted to be seen, and the revenge he took on a shirker in a Buckinghamshire village, for the sake of a dead English friend. It is a worthy story, but not first class, the best of it an interchange before it properly begins between Orton, an ex-soldier from Sydney, and Bevin, the smallholder who tells the main story:

'Have you started that Republic of yours down under yet?' said Bevin. 'No. But we're goin' to. *Then* you'll see.'

'Carry on. No one's hindering.'

The Australian scowled. 'No. We know they ain't. And – and – that's what makes us so crazy angry with you. . . What *can* you do with an Empire that – that don't care what you do?'

Kipling's original intention had been to visit the South Pacific and drop in on Robert Louis Stevenson on Samoa – odd that he, furious at intrusions on his own privacy, had broken in on Mark Twain's in America and was now intending to do the same to Stevenson. But for whatever reason – in *Something of Myself* he speaks glancingly of a drunken captain and a fruit-boat's uncertain sailing – he made for India, England, and marriage. On this steamer the Salvation Army's General Booth was travelling too. As well as reprimanding the elderly, grey-haired General about his lasses in India, Kipling also told him how shocking he had found it to see him beating a tambourine on the Adelaide quay to the weeping, singing crowd who had come to see him off. The General replied, 'Young feller, if I thought I could win *one* more soul to the Lord by walking on my head and playing the tambourine with my toes, I'd – I'd learn how.' 'And he had the right of it,' Kipling admitted later. Was General Booth a part of the model for his St Paul?

No more than Charlotte M. Yonge did Kipling need really to visit a place in order to write well about it. In his approach to the unvisited South Seas, he was ambivalent. On the one hand they – or part of them – belonged to the British Empire, as the South Wind boasted in 'The English Flag':

> 'Strayed amid lonely islets, mazed amid outer keys,
> 'I waked the palms to laughter – I tossed the scud in the breeze.
> 'Never was isle so little, never was sea so lone,
> 'But over the scud and the palm-trees an English flag was flown . . .

But this imperial approach has less feeling than do the temptations with which the South Seas tried to beguile McAndrew:

> I was not four and twenty then – Ye wadna judge a child?
> I'd seen the Tropics first that run – new fruit, new smells, new air –
> How could I tell – blind-fou wi' sun – the Deil was lurkin' there?
> By day like playhouse-scenes the shore slid past our sleepy eyes;
> By night those soft, lasceevious stars leered from those velvet skies,
> In port (we used no cargo-steam) I'd daunder down the streets –
> An ijjit grinnin' in a dream – for shells an' parrakeets,
> An' walkin' sticks o' carved bamboo an' blowfish stuffed an' dried –
> Fillin' my bunk wi' rubbishry the Chief put overside.
> Till, off Sambawa Head, Ye mind, I heard a land-breeze ca',
> Milk-warm wi' breath o' spice an' bloom: 'McAndrew, come awa'!'
> Firm, clear an' low – no haste, no hate – the ghostly whisper went,
> Just statin' eevidential facts beyon' all argument:
> 'Your mither's God's a graspin' deil, the shadow o' yoursel';
> 'Got out o' books by meenisters clean daft on Heaven an' Hell,
> 'They mak' him in the Broomielaw, o' Glasgie cold an' dirt,
> 'A jealous, pridefu' fetich, lad, that's only strong to hurt.
> 'Ye'll not go back to Him again an' kiss His red-hot rod,
> 'But come wi' Us' (Now, who were *They*?) 'an' know the Leevin' God,
> 'That does not kipper souls for sport or break a life in jest,
> 'But swells the ripenin' cocoanuts an' ripes the woman's breast.' . . .

> from 'McAndrew's Hymn'

There was something of that Calvinist Scot in Kipling. He knew the temptation of the ripening breast, but he believed that the languorous delights of the Southern Hemisphere should be indulged in only by such English gentlemen as were not quite-quite (or, as he sometimes put it 'but–but–'), and perhaps something worse than that:

> We took no tearful leaving,
>   We bade no long good-byes.
> Men talked of crime and thieving,
>   Men wrote of fraud and lies.
> To save our injured feelings
>   'Twas time and time to go –
> Behind was dock and Dartmoor,
>   Ahead lay Callao!. . .
>
> Day long the diamond weather,
>   The high, unaltered blue –
> The smell of goats and incense
>   And the mule-bells tinkling through.
> Day long the warder ocean
>   That keeps us from our kin,
> And once a month our levée
>   When the English mail comes in.
>
> You'll find us up and waiting
>   To treat you at the bar;
> You'll find us less exclusive
>   Than the average English are.
> We'll meet you with a carriage,
>   Too glad to show you round,
> But – we do not lunch on steamers,
>   For they are English ground. . .

That poem about 'The Broken Men' refers to Callao in Peru. It was written in 1902 and Kipling had never then been to South America, but he wanted to go, if his verse in the *Just So Stories* is to be believed.

> I've never sailed the Amazon
>   I've never reached Brazil;
> But the *Don* and *Magdalena*,
>   They can go there when they will!
> Yes, weekly from Southampton,
> Great steamers, white and gold,
> Go rolling down to Rio
> (Roll down – roll down to Rio!).
> And I'd like to roll to Rio
> Some day before I'm old!. . .

But it was not until 1927 that Kipling sailed to Rio de Janeiro, broken in health, and recuperating not adventuring. *Brazilian Sketches* trimmed up with light verse came out of that journey, but nothing of literary significance.

106

CHAPTER EIGHT

NORTH AMERICA

Take up the White Man's burden –
In patience to abide,
To veil the threat of terror
And check the show of pride . . .

from 'The White Man's Burden'

HE two separate sides of Kipling's head were seldom more at odds than when he had anything to do with Americans. The first American he knew well, Ted Hill, had enraptured him. But on the SS *Nawab* out of Singapore, he first met American globetrotters: 'I have met a lump of Chicago Jews and am afraid that I shall meet many more. The ship is full of Americans, but the American-German-Jew boy is the most awful of all'[1] – though among these Americans a precocious child of eight called Albert was to come in useful later. In Japan he was appalled by the works of the American missionaries. He wrote:

> Something should be done to America . . . The American is objectionable. And yet – this is written from Yokohama – how pleasant in every way is a nice American whose tongue is cleansed of 'right there,' 'all the time,' 'noos,' 'revoo,' 'around,' and the Falling Cadence.[2]

Yet it was only a couple of years ahead, and, presumably, with the other side of his head, that Kipling accepted that there were *'nine and sixty ways of constructing tribal lays,/And every–single–one–of–them–is–right!'* It was that side of his head which responded to the warm generosity of the Americans in the *City of Peking* from Yokohama to San Francisco, who, on 24 May 1889, dressed the ship with flags from stem to stern, with 'the chiefest of the bunting the Union Jack' in honour of the Queen of England's birthday, with a toast to the Queen proposed by an American.

Kipling was never able to reconcile his ambivalence towards the United States. Three of his journeys there were to be traumatic, for good and for ill.

1889: From Tideway to Tideway

Kipling got off on the wrong foot with Americans on his very first landfall. When the *City of Peking* steamed through the Golden Gate, he 'saw with great joy that the block-house which guarded the mouth of the "finest harbour in the world, Sir"

'*San Francisco is a mad city – inhabited for the most part by perfectly insane people whose women are of a remarkable beauty.*' (From Sea to Sea, *let. 23*)

could be silenced by two gun-boats from Hong Kong with safety, comfort, and despatch.'[3]

He wrote this to the *Pioneer*, and of course it came back to the Americans, as did the many other ruderies he sent to India. He wrote rudely (but so did most nineteenth-century English visitors) about the ubiquitous spitting. He was rude about American journalists when, on more than the professional practice of dog not eating dog, it behoved him to be grateful that journalists sought him out. He was rude about American clothes and drinking habits and manners and service: but every English ex-colonial had been spoiled in that last respect, and Kipling was never a man to prefer democracy to deference.

Yet, if stunned by culture-shock, Kipling was still, though always critically, excited by America and enthusiastically open to its new experiences. At San Francisco the Hills had left for Pennsylvania. Kipling, before he joined them, explored America on his own, though never far from the beaten tourist tracks on which he travelled for the rest of his life. First he turned north into Oregon, where he went fishing; Kipling occasionally presents himself as a fly-fisherman, but somehow never convincingly. Then he decided to go into British Territory for a while 'to draw breath', and took the steamer up Puget Sound for Vancouver. His biographers disagree as to whether it was then or later, when passing through on his honeymoon, that he bought, as he thought, potentially profitable land there, but as he was bilked, this former occasion seems more likely; Carrie would never have been taken in by a confidence trickster.

There is surprisingly little to be said about Kipling and Canada. Kipling came greatly to respect Canada, not least for her rejection of what he understood to be the American view of her, that she was 'a ripe plum ready to fall into Uncle Sam's mouth when he should open it'; and the more so on his 1907 visit there, after Canada had sent a contingent to the Cape, and England had come to seem to Kipling a country on which had settled a 'cross between canker and blight'.[4] (This was the trip he made to accept an honorary doctorate from McGill University, and was lent a private railroad car to hitch to any train he liked.) Kipling took to the Canadian people, with their open pride in their country and he was, of course, delighted by the Canadian Pacific Railway. But, for whatever reason, the country aroused the journalist in him rather than the artist, and one of the most attractive of his journalist's pieces was the account of the CPR passing through the Rockies in the April of 1892; with newspaper publication in the United States, England, and India:

> The place is locked up – dead as a frozen corpse. The mountain torrent is a boss of palest emerald ice against the dazzle of the snow; the pine-stumps are capped and hooded with gigantic mushrooms of snow; the rocks are overlaid five feet deep; the rocks, the fallen trees, and the lichens together, and the dumb white lips curl up to the track cut in the side of the mountain, and grin there fanged with gigantic icicles. You may listen in vain when the train stops for the least sign of breath or power among the hills. The snow has smothered the rivers, and the great looping trestles run over what might be a lather of suds in a huge washtub.

There is no doubt that Kipling had the best will in the world towards Canada, but his Daemon did not. He wrote – what a subject! – on the Canadian Preferential Tariff of 1897 in his poem 'Our Lady of the Snows'. Of course Canada received her due in the round-the-Empire poems, but white-hot inspiration is never in her verses.

Back in the United States in 1889, Kipling made his way east by train, across the Rockies where, on the most precipitous stretch, the train ran on a trestle 286 feet up in the air. On his way east, he stopped off at all the regular tourist sights. He went to Yellowstone Park, vociferously resenting the tourists there; he hardly thought of himself as one. He went to Salt Lake City where he found the Mormon women so ugly that he thought polygamy must be 'a blessed institution' for them, but that only 'spiritual power' could drive the men into it. There is a creepingly macabre meeting with an undertaker in Denver, and then on to Chicago where: 'Except in London – and I have forgotten what London is like – I had never seen so many white people together, and never such a collection of miserables.'

The train '. . . had been climbing steadily from San Francisco, and at last won to over four thousand feet above sea-level . . . Then . . . we came down . . . two thousand two hundred feet in about thirteen miles.' (From Sea to Sea, *let. 26*)

The whole of Kipling's first American journey as he told it in *From Sea to Sea* is worth reading, and worth more quotation than can be given here. One of its best passages is about the Judas steer which he encountered in the Chicago stockyards: to go and watch cattle and pigs being slaughtered was a regular tourist outing. As each new batch of cattle arrived,

'this red devil... slouched across the yard, no man guiding him. Then he lowed something to the effect that he was the regularly appointed guide of the establishment and would show them round. They were country folk, but they knew how to behave; and so followed Judas some hundred strong, patiently and with a look of bland wonder in their faces. I saw his broad back jogging in advance of them, up a lime-washed incline where I was forbidden to follow. Then a door shut, and in a minute back came Judas with the air of a virtuous plough-bullock...'

After Chicago, Kipling went 'for peace and rest' to Beaver, Pennsylvania, which he discreetly renames 'Musquash', and does not say that his visit there was to see Ted Hill at home, and to meet her father, Professor R. T. Taylor, the strict Methodist President of a small college, and her pretty younger sister Caroline.

Later in London, Kipling's insufficient and unorthodox religious views may have been the reason, or excuse, for his engagement to Caroline coming to nothing.

What, at any time in his life, Kipling's religious views 'really' were, we can only guess at, and small point in doing so because of his chameleon capacity of putting on any skin the moment's creation demanded: St Paul's, Teshoo Lama's, the Abbot of 'The Eye of Allah'. It may be that his comment that Freemasonry was the nearest thing to religion that he had was most lastingly true. Yet it still may be that what he wrote to Professor Taylor in 1890 was for the time being, or for longer, sincere. He believed in a personal God, he wrote, disbelieved in eternal punishment or reward, regarded reverently the mystery of the Trinity and the Doctrine of the Redemption, 'but I cannot give them implicit belief'. He ended, 'I believe in God the Father Almighty . . . and in One filled with His spirit Who did voluntarily die in the belief that the human race would be spiritually bettered thereby.'[5] The degree of credence we give to this must depend on knowing whether in 1890 after he had returned to London, Kipling still wanted to marry Caroline Taylor; and we do not know this.

But in 1889, Kipling was delighted with Pennsylvania, and with Caroline. 'I had the honour of meeting in the flesh, even as Miss Louisa Alcott drew them, Meg and Joe [sic] and Beth and Amy.' He was intoxicated, as many another Englishman, by 'the fresh, wholesome, sweet life' of the unmarried American girl, free to mix with boys as a sister with brothers, and therefore understanding what men are like before she picks one to marry, 'knowledge that does not come to her sister in England till after a few years of matrimony.'[6]

'*Every Englishman goes to the Chicago stockyard . . . As far as the eye can see stretches a township of cattle-pens . . . Women come sometimes to see the slaughter, as they would the slaughter of men.*' (From Sea to Sea, *let. 35*)

Mark Twain: '. . . a man with . . . a mane of grizzled hair, a brown moustache covering a mouth as delicate as a woman's, a strong, square hand shaking mine.' (From Sea to Sea, let. 37)

Kipling tells us nothing of his visit to New York where he met his uncle, Harry Macdonald. He ends the letters, which were reprinted in 1899 as *From Sea to Sea*, with his side-trip, or pilgrimage, to Elmira in New York State. He wrote to his *Pioneer* readers:

> You are a contemptible lot, over yonder. Some of you are Commissioners, and some Lieutenant-Governors, and some have the V.C., and a few are privileged to walk about the Mall arm in arm with the Viceroy; but *I* have seen Mark Twain. . .'

Mark Twain received the uninvited visitor with a kindness that Kipling, in similar circumstances, would never have bestowed, and talked with him for over two hours, about copyright, about whether Tom Sawyer married Judge Thatcher's daughter, and about conscience. 'Once he put his hand on my shoulder. It was an investiture of the Star of India.'[7]

The next time the two men met was in 1907, when Rudyard Kipling, Mark Twain, and General Booth walked together in capped-and-gowned procession to receive Honorary Degrees from the University of Oxford. 'Young feller,' the General asked Kipling, 'how's your soul?'

1892–6: Home in Vermont

'I love this People,' Kipling had written on his first American visit. 'My heart has gone out to them beyond all other peoples.' So in 1892, after the honeymoon journey had failed at Yokohama, it must have seemed natural to settle at Brattleboro in Vermont, where some of Carrie's family lived, and where the young couple had visited on their way out. After all, Rudyard Kipling had nowhere of his own he could call home.

Carrie's grandmother, 'Madam' Balestier, had a substantial summer estate outside Brattleboro and offered Rudyard and Caroline the lease of a simple hiredman's house, Bliss Cottage, for $10 a month. Until they had recouped their finances, the Kiplings lived at Bliss Cottage in happy simplicity, and there, in December 1892, their first child, Josephine, was born. Carrie's feckless, rumbustious, often drunk brother, Beatty had been given a farm on the Balestier estate and Rudyard bought something over ten acres of land from him. On this the Kiplings built their house, Naulakha, a long wooden dwelling; but, says Lord Birkenhead who saw it in deserted desolation in the 1940s, with 'chilling interior decoration'. While Beatty and his wife Mai over at Maplewood kept open house, Carrie, though she said she did too, was already practising the mean economies that were to distinguish her housekeeping. With this, she was pretentious, setting up, to the neighbours' derision, a carriage with liveried groom, insisting on caps for the

---

The pretentious turn-out that riled the Brattleboro neighbours: Carrie, with the liveried, cockaded coachman Matt Howard up behind, driving, probably, the thoroughbreds Nip and Tuck.

Naulakha, Brattleboro, named in memory of Wolcott. The ground floor ran from kitchen, at one end, through dining-room and lounge to Carrie's sitting-room where she sat guarding Rudyard's study, last room in the line.

servants, dressing for dinner and making Rudyard do so too; it is true that dressing for dinner at home was English gentry practice right up to the Second World War, but even in the 1890s it was ridiculously pretentious for a young couple living in a log house in the Vermont countryside. Add to this that Kipling himself, though courteous to the farming neighbours, hated intrusion, and was not prepared to give journalists even that discreet modicum which would keep them at friendly bay, and this hand of cards was clearly dealt for disaster.

But there were happy times first. Kipling delighted in the countryside and the climate, the vivid New England autumns and clean icy winters, and at all seasons, the amazing views of Mount Monadnock from Naulakha's windows; and he wrote profusely and well. *The Jungle Books* were written in Vermont, and some other good stories and poems; and some names collected that would later make a jingle for the Just So Story about the whale. It should be chanted (as it was to me) at a now-dismantled suburban railroad station in Boston, and it runs: 'Change here for Winchester, Ashuelot, Nashua, Keene, and stations on the *Fitch*burg Road.'

By 1894 there was enough money for a winter cruise to Bermuda, which helped to provide, some forty years later, a doggedly farcical story, 'A Naval Mutiny', about lower-deck parrots in revolt, and with it a jolly doggerel in which some derelict Jacobean sailors, begging their way to London, chance on a Southwark inn and on a company of players there, and for a 'bite and a sup, and a bed of clean straw', spin them yarns about the Bermudas until midnight:

Seven months among Mermaids and Devils and Sprites,
And Voices that howl in the cedars o' nights,
With further enchantments we underwent there.
Good Sirs, 'tis a tale to draw guts from a bear!

Finding one of the players especially greedy for marvels, the sailors passed from 'plain salted truth' to flat lying. But that player, when he paid them off, said,

. . . 'Never match Coins with a Coiner by trade,
Or he'll turn your lead pieces to metal as rare
As shall fill him this globe, and leave something to spare . . .'

This poem, 'The Coiner', is dated 1611, the date usually given to Shakespeare's play, *The Tempest*.

Despite the fact that Beatty Balestier had messed up the accounts in their absence, there was still enough for a brief trip to England to see Lockwood and Alice. Lockwood's official retirement dated from May 1893, but he had had six months special leave from the previous October, and it was presumably then that he had visited Naulakha and had carved on its still unfinished mantelshelf 'The Night cometh when no man can work'; he and Rudyard had gone off together on a brief trip into Canada.

Other good friends came visiting: Arthur Conan Doyle from England, Charles Eliot Norton from Harvard, and from Brattleboro a new friend, the local doctor, James Conland.

Conland, who delivered the two daughters born in Vermont, had served in the fishing fleet based on Gloucester, Massachusetts, and it was he who gave Kipling the factual material for his novel, *Captains Courageous*. Conland took Kipling to the Annual Memorial Service at Gloucester for fishermen lost at sea the previous year; he demonstrated the gutting of cod, and he took Kipling out on a pollock-fisher where Kipling was, as so often, seasick.

All devoted readers of Kipling are likely to mark down some work as unjustly neglected. For me – together with some parts of *The Light that Failed* – such a work is *Captains Courageous*. It is, of course, a young person's story, but many such serve adults well.

Morally, the story is, like *The Secret Garden*, about the turning of poor character into good. Kipling's Harvey Cheyne, an older version of the horrible Albert of the SS *Nawab*, is the spoiled-rotten son of a self-made millionaire. Crossing the Atlantic with his silly, doting mother, Harvey is washed overboard, picked up by the Gloucester fishing-schooner, *We're Here*, and during the passage to the Newfoundland Banks and back, learns (perhaps too quickly and readily) respect for work and the men who do it. There are some superb set-pieces in the book; Uncle Abishai's ramshackle boat, a Marblehead 'heel-tapper', which was 'run-under' by her drunken crew who 'sailed [it] into a patch of watery sunshine . . . dropped into a hollow and – was not'; the gathering of the Banks fishing fleet by the shoal called

the Virgin, where social life was in 'Every dialect from Labrador to Long Island, with Portuguese, Neapolitan, Lingua Franca, French, and Gaelic'; the faceless corpse hooked on to Harvey's line who had come for his knife which Harvey had bought at a sale of the dead man's goods. Richest of all (at least to the railroad-devotee), is the saga of the railroad journey from San Diego on the California coast to Gloucester on the Atlantic, made by the millionaire and his wife in their private car when they hear that their lost son is alive.

A railway magnate friend of Kipling's, when asked for help, sent 'a fully worked-out time-table with watering halts, changes of engine, mileage, track conditions and climates, so that a corpse could not have gone wrong,' Kipling later wrote gratefully.[8] But the magic, of course, is in what he himself built on that timetable, the journey of Cheyne's private car, the 'Constance', from San Diego, drawn by 'specials' to Chicago, hitched there on to the Limited for Buffalo, and the New York Central and Hudson Line, 'who slid her gracefully into Albany, where the Boston and Albany completed the run from tide-water to tide-water – total time, eighty-seven hours and thirty-five minutes, or three days, fifteen hours and one-half. Harvey was waiting for them.'

(Another railway magnate, having read the book, took his own private car over the same route to see if he could break that timing, and just succeeded. In 1983, the run over scheduled routes would have taken three days, nineteen hours and thirty-five minutes from San Diego to Boston, though two and a half hours are wasted by a bad connection at Los Angeles.)

Before *Captains Courageous* was published in 1897, the Kiplings had left Naulakha for good. Troubles had been building up between Beatty and Carrie; over the land deal and the house-building, over monies lent and not repaid, over Carrie's bossiness and prim censoriousness and Beatty's often drunken expansiveness. At last, in May 1896, Rudyard, out on a bicycle ride, was physically threatened by Beatty, and, idiotically ill-advised, had Beatty arrested and charged with assault. Beatty was popular in the neighbourhood, Carrie was not, and Rudyard had been accepted only on a sufferance dissipated by this petulant and timid response. The formerly rebuffed journalists swarmed to Brattleboro and gleefully smeared Kipling all over the press. He could not ride it out. In August, the Kiplings packed up and left. Their first attempt to make a home had failed.

1899: New York

So far as business was concerned, Kipling had no need to go to America again. He had met his lastingly right publisher there, F. N. Doubleday (known from his initials as Effendi), and Carrie and his agent could look after any needed decision-taking. But one unnecessary and finally tragic journey was made.

In the winter of 1898–9, when the Kiplings were living at Rottingdean, Carrie decided that she wanted to go to America to see her mother, and to collect this and that from Naulakha; and there was some problem about Rudyard's copyrights which hardly needed his presence to sort out, but which, no doubt, provided enough excuse for his going too. They decided to take the children, Josephine, Elsie, and John.

Alice Kipling protested that this was not a wise thing to do in mid-winter, and Rudyard was anxious about it, but Carrie was resolved. The voyage was dreadful, and the little girls developed bad colds, exacerbated by a long, chilly wait in the

---

New York – 'I'm going to where the sun shines and oysters is cheap . . . and I shall have grapefruit for breakfast and nineteen different kinds of bread,' Kipling wrote, before the disastrous trip of 1899. (Birkenhead, p.194)

New York customs-house. Blizzards raged, while the family cowered in the Hotel Grenoble on West 56th Street.

Carrie's sister Josephine, now married to a doctor, had met the Kiplings in New York, and fortunately so, for soon Rudyard fell ill too, and developed pneumonia in both lungs. The children, Josephine with a high fever, were sent to the home of old friends, the De Forests, on Long Island. Dr Conland came down from Brattleboro to help Dr Dunham, and with skill and unceasing care the two doctors pulled Kipling through.

His dangerous condition had proved to be major international news. Goodwill messages came from all over the world, including one from the Kaiser, though that gave Kipling no pleasure, for his fear of the Kaiser's Germany was already kindled.

This appalling time showed Carrie at her best, in courage and in care for Rudyard. On 4 March he had come out of a long delirium, desperately weak, barely alive. On 6 March Josephine died, just seven years old. She was buried on Long Island, and Carrie, coming straight from the funeral to her husband, realized that her black dress might tell him what must still be kept from him. She snatched up a red shawl, put it round her shoulders before she went into Rudyard's room, and so was able to keep the death from him for a few more necessary days. When he knew, he endured it, but he never got over it. Angela Thirkell, daughter of his cousin, Margaret Mackail (*née* Burne-Jones) wrote, 'Much of the beloved Cousin Ruddy of our childhood died with Josephine, and I feel that I have never seen him as a real person since that year.'[9]

*   *   *

Kipling did not go to America again. 'Nothing but Gehenna would make me go to New York,' he wrote to a friend in 1930. This was the year that the Kiplings, both ailing now and old for their years, took a winter cruise to the West Indies, and Caroline, already with diabetes and chronic rheumatism, developed appendicitis in Bermuda. To Kipling's now almost paranoid revulsion from America was added disgust at the American tourists who, in those Prohibition days, came to Bermuda to get drunk. The suggestion that Carrie might be operated on in the United States was unacceptable: the United States, Kipling wrote to Frank Doubleday, was 'not a civilized country for the sick'. The Kiplings decided to come home via Montreal, where Dr Dunham came up to see them. The operation proved unnecessary. The Kiplings did not cross the Atlantic again.

*   *   *

Without the American experiences Kipling's work would have been a good deal the poorer. Much of the American dimension is deftly integrated into stories that are not about America at all; it is, however, worth noting that whenever Americans *speak*, Kipling's marvellous ear got the requisite dialect right; he could 'do' several dialects in his own native English as well; Mark Twain, too, had prided himself on this capacity; there were seven distinct dialects in *Huckleberry Finn*, he claimed, and recent scholarship has justified the claim.*

Few of Kipling's stories are wholly based on America, but many are about Americans, and one such, not very good but curious in view of the Brattleboro disaster, is 'An Error in the Fourth Dimension' of 1893, about an American millionaire who settles in England, and is first pursued by English law and then treated as insane because he flagged down an English express train, just as he would have back home, when he was in a hurry to get to London. In contrast, there is the charming (if rather patronizing) story 'An Habitation Enforced' of 1905 which tells of yet another American millionaire, who buys a beautiful, neglected Sussex house, and merges into England: but the wife's family, as we and she eventually learn, had come from that very house long ago.

On a holiday in Washington in 1895, Kipling had met Theodore Roosevelt, then head of the Civil Service Commission, and the two men became lifelong if, of necessity, largely epistolary friends. But despite Roosevelt's attempts to persuade Kipling that the immigrant populations of America needed England as an enemy against whom they could unite, Kipling seems always in his heart to have seen the United States as rebellious colonies who must one day see that the Mother Country knew best, be grateful for her good advice, and recognize the superiority of her ways. Yet, as always, the Daemon could transcend the Kipling limitations, and his poem 'Philadelphia' of 1910 is nearly faultless. It was written to accompany 'Brother Squaretoes', a story of the American War of Independence, in *Rewards and Fairies*. Almost all the people in it are real people, all the places, real places. Philadelphia was the first capital of the United States, and Count Zinzendorf's Moravian Church is still standing there:

> If you're off to Philadelphia in the morning,
>   You mustn't take my stories for a guide.
> There's little left, indeed, of the city you will read of,
>   And all the folk I write about have died.
>
> Now few will understand if you mention Talleyrand,
>   Or remember what his cunning and his skill did;
> And the cabmen at the wharf do not know Count Zinzendorf,
>   Nor the Church in Philadelphia he builded.
>
>> It is gone, gone, gone with lost Atlantis,
>> (Never say I didn't give you warning).
>> In Seventeen Ninety-three 'twas there for all to see,
>> But it's not in Philadelphia this morning.
>
> If you're off to Philadelphia in the morning,
>   You mustn't go by anything I've said.

---

*David Corkett quoted in *The Times Literary Supplement* 9 May 1986, 440/1.

Bob Bicknell's Southern Stages have been laid aside for ages,
    But the Limited will take you there instead.
Toby Hirte can't be seen at One Hundred and Eighteen
    North Second Street – no matter when you call;
And I fear you'll search in vain for the wash-house down the lane
    Where Pharaoh played the fiddle at the ball.

    It is gone, gone, gone with Thebes the Golden,
    (Never say I didn't give you warning).
    In Seventeen Ninety-four 'twas a famous dancing floor –
    But it's not in Philadelphia this morning.

If you're off to Philadelphia in the morning,
    You must telegraph for rooms at some Hotel.
You needn't try your luck at Epply's or 'The Buck,'
    Though the Father of his Country liked them well.
It is not the slightest use to inquire for Adam Goos,
    Or to ask where Pastor Meder has removed – so
You must treat as out of date the story I relate
    Of the Church in Philadelphia he loved so.

    He is gone, gone, gone with Martin Luther
    (Never say I didn't give you warning).
    In Seventeen Ninety-five he was (rest his soul!) alive,
    But he's not in Philadelphia this morning . . .

Kipling was never able to settle to a calm certainty in his feelings towards the United States, but veered between a contemptuous hatred and an enthusiastic affection. So far as practical matters went, the Americans recognized his quality and were prepared to treat him as a great writer while England, which had barely heard of him, reserved judgment; but the Americans had no scruples about pirating his works, and Kipling was not the only English writer who found this piracy intolerable. Many Americans were and always remained his good friends: the Nortons, Dr Conland, 'Effendi' Doubleday, and many others. But certainly he suffered greatly in America, both in Vermont where some people who happened to be Americans could fairly be blamed for it, and in New York where Josephine died and no American could conceivably be blamed, but which made American associations thereafter largely intolerable.

Yet Kipling's ambivalence about Americans went right back to his first meetings with them on the boats out of India, about America from the moment he first landed in San Francisco. I think the simplest explanation of his attitude to America and Americans is that he was jealous of them. This is not an uncommon attitude among English people, and it does not preclude either affection or disdain, both of which are apparent in Kipling's creative work about the United States. In the best of it, the affection is paramount.

CHAPTER NINE

LE PAYS DE TENDRE: II
ANIMALS AND CHILDREN

The toad beneath the harrow knows
Exactly where each tooth-point goes;
The butterfly upon the road
Preaches contentment to that toad.

from 'Pagett, M.P.'

OHN Lockwood Kipling, Rudyard Kipling's father, published his book *Beast and Man in India* in 1891. Lavishly illustrated by both Lockwood and Indian colleagues and with some chapter headings written by Rudyard, it describes in absorbing and dispassionate detail the lives of many animals common in India, both domesticated and wild: the legends about them, the facts about them, and their treatment and use by Indians and by English. I am told that *Beast and Man in India* is unlikely to be reprinted because too realistically harsh in some of its reports.

Rudyard Kipling reserved realism and harshness for humans. Hardly ever did he write restrainedly and respectfully about animals as animals, and this is almost the only way I care to read about them. So, many readers are likely to find unsympathetic my treatment of Kipling's generally much-loved work on animals.

His approach to them was manifold. The four-line epigram that heads this chapter exemplifies a couple of them, viz, that animals are capable of 'knowing' as we are, and so can, in art, be substituted for humans; and that animals can be used to point moral lessons, though the lesson implied here is surprisingly revolutionary, given Kipling's general belief that the right attitude for lower orders is submission.

There are many other ways of making stories about animals. One, surely almost as old as mankind, is to explain the nature of animals, as of other aspects of the world, by means of fables. Another, which must be as old if not older, is to treat animals as gods.

All these ways were used by Rudyard Kipling. The treatment which is strangest now to Europeans must be the last, though perhaps less strange to the many Americans who know the still-living American-Indian myths. Kipling, of course, took this approach from the Indians of India, though he did not use it much. The *punchayet* or conference of the beast-gods in 'The Bridge-Builders' is the best case in point. Finlayson the engineer is marooned on an island in the flood, and hears the beasts talking; or fantasizes that he hears the beasts talking because of the opium-pill his Indian foreman gave him against the chill; which does not matter. What matters is that the beasts are the gods of the Hindu pantheon, Hanuman the Ape, Shiv the Bull, Ganesh the Elephant, with several others and among and above them the young cow-herd god, Krishna the Well-beloved. Animals who are gods cannot easily be judged by Europeans now. We have the word of the Indian writer N. C. Chaudhuri that this passage is satisfactory.

Similarly, the *Just So Stories* are not really animal stories, but myths of a very old kind. Almost all cultures have tales about how the robin got his red breast, the rabbit his long ears, and such like, and Kipling's stories about 'How the Whale got his Throat' and 'How the Camel got his Hump' are of this kind. But they are not about animals in their own natures.

The *Just So Stories* appear at their best when recited in appropriately incantatory voices, as we are told that Kipling himself recited them to the children of the family in the late 1890s. Spoken in this way, some of them can make a good noise, and notably 'Old Man Kangaroo', but in my judgment they carry no conviction as fables, being self-consciously mannered and written with an ear to the grown-ups who can appreciate their clever touches, too far removed from the artlessness of their primitive predecessors. I am not decrying the genre of fable; only intimating that I think that Aesop and La Fontaine could bring off the made, as opposed to the

popular, fable, and Kipling could not. The *Just So Stories* are dearly loved by many people but they do no justice to animals.

Nor do *The Jungle Books*, excellent reading though they are. The tragedy of a lost child reduced to jungle life is nothing to do with a boy liberated from an Indian village to a wider world where the beasts are wiser and better parents and tutors than his own could possibly have been. *The Jungle Books* are tales about right training for a little white Sahib, about the need for obedience (' –

Rudyard Kipling's fine illustration for 'The Cat That Walked by Himself'. In a 1986 paper for the Kipling Society, Lisa A.F. Lewis maintains that Kipling respected cats, although cats used to count as girls' pets, not boys'.

Rudyard Kipling on the way to Cape Town on a Union Castle liner. He is said to be telling a Just So *story to Elsie and John and some other children.*

the head and the hoof of the Law and the haunch and the hump is – Obey!'), and about the need to avoid contamination by jabbering rabble-rousers or dreamy intellectuals, here personified by the Monkey-Folk, the Bandar-Log:

> Here we sit in a branchy row,
> Thinking of beautiful things we know;
> Dreaming of deeds that we mean to do,
> All complete, in a minute or two – . . .
>
> All the talk we ever have heard
> Uttered by bat or beast or bird –
> Hide or fin or scale or feather –
> Jabber it quickly and all together!
> Excellent! Wonderful! Once again!
> Now we are talking just like men.
> > Let's pretend we are . . . Never mind!
> > *Brother, thy tail hangs down behind!*
>
> from 'Road-Song of the *Bandar-Log*'

But no criticisms can stand against the fact that the animals of *The Jungle Books* are entirely acceptable, even entirely delightful to most readers. No matter that, viewed dispassionately, there is almost nothing that is truly beast-like about them.

The twin brothers, Maurice and Edward Detmold, made some magnificent illustrations for the 1908 edition of The Jungle Book; *this one, for the story 'Tiger! Tiger!', reproduces well in black and white.*

Certainly Kaa can change his skin and glide not walk, Bagheera lie along a branch and lower his eyes before man's, and the Bandar-Log chatter and skitter in ways which may recall but are not really like those of the intellectuals whom Kipling had come to hate. But the purpose of *The Jungle Books* is not to bring comprehension of animals. It is to set up some simplified archetypes of humans, made more comprehensible and more – or less – attractive by being typified as animals. The lessons are hammered home: respect the family, the teachers, the overlords, and despise the talkers who never get anything done. It is no surprise that Kipling's friend Robert Baden-Powell based the junior Boy Scouts, the Wolf Cubs, on *The Jungle Books*, or that Kipling greatly admired the Scout and Guide movements.

There are several other famous 'animal' stories which are not really about animals. One such, much loved and often reprinted, is 'The Maltese Cat' of 1895. The Cat is one of the cheap ponies of the poor men's polo team, the Skidars, able, through his understanding of the game to coach his team-mate ponies to victory over the crack Archangels. Only at one moment does the Cat come to life as a pony and this is in the mess at two o'clock in the morning when 'a wise little, plain little, grey little head looked in through the open door', and the *sais* (the groom) brought in the Maltese Cat, now lamed for life.

The moral here, one of Kipling's most usual morals, is the value of team work, the need for individuals to train for their jobs and subordinate themselves to the

124

common good. It was a moral often implicit in his stories about humans, but as a direct lesson rather than an implication he was not so good at it with us. Where he could hammer it home was where he transferred it to the beasts, as in the Mowgli stories, as in 'The Maltese Cat', as in 'The Mother Hive' of 1908 in which a healthy hive is penetrated by a socialistic wax-moth and saved by a few loyal bees. Kipling also presented similar lessons by way of anthropomorphized machines, like 'The Ship that Found Herself' where the grumbling individualistic parts of a new ship discovered, after a rough ocean crossing, that the need was to speak in one big voice, the voice of the ship; or '·007' in which a timorous eight-wheeled new American locomotive gains guts and confidence and his rightful respect in the yard.

The moral properties of these stories can most fairly be appreciated if we translate them back into human terms. Let us take 'A Walking Delegate' of 1894, set in Vermont. A walking delegate is a peripatetic union organizer, in this story a mean yellow horse sent up to board from a livery stable, and grazing in the field with several others, among them the Kiplings' own carriage horses, Nip and Tuck. The yellow horse tries to convince the others that they are being exploited and should rise against Man the Oppressor. Some momentarily waver. The majority are loyal servants of their men, and the yellow horse is put in its place. Told about people, the story would not be worth telling. As a study of American regional dialects, it is first-class.

Most of the animals that had once been near to Kipling gradually passed out of his life. The Indian animals were left a long way behind, and Kipling's ready devotion to motor-cars phased out the horses. Eventually the only animals left were the dogs:

> Master, this is Thy Servant.
>   He is rising eight weeks old.
> He is mainly Head and Tummy.
>   His legs are uncontrolled.
> But Thou hast forgiven his ugliness,
>   and settled him on Thy knee...
> Art Thou content with Thy Servant?
>   He is *very* comfy with Thee...
>
> from "'His Apologies'"

The proud entry into the mess-room of the trium-phant pony who had begun his working life pulling a vegetable cart in Malta: Lockwood Kipling's illustration to 'The Maltese Cat' for the Outward Bound edition.

This poem was later than but could well have gone with a story called 'The Woman in His Life', a post-war story about an ex-officer constantly on the verge of a nervous breakdown, succoured and eventually cured by Dinah, an Aberdeen puppy his batman introduces into his life. Kipling clearly came to believe that it was with the dog that the most perfect human/animal relations could be forged, the dog who knew his place ('Four-Feet trotting behind') as the cat who walked by herself did not, the dog the perfect servant. This series of imaginative forays culminated in *Thy Servant A Dog* of 1930, a dog its titular hero and second-remove Narrator. An extract should enable every reader to know straightaway whether this is his or her book. This is the beginning of its second paragraph:

> There is walk-in-Park-on-lead. There is off-lead-when-we-come-to-the-grass. There is 'nother dog, like me, off-lead. I say: 'Name?' He says: 'Slippers.' He says: 'Name?' I say: 'Boots.' He says: 'I am fine dog. I have Own God, called Miss.' I say: 'I am very fine dog. I have Own God called Master.'

This manner continues throughout the ninety pages of text.

There are several ways of liking animals. Kipling's was peculiarly English, an approach shared with varying degrees of success by Beatrix Potter, by Kipling's great admirer, T. S. Eliot and, where the animals are stuffed, A. A. Milne; and for personified machines, the Reverend W. Awdrey and Graham Greene. Some readers may find Kipling's attitudes to animals harder to respond to than his attitudes to Empire, especially since, like many other English writers, he was as ready to write about the delights of hunting them down. But for those whose fondness and respect is given to some animals *as* animals, Kipling has just a few good stories and some touching verses to offer. The verses are '"The Power of the Dog"' and its first stanza goes:

> There is sorrow enough in the natural way
> From men and women to fill our day;
> And when we are certain of sorrow in store,
> Why do we always arrange for more?
> *Brothers and Sisters, I bid you beware*
> *Of giving your heart to a dog to tear...*

The story of 1909 that the verses belong to, 'Garm – a Hostage', opens with the Narrator saving the soldier Stanley from the punishment that must follow yet another of his drunken bouts. In gratitude, and as pledge for future abstemiousness, Stanley gives to the Narrator his bull-terrier. The Narrator protests, '"That dog's worth more than most men, Stanley," I said. "'E's that and more," said Stanley', and so he is. But neither soldier nor dog can live without the other, and this time it is realistically and pitifully that Kipling recounts the pain of the dog that has lost its own man, never adding more to it that a human observer could have seen.

But if, in my view, Kipling's Daemon slept through most of his work on animals, he could sometimes be awakened, and so he was for 'The Conversion of St. Wilfrid', one of the stories in *Rewards and Fairies*. It tells of the Northumbrian Wilfrid who converted most of the South Saxons, but failed with the Sussex landowner Meon who had a pet seal Padda. Eddi, Wilfrid's chaplain, was scared stiff of Padda, and outraged when Meon said he'd be baptized only if Padda were baptized too. But the lives of all three men were saved by Padda the seal, acting only, as Eddi came to understand, in his nature as a seal, and when Meon at last offered himself for baptism, Eddi, when he thought Wilfrid wasn't looking, 'made a little cross in holy water' on Padda's wet muzzle. The poem that goes with the story is better still. Eddi, now priest of a little Sussex chapel, is preparing to celebrate mass there on Christmas Eve. But 'the Saxons were keeping Christmas' in their own way, and no one came to the service, until, at the open door, there wandered in 'an old marsh donkey' and 'a wet yoke-weary bullock'.

> 'How do I know what is greatest,
>   How do I know what is least?
> That is my Father's business,'
>   Said Eddi, Wilfrid's priest. . .
>
> And he told the Ox of a Manger
>   And a stall in Bethlehem,
> And he spoke to the Ass of a Rider
>   That rode to Jerusalem. . .
>
> from 'Eddi's Service'

Both the story and the poem have the acceptable simplicity of the old English legends about the English saints and the beasts they often loved and tended. But not all the animals Kipling treated as animals are endearing. Bimi, the jealous chimpanzee of the chilling story 'Bertram and Bimi' *(described on page 143)* is quite literally beastly.

*   *   *

> . . . God's mercy is upon the young,
> God's wisdom in the baby tongue. . .
>
> from 'Tod's Amendment'

Several of Kipling's animal stories were written for children, and many for his own children. He had three: Josephine, born in Vermont in 1892; Elsie, also born in Vermont in 1896; and John, born in 1897 at the Burne-Joneses' home in Rottingdean. Josephine, by photographs and all accounts, was the prettiest and most enchanting. She was her father's angel, and her death was an open wound to him all his life. Two of his writings are said to have had her in mind. One is the poem that comes at the end of the two Stone Age tales in the *Just So Stories*, about the child, Taffy and her father Tegumai. Taffy is flitting ahead on the trail that runs over Merrow Down; lighting a damp-wood smoke to show him the way:

'My daughter is growing into a beauty,' Kipling said of Josephine, and so she was. With her death, his younger daughter wrote later, 'a light had gone out that could never be rekindled'.

For far – oh very far behind,
  So far she cannot call to him,
Comes Tegumai alone to find
  The daughter that was all to him!

from 'Merrow Down'

The other direct recall of Josephine is said to be in the story 'They' of 1904. This is a Sussex story in which the Narrator, on a meandering motor-car exploration of the Downs, willingly loses himself and falls upon an old garden and an old house hidden in a valley. The blind woman who owns the house invites him in. Everywhere he hears the noises of happy children and once or twice, catches a glimpse of a waving hand, a 'bright head', a boy's blue blazer. A month or so later, knowing the way now, he calls again, and then again, and this third time he is sitting withdrawn by the fire on the brick hearth while the blind woman talks to one of her tenant farmers. It seems that someone has slipped round the leather screen behind him, for he feels his hand taken between the soft hands of a child and thinks that now, at last, he need only turn round to see, properly, one of the children whom so far he has only heard and glimpsed –

> The little brushing kiss fell in the centre of my palm – as a gift on which the fingers were, once, expected to close: as the all-faithful half-reproachful signal of a waiting child not used to neglect even when grown-ups were busiest – a fragment of the minute code devised very long ago.
> Then I knew...

Both Elsie and John Kipling were conventionally brought up. John went to a boarding prep-school at Rottingdean and then to Wellington. His poor eyesight prevented him from taking up the Naval Cadetship promised by Sir John Fisher, the First Sea Lord, and Wellington doubted his being able to pass the Army's entrance exams. So he was sent to a crammer, and there he was at the outbreak of war in 1914.

In 1983 there was published a book of Kipling's letters to his children, called *O Beloved Kids*. Most of the letters are as jocular as the address that is the title. As the poet Craig Raine has said of it, it shows that 'though Kipling was a master at writing for children, he was less good at writing *to* children'.[1] Kipling's surviving children seem to have been, as children, ordinary, untouched by any of the elfin sparks the father had perceived in Josephine. Even as Dan and Una, the useful devices for asking for explanations in *Puck of Pook's Hill* and *Rewards and Fairies*, the Kipling children come to no larger life of independency. But the letters are untouched by the Daemon (Craig Raine quotes 'This is the doom of the Makers – their Daemon lives in their pen./If he be absent or sleeping, they are even as other men...'). It cannot have been easy being Kipling's children, even though we do not know that John and Elsie ever resented the dreadful screen of hilarity through which their father addressed them. 'Oh you Awful Kid', one letter to Elsie begins, though it contains perhaps the nearest expression of direct affection in any of them – 'I too sometimes, want to see you – most dreffle! You see, I love you!'

John, certainly, at least once he had gone into the Army found Kipling's 'knowingness' irksome. He puts his father right pretty sharply on the impracticality of his suggestion of rabbit wire, or at a pinch, tennis netting, slung over a trench to stop lobbed hand grenades.

For all the persistent joking, the intrusive solicitude of those letters, no one can doubt Kipling's deep affection for his children, and his real and constant worrying over them; and, especially for John, his worries about homosexuality, though there is no reason to suppose they were needed.

Kipling had always hated and feared homosexuality, perhaps to a disturbing extent. Even in *Stalky & Co.*, he cannot help reassuring the adult reader about the essential innocence of the boys at Westward Ho! and that nothing of *that* kind went on there. In the story 'The Moral Reformers', the well-liked Padre, the Reverend

John, visits Stalky, M'Turk and Beetle in their study, and Beetle comments that the Padre had come through their dormitory the previous night – he had recognized that particular 'baccy'.

> 'Good heavens,' said the Reverend John absently. It was some years before Beetle perceived that this was rather a tribute to innocence than observation. The long, light, blindless dormitories, devoid of inner doors, were crossed at all hours of the night by masters visiting one another; for bachelors sit up later than married folk. Beetle had never dreamed that there might be a purpose in this steady policing.

In *Something of Myself*, Kipling is more explicit, and by later lights, embarrassingly so. But unless young John shared his father's outlook, he must have been made uneasy, especially in the light of the mild homosexuality likely at any boys' boarding school, to receive such warnings as this; written in 1912, when John was thirteen –

> What really bothered me most was not being able to have a last jaw with you. I wanted to tell you a lot of things about keeping clear of any chap who is even suspected of beastliness. There is no limit to the trouble possible if one goes about (however innocently) with swine of that type. Give them the widest of wide berths. Whatever their merits may be in the athletic line they are at heart only sweeps and scum and *all* friendship or acquaintance with them ends in sorrow and disgrace.

Kipling ends this part of the letter with 'More on this subject when we meet.' What more could there have been?

$$\ast \qquad \ast \qquad \ast$$

Even before he had children of his own, Kipling had had a line in Anglo-Indian children of more or less insufferable sentimentality. There was 'His Majesty the King' of 1888, a neglected six-year-old, who knew his mother only as Memsahib, and spoke like this – he is describing his mother's 'escort', 'the Captain Man': 'He *doesn't* laugh. He only makes faces wiv his mouf, and when he want to o-muse me I am *not* o-mused.' There was Wee Willie Winkie of the same year and similar vocabulary, who saved an admired officer's fiancée from murderous tribesmen. There was Tod of the earlier story, 'Tod's Amendment' who knew the vernacular and listened to the servants talking with their friends, and so was able to put to rights the Legal Member of the Supreme Legislative Council on the drafting of a Bill on land tenure.

Only a couple of these early stories about children are likely to appeal to modern readers, and these are not about middle-class Anglo-Indian children. One, 'The Drums of the Fore and Aft', is about two fourteen-year-old drummer-boys, stunted, foul-mouthed, sweepings of the London streets, who, not from native courage but because they are drunk, are able to rally a frightened, inexperienced regiment under fire; and die for it. This story takes far too circuitous a way to its climax, but the end is worth the journey.

Shirley Temple as Wee Willie Winkie in John Ford's film of 1937, about the Colonel's child who outfaced the Bad Men across the frontier and saved the subaltern's fiancée.

The other, and better tale is 'The Story of Muhammad Din'. Muhammad Din is the child of Iman Din, the Narrator's *khitmatgar* or butler, 'a tiny, plump figure in a ridiculously inadequate shirt which came, perhaps, half-way down the tubby stomach'. With the Sahib's permission he takes possession of such throw-outs as an old polo ball, a broken soap-dish, a gaily spotted sea-shell deliberately dropped, and with these, and some shrivelled marigold flowers and bits of red brick, Muhammad Din builds grottos in corners of the garden. One day the Narrator learns that the child has a fever, and he sends quinine and an English Doctor. But a week later, 'I met on the road to the Mussulman burying-ground Iman Din, accompanied by one other friend, carrying in his arms, wrapped in a white cloth, all that was left of little Muhammad Din... "They have no stamina, these brats," said the English Doctor.' Hardly ever when writing about Indians, did Kipling fall into sentimentality.

Of all Kipling's writings for or about children, the most substantial and important are *Puck of Pook's Hill* and *Rewards and Fairies*. But only nominally are those *for* children – very few children enjoy them. These stories find their places elsewhere in this book.

CHAPTER TEN

AFRICA

On your feet and let them know
This is why we love her!
For she is South Africa.
She is Our South Africa.
Is Our Own South Africa,
Africa all over!

from 'South Africa'

OR his time in India, Kipling had been a watcher, as much of the Whites as of the Indians. In Vermont, he would have been glad to belong, if accepted on his own terms; but he was not accepted, and he went away again. Africa, or rather and specifically, South Africa, was the object of a love-affair which flared to a climax, flamed for a while, then almost died away.

Kipling first went to South Africa in 1891 on his recuperative way to the Antipodes. He landed at Cape Town on 10 September and stayed there until the 25th, delighted with what he later described as:

> a sleepy, unkempt little place, where the stoeps of some of the older Dutch houses still jutted over the pavement. Occasional cows strolled up the main streets, which were full of coloured people of the sort that my *ayah* had pointed out to me were curly-haired (*hubshees*). . . there were also many Malays who were Muslims of a sort and had their own Mosques, and whose flamboyantly-attired women sold flowers on the curb, and took in washing. . .[1]

On the SS *Mexican* Kipling had met a congenial Navy Captain, whom he had accompanied at Madeira on a wine-buying expedition for the Captain's new command at Simons Town, the naval base. This friendship gave Kipling entry to the Navy Club of the Cape Station, whose Admiral kept tethered turtles on the swim in case he wanted turtle soup.

There is no indication that Kipling, still young, unmarried, footloose, thought then of South Africa as somewhere to belong. But one day in a restaurant, just before he left for Australia, Kipling claimed to have seen the man who would, for a time, make South Africa home for him: Cecil Rhodes. 'It never occurred to me to speak to him; and I have often wondered why –' Kipling wrote in 1936,[2] but surely to have done so then would have been to make the kind of intrusion that he himself most resented. Primrose, however, thinks this reported sighting of Rhodes a

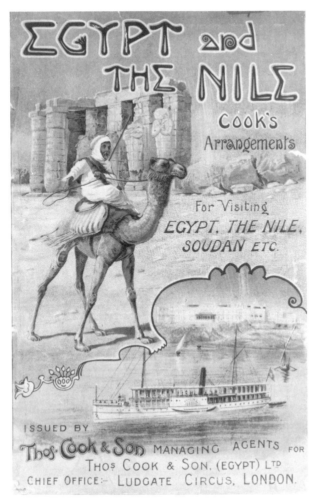

A Thomas Cook poster of 1905-6, and one as tempting and attractive for Nile tourists still as when it was first issued.

fantasy; on 13 September Rhodes left Cape Town for a trip to Matabeleland, and did not return before Kipling left.[3]

There was, however, more of Africa to visit and write about. It was not, after all, usual to travel between England and India without touching Egypt on the way, and almost at the end of his life Kipling still claimed some muddled memories of his second journey to England when he was five:

– a time in a ship with an immense semi-circle blocking all vision on each side of her. (She must have been the old paddle-wheel P&O *Ripon*). There was a train across a desert (the Suez Canal was not yet opened) and a halt in it, and a small girl wrapped in a shawl on the seat opposite me –[4]

Egypt, since 1878 an Anglo-French condominium, did not inspire Kipling, though he wrote some unmemorable verses on Araby Pasha's revolt and defeat in 1882. However, in 1913 the Kiplings chose Egypt and the Nile River trip for their winter holiday and Kipling described the trip in seven 'Letters' for *Nash's Magazine* and the *Cosmopolitan*; they were reprinted in *Letters of Travel* of 1920. In them Kipling grumbled testily at the deficiencies of the single-screw P&O boat which took them to Port Said, and marvelled, as all tourists do, at the narrowness of the strips of green which separate the Nile from the desert in the south. Much is tiresome, like the jocular chats with long-dead Egyptians, but there is sharp observation too; for instance, the alternation of West and East in sophisticated women in Cairo. And there is, as I think, a moment of tragedy when remembered similarities culminate in recognition of the smells of foods cooking in the court-yards ('them spicy garlic smells'), 'and I found myself saying, as perhaps the dead say when they have recovered their wits, "This is my real world again."'[5]

The Sudan, though Kipling never went south of Halfa, did a little better by the Daemon. For one thing, it served him as background for the battle scenes in *The Light that Failed*, though hardly evocative of the country, or needing to be. Then in 1890 there had been a well-known, if now unlikeable tribute to the Sudanese – the Fuzzy-Wuzzies – whom we English defeated, with difficulty, in 1885 at Abu Klea, though not in time to save General Gordon, besieged in Khartoum:

> So 'ere's *to* you, Fuzzy-Wuzzy, at your 'ome in the Soudan;
> You're a pore benighted 'eathen but a first-class fightin' man;
> An' 'ere's *to* you, Fuzzy-Wuzzy, with your 'ayrick 'ead of 'air –
> You big black boundin' begger – for you broke a British square!

from '"Fuzzy-Wuzzy"'

A far better piece on the Sudan, though unrecommendable to campaigners against blood-sports, is a well-made story, the 'Little Foxes', of 1909, about an English governor in the Sudan who introduced fox-hunting, made it the basis of his rule, and arranged public humiliation for the heart-bleeding Liberal MP who came out to investigate reported ill-treatment of the natives. Kipling maintained that this was basically a true story, which had been told to him by one of the fox-hunting administrators; and later, he said, he met another of them who said that he had got it just right.

Central Africa, where Kipling never stopped off, produced a story based on Strickland, the Indian policeman (*see page 39*), now retired and living at Weston-super-Mare. His young son Adam, Assistant-Commissioner in a Central African Protectorate, has been sent home on sick leave, wasted after bad fever, heavily dependant on his Indian bearer Iman Din. To a group of old friends, including Stalky and the Narrator, Adam tells of the cannibalism in his district – 'When a Sheshaheli offers you four pounds of women's breast, tattoo marks and all, ske-wered up in a plantain leaf –' and of the good fortune that enabled him, though

'This is the Elephant's Child having his nose pulled by the Crocodile. . . he is talking through his nose and saying, "Led go! You are hurting be!"' (from Kipling's own caption to his own illustration)

nearly prostrate with fever, to fine a slave-dealer enough to finance the cotton-growing by which Adam hoped to rehabilitate his erring district.

But the old friends are fly old birds, and once young Adam has gone to bed, they demand the true story from Iman Din. As they suspected, both slave-dealer and servant had conspired, for love of the young man (we recall the model young subalterns in India), to get the required cash into Adam's hands. 'A Deal in Cotton' (1902) is a clever story, but the patronising deceiving of the adored young man is offensive.

Mozambique had set Kipling's first naval story, 'Judson and the Empire', in 1893, which is, as his comic stories go, better than many. In 1900 Mozambique was to be the end of the journey for a more important character, the Elephant's Child of 'satiable curiosity, who, in order to discover what the Crocodile had for dinner,

> went from Graham's town to Kimberley, and from Kimberley to Khama's Country, and from Khama's Country he went east by north, eating melons all the time, till he came to the banks of the great grey-green, greasy Limpopo River, all set about with fever-trees. . .

Kipling had himself taken some part of that journey in 1898 (and some of it on a bicycle), when, at Rhodes's suggestion, he had visited the new province of Rhodesia, but (apart from a much later winter trip to Egypt again, and another to Algeria) this was as far 'North of South' as he ever went.

It was when Kipling went back to Cape Town early in 1898 with his wife and children that he met Cecil Rhodes, premier of Cape Colony, a millionaire from Kimberley diamonds and Rand gold. Kipling and Rhodes discovered they shared a dream, South Africa as a white man's land where the English could settle and make fortunes. This was a dream over-enthusiastically shared too by the adventurer Dr Leander Starr Jameson, who in 1893 had crushed the Matabele, and made their land into Rhodesia, and in 1896 had made his notorious raid into the Transvaal. No one, not even the Liberals in England, considered the black people of these regions. The niggers in the woodpile then were the Boers, the deeply religious, deeply conservative descendants of the original Dutch settlers, who did not dream the English dream and feared for their own way of life, with the intrusion into 'their' Transvaal of the British *uitlanders* who were making big money there. British and Boer aims and values were incompatible. Attempts at negotiation – the British side headed by Alfred Milner, the Boers by Paul Kruger – broke down. In 1899 war broke out, the Boers of the Transvaal and the Orange Free State against the British of the Cape Province, and the Boers, initially, with substantial superiority in men and artillery.

When the war began, Kipling was in England, an England deeply divided on the moral rightness of this war. The Liberals were outraged by it, and they included Aunt Georgie Burne-Jones. Kipling was vehemently pro-war from the start, seeing it as not only necessary to the fulfilment of his and Rhodes's dreams, but a golden opportunity for the British to rehearse for that coming war against the Germans that he was already so presciently aware of. As he made the British general say in his story, 'The Captive' of 1902:

It's a first-class dress-parade for Armageddon. With luck, we ought to run half a million men through the mill. Why, we might even be able to give our Native Army a look in –

In Rottingdean, where he was then living, Kipling began his war work. He set on foot a movement for rifle-clubs in the villages, which undoubtedly paid off when, in 1914, Armageddon came. And to raise money for the Soldiers' Families' Fund, he wrote some verses, which, he said, with mock modesty, 'had some elements of direct appeal, but, as was pointed out, lacked "poetry"'. Here is the first stanza of 'The Absent-Minded Beggar' – 'beggar', of course, as usual, a euphemism:

When you've shouted 'Rule Britannia,' when you've sung 'God Save the Queen,'
   When you've finished killing Kruger with your mouth,
Will you kindly drop a shilling in my little tambourine
   For a gentleman in khaki ordered South?
He's an absent-minded beggar, and his weaknesses are great –
   But we and Paul must take him as we find him –
He is out on active service, wiping something off a slate –
   And he's left a lot of little things behind him!
Duke's son – cook's son – son of a hundred kings –

Left: Kipling among the war correspondents at Glovers Island. Of his work on The Friend *he said, 'Never again will there be such a paper. Never again such a staff. Never such fine larks.'*
Right: Cecil Rhodes, model imperialist, anathema to Liberals, wanted to federate South Africa under British rule. 'What is your dream?' he asked Kipling, who replied that Rhodes was part of it.

(Fifty thousand horse and foot going to Table Bay!)
Each of 'em doing his country's work
    (and who's to look after their things?)
Pass the hat for your credit's sake
      and pay – pay – pay!. . .

These verses were printed first in Alfred Harmsworth's jingoist *Daily Mail*, reproduced on cotton for handkerchiefs, in silk for 'benefit' programmes, set to catchy music by Sir Arthur Sullivan, ground out on hundreds of barrel-organs. They raked in a quarter of a million pounds.

The South African War was, for Kipling, his very own war. Rhodes called on his willing services, as did Lord Roberts who arranged for Kipling to join the staff of *The Friend*, the first Army newspaper issued specifically for the troops in the field.

The Boer War provided the first occasion when Kipling actually saw troops under fire and, indeed, came under fire himself; this at a small engagement at Karee Siding. Kipling came to respect Piet, as he called the Boer fighting man, and he supposed that the soldiers did too: 'I'd just as soon as not/Respect the man I fight,' he had a 'Regular of the Line' say in his poem 'Piet', and 'I've known a lot o' men behave a dam' sight worse than Piet.' But he hated what he saw as the treacherous Boer civilians, who would shoot from farmhouses flying the white flag; what he was castigating as less than fair fighting was, of course, guerrilla warfare.

Several stories came out of that war: 'A Burgher of the Free State' which appeared in the *Daily Express* in 1900, but was so much disliked by Georgie Burne-Jones that it was not published in any collected edition in Kipling's lifetime; 'The Captive' about an engaging American arms dealer on the make; 'The Comprehension of Private Copper' in which an English private out-tricks an arrogant half-caste Boer; and 'A Sahib's War' *(see page 103)*. The last three stories were collected in *Traffics and Discoveries* of 1904, and there too is the outstanding if puzzling story 'Mrs. Bathurst'. That story, among its other merits shows Kipling's eye for a landscape of quite a different palette from India's:

> . . . a bay of drifted sand and a plank-platform half buried in sand not a hundred yards from the edge of the surf. Moulded dunes, whiter than any snow, rolled far inland up a brown and purple valley of splintered rocks and dry scrub. A crowd of Malays hauled at a net beside two blue and green boats on the beach; a picnic party danced and shouted barefoot where a tiny river trickled across the flat, and a circle of dry hills, whose feet were set in sands of silver, locked us in against a seven-coloured sea. . .

Of Kipling's many poems about this war, a few, of very different kinds, are unforgettable. There is 'Lichtenberg' *(see page 103)*. There is the famous 'Boots', as fine an example as any – and yet only one of many – of Kipling's mastery of rhythm:

> We're foot–slog–slog–slog–sloggin' over Africa –
> Foot–foot–foot–foot–sloggin' over Africa –
> (Boots–boots–boots–boots–movin' up and down again!)
>   There's no discharge in the war!. . .
>
> Don't–don't–don't–don't–look at what's in front of you.
> (Boots–boots–boots–boots–movin' up an' down again);
> Men–men–men–men–men–go mad with watchin' 'em,
>   An' there's no discharge in the war!. . .

Of a different quality, there is 'The Hyaenas', written much later for the aftermath of the Great War, but based on Boer War experience:

> After the burial-parties leave
>   And the baffled kites have fled;
> The wise hyaenas come out at eve
>   To take account of our dead. . .
>
> They whoop and halloo and scatter the dirt
>   Until their tushes white
> Take good hold of the Army shirt,
>   And tug the corpse to light,
>
> And the pitiful face is shewn again
>   For an instant ere they close; . . .

Kipling could not write good verse to order. There were two deaths in Africa for which he would have wished to do his best: that of Mary Kingsley, who caught the fever from the soldiers she nursed in Simons Town hospital, and died in 1900; and, when the war was petering out in March 1902, the death of Cecil Rhodes. For both, Kipling's verses were only mediocre; though the latter poem was read over Rhodes's grave in the Matoppos Hills and some lines from it carved on the Rhodes Memorial on Table Mountain.

Rhodes had been suffering from heart disease for some time, but already during the war he had built on his country estate of Grote Schuur a little house called the Woolsack for visiting artists or men of letters. The Woolsack was always available to the Kiplings; Carrie and the children wintered at the Cape throughout the war, and from the time the Woolsack was finished until they gave up their South African winters in 1908, this was where they stayed. Here the children knew barefoot freedom with all kinds of beasts, including a lion-cub hand-reared by Carrie. It was to the Woolsack that Rhodes came to talk about a new dream, that of the Rhodes Scholarship for men from the Dominions and Colonies (and, oddly, from America and Germany) to go to Oxford, and it was Carrie who persuaded him that his proposed £250 a year for a student was not enough and should be raised to £300. When in 1917 the Rhodes Trust was set up, Kipling was happy to be made one of the Trustees, and remained so until 1925 when he resigned in protest at the appointment of the 'Liberal' Philip Kerr, the future Lord Lothian. And it was here that the often inarticulate Rhodes would call on Rudyard for words to clothe his ideas. (His Prime Minister cousin Stanley Baldwin, though far from inarticulate, was to do the same later on – it was Kipling who supplied Baldwin with the famous words for castigating the ambition of the press-lord, Beaverbrook for 'power without responsibility' as 'the prerogative of the harlot throughout the ages'. More benignly, Kipling helped to write King George V's Christmas broadcasts.)

On the face of it, the English won the Boer war, to the great satisfaction of most of the English people, whose hysterical celebration of the relief of Mafeking in 1900 had added the verb 'maffick' to the language. (It is said that Colonel Robert Baden-Powell, commanding at Mafeking, so much enjoyed the siege that he looked for another town to be besieged in; and was only with difficulty diverted.) The Liberals, however, remained unhappy. When the Peace of Vereeniging was signed in May 1902, Georgie Burne-Jones hung from the window of her Rottingdean house a black banner on which was written: 'We have killed and also taken possession.' A protesting crowd gathered and Rudyard, hurrying over from his home across the green, had some difficulty in persuading them to disperse.

He himself was unhappy about the peace, though for different reasons. He worried about the returning soldiers. Having seen South Africa, how could England content them?

> Me that 'ave rode through the dark
> Forty mile, often, on end,
> Along the Ma 'ollisberg Range,
> With only the stars for my mark

London on Mafeking night. The Oxford English Dictionary states that the verb maffick *was originally used 'to designate the behaviour of the crowds . . . that celebrated with uproarious rejoicing the relief of the British garrison'.*

An' only the night for my friend,
An' things runnin' off as you pass,
An' things jumpin' up in the grass,
An' the silence, the shine an' the size
Of the 'igh, unexpressible skies –
I am takin' some letters almost
As much as a mile to the post,
An' 'mind you come back with the change!'
Me!. . .

from 'Chant-Pagan'

In another poem of the same year, Kipling gave a Cockney's answer:

If England was what England seems,
An' not the England of our dreams,
But only putty, brass, an' paint,
'Ow quick we'd drop 'er!   But she ain't!. . .

from 'The Return'

Kipling worried also because he was unsure that we had, in any real sense, won a victory:

Let us admit it fairly, as a business people should,
We have had no end of a lesson: it will do us no end of good . . .

140

It was our fault, and our very great fault, and *not* the judgment of Heaven.
We made an Army in our own image, on an island nine by seven,
Which faithfully mirrored its makers' ideals, equipment, and mental attitude –
And so we got our lesson: and we ought to accept it with gratitude . . .

from 'The Lesson'

But we did not, and here was Kipling's major worry. The war had not taught us enough. It had not even taught us enough about the proper care of our soldiers; in South Africa as in India, Kipling had been appalled by the casual health and sanitary arrangements – were these being rectified? Above all, had we taken sufficient warning that, in what little time might remain, we should be getting ready for a greater, more terrible war?

Ever more desperately Kipling tried to awaken England. He tried in a sub-Wellsian story 'The Army of a Dream' (1904) to convince his unheeding country-men of the social gains of conscription. He tried in 'The Islanders' of 1902, a poem that gave much offence, to insult his countrymen into action, abusing them as 'the flannelled fools at the wicket' and 'the muddied oafs at the goals'. A finer poem, 'The Dykes', of 1903, gave symbolic warning of the perils of inertia:

We have no heart for the fishing – we have no hand for the oar –
All that our fathers taught us of old pleases us now no more.
All that our own hearts bid us believe we doubt where we do not deny –
There is no proof in the bread we eat nor rest in the toil we ply . . .

We were born to peace in the lee of the dykes, but the time of our peace is past . . .

The untended dykes are breached, and the waters pour in:

Now we can only wait till the day, wait and apportion our shame.
These are the dykes our fathers left, but we would not look to the same.
Time and again were we warned of the dykes, time and again we delayed:
Now, it may fall, we have slain our sons, as our fathers we have betrayed . . .

On the Continent there was stirring a new way of conceptualizing society, of thinking in terms of mutually hostile generations. Kipling was by many years the first writer to express this in England; and rage at the old men's inertia, their blindness to England's danger, their lack of heed for their sons, imbues another poem of 1903, 'The Old Men':

The Lamp of our Youth will be utterly out, but we shall subsist on the smell of it;
And whatever we do, we shall fold our hands and suck our gums and think well of it.
Yes, we shall be perfectly pleased with our work, and that is the Perfectest Hell of it! . . .

No one much listened to Kipling's warnings. The Boer War was over, and even Kipling began to forget it, to live in the pleasant present of a new life in Sussex. But from time to time he would repeat his warnings about the powers that were single-mindedly making ready for war.

CHAPTER ELEVEN

'THE HIGH AND NARROW SEAS'

If blood be the price of admiralty,
Lord God, we ha' paid in full!...

from 'The Song of the Dead'

IPLING'S passion for, his infatuation with, the sea has origins impossible to know. As a child, he was never a one for – in Kenneth Grahame's phrase – 'messing about in boats'; at school he had been keen on swimming, but his interest in the sea went no further. As a traveller, his chosen transport was the most comfortable steamer available, and even so, if the sea was at all rough, he was usually seasick. Like all Englishmen, he was, of course, aware that he came of an island people, a seafaring race, and that Britannia still ruled the waves, but though Kipling wrote proudly in prose and verse of the seven seas of the British Empire, he was as much moved by lonely seas, the habitat not of men but seals and sea-serpents; and he used the sea and ships on the sea as metaphors for almost anything, from pirating publishers to England in near-terminal peril. There is no obvious explanation. As so often with Kipling, we must simply accept the facts as they are, with, in this case the realization that if he had never written about anything *but* the sea, he would still be among our more important writers.

The first material for Kipling's maritime writing plopped into the well of his unconscious in March 1889, when he left Calcutta by way of the shifting estuary of the Hoogly, through which ships were guided by the highly skilled, proudly exclusive brotherhood of Hoogly pilots. That experience floated up again six years later as 'An Unqualified Pilot', a story, really, for older children and a good one, about the Hoogly pilot's young son who had the guts and the impertinence to work a Chinese junk up the estuary at a cut price.

The next steamer, the *Africa* from Rangoon to Singapore, provided, or led to the invention of the German naturalist for whom he pinched the name Hans Breitmann from the popular American *Hans Breitmann's Ballads* by Charles G. Leland, which Kipling had enjoyed as a boy, and had parodied in 1888 in India. The two stories Kipling gives to Breitmann to tell are not stories *of* the sea, but that sub-genre of stories told *on* the sea, typically in the smoking-rooms of liners, though in this case one is told in the ship's bows among the Lascars on a night of great heat, the other at tea-and-beer-drinking time on deck. Unfortunately Kipling reproduces Breitmann's German-accented English in phonetical spelling as nearly unreadable as that of the original *Ballads*, and one cannot but recall George Orwell's suggestion about the greater acceptability of Kipling's Cockney work if it were to be transcribed into standard English.

Here, the difficulty is a pity, for both stories are economical, brutish, and good. 'The German Flag' of the one story is an extremely poisonous coral-snake caught in Uruguay by the naturalist Reingelder, at a time when Breitmann, another collector-naturalist, was after orchids there. Reingelder disregarded warnings, so, Breitmann ends laconically, 'I took der coral-snake – dot Sherman Flag – so bad and dreacherous, und I bickled him alife. So I got him: und so I lost Reingelder.'

This story was short of incubation: it appeared in the *Gazette* in April 1889. 'Bertran and Bimi' did not appear before it was printed in *Life's Handicap* in 1891. It is longer and more serious, the story of a French naturalist and Bimi, his extremely clever chimpanzee. This is one of those stories it would be a pity to enlarge on for fear of tempering the finally atrocious impact it makes on the reader.

Wharf at Calcutta. The passage of 'the uncertain Hugli' was plotted by the Port Office, whose elite service of pilots guided annually some 2 million tons of shipping up and down the estuary.

The steamer on which those stories are told gives the impression of being a somewhat more casual and disreputable boat than, surely, the one that carried Kipling, the Hills and the American tourists. The steamer of the story 'A Matter of Fact' was undoubtedly a tramp. In 'A Matter of Fact', three journalists, an American, a Dutchman, and the Narrator, are all taking this cheapest possible way from Cape Town to Southampton. One day something goes hideously wrong with the sea. There is a gigantic wave, a filthy smell, an icy coldness:

> . . . a silver-gray wave broke over the bow, leaving on the deck a sheet of sediment – the gray broth that has its place in the fathomless deeps of the sea. . . The dead and most untouched deep water of the sea had been heaved to the top by the submarine volcano.

Then –

> Some six or seven feet above the port bulwarks, framed in fog, and as utterly unsupported as the full moon, hung a Face. It was not human, and it certainly was not animal, for it did not belong to this earth as known to man. The mouth was open, revealing a ridiculously tiny tongue – as absurd as the tongue of an elephant; there were tense wrinkles of white skin at the angles of the drawn lips, white feelers like those of a barbel sprung from the lower jaw, and there was no sign of teeth within the mouth. But the horror of the face lay in the eyes, for these were sightless – white, in sockets as white as scraped bone, and blind. Yet for all this the face, wrinkled as the mask of a lion is drawn in Assyrian sculpture, was alive with rage and terror. One long feeler touched our bulwarks. Then the face disappeared. . .

The Thing (the terrifyingly strange was often called 'the Thing' in those days) reappears. It is a Sea-Serpent and it is mortally wounded. Then there is a 'dot on the horizon and the sound of a shrill scream, and it was as though a shuttle shot all across the sea in one breath, and a second head and neck tore through the levels –'. This is the mate of the first Thing, and in Kipling's description of the agony of these beasts there is a matching agony of pity I think he never achieved again.

The story ends with a naughty European kick-in-the-tail at the American journalist who in humiliation learns that the best method of publishing the truth may be by way of a lie.

A sea-story often counted among Kipling's best is '"The Finest Story in the World"' of 1891, in which the Narrator, living in London, picks up a bank-clerk called Charlie Mears who wants to write, and usually wants to write trash, but sometimes slips into recounting memories of earlier incarnations: he had been a Greek galley slave; he had been a Norseman who had sailed with Eric the Red to Furdurstrandi, the distant beaches, which are in Vineland which is America. Kipling has to convince us (and very nearly does) that he himself has somehow acquired praeternatural knowledge of a galley-slave's life and conditions, exactly how he is chained to his oar, exactly how the sunlight comes 'squeezing through between the handle and the hole and wobbling about as the ship moves', how the overseer disposes of the bodies of the men from the lowest deck who work in the

'The two things met . . . Male and female, we said, the female coming to the male. She circled round him bellowing, and laid her neck across the curve of his great turtle-back. . .' (From an illustration to 'A Matter of Fact')

dark and go mad. For the Furdurstrandi incarnation, Kipling lets us know the source, which is the Saga of Thorfin Karlsefne, and though this is a grand story for anyone to retell (it was charmingly retold in 1968 by the American Harry Harrison in *The Technicolor Time Machine*) the intended element of praeternaturality is absent: we can see how the trick is done.

Of course the Narrator in the story hopes for more, and more. But then, as Grish Chunder, the Bengali law student, had predicted, Charlie falls in love, and the present closes him in.

It is a good story, and nearly excellent, but it is flawed. The incarnations are, as indicated, of uneven quality. We are irked, once again, by the knowing Narrator; and we can hardly believe that this narrator would have offered such patient kindness to the vulgar little bank-clerk that was Charlie before his gift broke through. Did one side of Kipling's head see himself as a Charlie?

Already by the 1890s Kipling was writing rollicking verses which were ostensibly about the sea but really about something else, as 'The Rhyme of the Three Captains' was about American pirating of English works *(see page 80)*, and 'The Three-Decker' of 1894 was a defence of the old-fashioned three-volume romantic novel against more modern practices in fiction:

> We asked no social questions – we pumped no hidden shame –
> We never talked obstetrics when the Little Stranger came . . .

> I left 'em all in couples a-kissing on the decks.
> I left the lovers loving and the parents signing cheques.
> In endless English comfort, by county-folk caressed,
> I left the old three-decker at the Islands of the Blest!. . .

This kind of thing is jolly enough, if hardly important. But a few of the earlier sea poems are outstanding, like 'The Sea and the Hills' originally a chapter-heading for *Kim* in 1901; this became, with some changes, the second of four verses of a poem in *The Five Nations* of 1903. Here are the original seven lines from the head of Chapter 13 of *Kim*:

> Who hath desired the Sea – the immense and contemptuous surges?
> The shudder, the stumble, the swerve ere the star-stabbing bowsprit emerges –
> The orderly clouds of the trade and the ridged roaring sapphire thereunder –
> Unheralded cliff-lurking flaws and the head-sails' low-volleying thunder?
> His Sea in no wonder the same – His Sea and the same in each wonder,
>   His Sea that his being fulfils?
> So and no otherwise – so and no otherwise hillmen desire their Hills!

The other important early poems are two companion pieces, two long monologues. The first, from which we have already had several quotations (*see pages 99 and 105*), is 'McAndrew's Hymn' of 1894, the justification of a Calvinist Scottish Chief Engineer. 'Lord, send a man like Robbie Burns to sing the Song o' Steam,' McAndrew cries, but most people who have read his Hymn will believe that Kipling was the man he sent.

McAndrew was 'Third on the *Mary Gloster*' when he was tempted by the 'soft, lasceevious stars' of the South Seas, and the *Mary Gloster*, whose name titles the second poem, was the freighter that the self-made millionaire ship-owner, Sir Anthony Gloster, had built and named for his loved wife Mary.

Now Mary is dead, buried at sea. Sir Anthony is dying, and all the family he leaves is a no-good wastrel of a son:

> Harrer an' Trinity College! I ought to ha' sent you to sea –
> But I stood you an education, an' what have you done for me?
> The things I knew was proper you wouldn't thank me to give,
> And the things I knew was rotten you said was the way to live.
> For you muddled with books and pictures, an' china an' etchin's an' fans,
> And your rooms at college was beastly – more like a whore's than a man's. . .

But there's no one else, so it must be this weakling who will go out to the Java Seas in the *Mary Gloster*, with McAndrew and the coffin, to carry out his last wishes:

> *I* believe in the Resurrection, if I read my Bible plain,
> But I wouldn't trust 'em at Wokin'; we're safer at sea again. . .
> An' Mac'll take her in ballast – an' she trims best by the head –
> Down by the head an' sinkin'. . .
> 'Never seen death yet, Dickie? – Well, now is your time to learn!

146

Left: McAndrew, as envisaged by Howard Pyle in Scribner's Magazine, *December 1894, where 'McAndrew's Hymn' was first published.*
Right: Kipling dreaming of the Navy. The two visits he made to the Channel Squadron in 1898 were written up and published that autumn as A Fleet in Being.

This poem, published in 1896 and perfectly transmuted from whatever experiences lay behind it, still gives rise to some queries relating to Kipling's life. The contemptuous references to 'Harrer an' Trinity College', remind us that Harrow School and Trinity College, Cambridge, had educated Stanley Baldwin, and that Rudyard was understandably bitter that his own education was both socially inferior and truncated. 'I'd give anything to be in the Sixth at Harrow as he is, with a University Education to follow,' he wrote to one of his aunts when he left school to go to India.

It was off the Little Paternosters that Sir Anthony Gloster's wife had been committed to the deep, and it was there that Sir Anthony was coming to join her 'in my private carriage'. The Paternoster Islands are in the Strait of Makasar with Java to the south, Borneo to the west, and only once could Kipling have come this way, on the P & O boat that took him from Australia to Ceylon in late 1891. His account of this journey is confined to his brushes with General Booth and he has nothing to say about the route, but if this was the way he came, it served him well for several good poems and stories. It was to the south-east of the Paternosters, in the Flores Straits, that the Keeper of the Wurlee Light saw streaky water upon streaky water and went mad; this was 'The Disturber of Traffic', though that story, already published in America before Kipling left Cape Town, must have been written in anticipation not recollection of the journey. Here too, but later, was set 'The Devil and the Deep Sea' published in 1896, a true comedy, and not, as Kipling's comedies often so unfortunately are, a topple into farce. 'The Devil and the Deep Sea' tells of a 900-ton tramp who frequently needs to change her name – from *Aglaia* to *Guiding Light*, to *Julia M'Gregor*, to *Shah-in-Shah*, to *Martin Hunt* – because of the piratical exploits of her devil-may-care crew. But the *Haliotis*, as she then is, gets what seems to be her final come-uppance when caught pearl-smuggling in these self-same seas, and the devoted expertise by which the Chief gets up steam in the ruined ship and slips port is, of all Kipling's expertise stories, the most exciting, because the use of special knowledge is in no way show-off, but essential to the story's suspenseful development. I have suggested earlier *(page 101)* a possible source for what seems to be Kipling's intimate knowledge of these tough, rough little ships.

*   *   *

At Cape Town in 1891 Kipling had had his first contacts, social and unofficial, with the Royal Navy, and these had clearly predisposed him to accept the invitations the Navy gave him in England in 1897 to go out with them; Kipling's second outing with the Navy the following year was, incidentally, the only time he ever landed in Ireland. Thereafter Kipling frequently visited the Navy. And as once with the Army, so now with the Navy, Kipling fell in love:

> That was a Royal progress . . . the leisurely, rolling slow-march of the overlords of all the seas. And the whole thing was my very own (that is to say yours); mine to me by right of birth. Mine were the speed and power of the hulls, not here only but the world over; the hearts and brains and lives of the trained men; such strength and such power as we and the World dare hardly guess at. And holding this power in the hollow of my hand; able at the word to exploit the earth to my own advantage, to gather me treasure and honour, as men reckon honour, I (and a few million friends of mine) forebore because we were white men.
>
> from *A Fleet in Being*

It is passages like this which make one wonder if the Daemon was apt to doze off while Kipling judged what to obliterate with the Indian ink.

These visits, and others made later, especially those of 1915 and in 1916 constituted a substantial achievement by the Royal Navy, for from 1896 onward Kipling was the Navy's enthusiastic publicist. Small books like *A Fleet in Being* of 1898, *The Fringes of the Fleet* of 1915 about minesweepers and submarines, and *Destroyers at Jutland* of 1916, were good journalism (if we can put up with their self-conscious jocularity) and good propaganda.

Kipling wrote some dreary farcical stories based on a Chief Petty Officer called Pyecroft, though he once used Pyecroft seriously and well, as part-narrator of 'Mrs.

Bathurst'. But unlike the Army in India, with the Navy he was better with the officers, and one wartime story, 'Sea Constables' of 1915, is good. Four 'temporary' naval officers talk together on shore over an hotel meal, piecing together between them the full account of how they hounded a neutral skipper and finally refused the request that would have made it possible he might live. Ethically, Carrington says, this is a deplorable tale. But it is probably enough to comment that it has the cold cruelty appropriate to the situation.

Even those who often re-read *Puck of Pook's Hill* and *Rewards and Fairies* may still be surprised if they tot up how many of those historical stories are, one way and another, about the sea; and almost all of them splendid. There are stories only indirectly about the sea, like 'The Wrong Thing', with niggardly King Henry VII wanting his gold scrollwork for the *Sovereign* on the cheap, and 'Gloriana', where the Queen – 'Gloriana – Belphoebe – Elizabeth of England' – entices two noble youths to sneak their ships dangerously against the Spaniards, without ever admitting her encouragement. ('I don't think you know really what you wanted done,' said flat-footed Una.) There are genuine sea stories: 'The Knights of the Joyous Venture', a Viking journey to Central Africa where Devils are fought for gold, and 'Simple Simon'; and '"A Priest in Spite of Himself"', a tale of Napoleon and Talleyrand, and of the French and the British smugglers who kept up their trade, come hell or high water:

> Twix' the Lizard and Dover,
> We hand our stuff over,
> Though I may not inform how we do it, nor when.
> But a light on each quarter,
> Low down on the water,
> Is well understood by poor honest men . . .
>
> from '"Poor Honest Men"'

Progressively, as he wrote these stories, Kipling allowed himself to forget that they were intended even nominally for children, built up, as they were, in layer upon layer of knowledge and meaning, and one of the most impressive, if ostensibly, one of the simplest, is '"Dymchurch Flit"'. The Widow Whitgift lives at Dymchurch on the Marsh, which is Romney Marsh, and she can, like all the Whitgifts, see further through a millstone than most, and 'read signs and sinnifications out o' birds flyin', stars fallin', bees hivin' an' such.' To her one night came the Pharisees (which is Sussex speech for fairies). Because of the Reformation, they must leave England. 'Farewell, Rewards and fairies –' wrote Bishop Corbett in his 'proper new ballad, entitled the Fairies' farewell' in 1647. What the Pharisees want of the Widow Whitgift is the loan of a boat and of her two sons, one born blind and the other struck dumb. Unwillingly, but at last, though grudgingly, with the 'Leave and Goodwill' without which they cannot depart, the Widow loans her sons and her boat:

– the Pharisees just about flowed past her – down the beach to the boat. *I* dunnamany of 'em – with their wives an' childern an' valooables, all escapin' out of cruel Old England. Silver you could hear clinkin', an' liddle bundles hove down dunt on the bottom-boards, an' passels o' liddle swords an' shields raklin', an' liddle fingers an' toes scratchin' on the boatside to board her when the two sons pushed off. That boat she sunk lower an' lower, but all the Widow could see in it was her boys movin' hampered-like to get at the tackle. Up sail they did, an' away they went, deep as a Rye barge, away into the off-shore mistës. . .

'"And, of course, the sons were both quite cured?"' Una asked – she *would*. But Tom Shoesmith (it seems to be he) who tells the story, says, and surely rightly, '"No-o. That would have been out o' Nature. She got em back *as* she sent 'em."'

The last good poem that Kipling wrote was 'The Storm Cone', a poem which powerfully used the metaphor of a ship on a lee coast in a storm:

> This is the midnight – let no star
> Delude us – dawn is very far.
> This is the tempest long foretold –
> Slow to make head but sure to hold. . .
>
> If we have cleared the expectant reef,
> Let no man look for his relief.
> Only the darkness hides the shape
> Of further peril to escape.
>
> It is decreed that we abide
> The weight of gale against the tide
> And those huge waves the outer main
> Sends in to set us back again. . .
>
> She moves, with all save purpose lost,
> To make her offing from the coast;
> But, till she fetches open sea,
> Let no man deem that he is free!

The poem's date of 1932 would make it seem that Kipling, sensitive always to peril for England, was warning of the rise of Hitler. But I have been told by someone who remembered the poem's first publication in the *Morning Post* that its purpose was the encouragement of the National Government of Ramsay MacDonald, formed after his Labour Government had resigned on 29 August 1931.

150

CHAPTER TWELVE

TRAVELS IN
TIME AND SPACE

Cities and Thrones and Powers
  Stand in Time's eye,
Almost as long as flowers,
  Which daily die:
But, as new buds put forth
  To glad new men,
Out of the spent and unconsidered Earth
  The Cities rise again...

from *Puck of Pook's Hill*

THE writer may enter time at any point he chooses, the future, the present, and the past, and Kipling worked in all three. His few stories of the future could fairly be called by our modern name of science fiction, though the genre is a good deal older than the name. In Kipling's youth, its best-known exponent had been Jules Verne, and one of the ways Kipling's father had made Rudyard learn French had been to give him Verne's *20,000 Leagues Under the Sea* in English at the start of the Paris trip of 1878, and then, when the boy was well into it, Lockwood took the English version away and left Rudyard with the French original. It is small wonder that Rudyard mastered both French and the craft of writing about technological futures.

Most of Kipling's work was set, as it superficially seems to us, in the present, but in fact, like many Victorians, Kipling tended to work a little way back into the past. Many of the Victorians would set their stories a generation or so before their own times – George Eliot is a good example – and so did Kipling. I have already pointed out *(page 27)* how many of the Simla stories told of days before Kipling went to India – of 'an almost pre-historic era in the history of British India' before lawn-tennis was born, before croquet was invented, and archery 'was as great a pest as lawn-tennis is now', he wrote in one of the *Plain Tales*. But in addition to this small and normal move backwards in time, Kipling often worked in what can more conventionally be called history, and it is such work that is part of the subject of this chapter.

Yet no imaginative writer is necessarily tied to our linear time. He can move outwards and upwards and downwards in time, and this Kipling did.

Left: 'The time is near . . . when the most extreme distances will be brought within the compass of one week's . . . travel,' Kipling told the Royal Geographical Society in February, 1914.
Right: 'The Night Mail flies over a hospital ship where they are singing the morning hymn.' This illustration is from the story's first publication in the Windsor Magazine *of December, 1905.*

I start with what can be called the conventional future, that of our own community as it might turn out to be. Typically, communities of the future are ideal communities, and usually ones of loving egalitarianism: the lion lies down with the lamb and little children lead them, whether in biblical times or modern science fiction. But, very rarely we find 'right-wing', hierarchical future societies, invented not as cacotopias, or horrid warnings, but shown as ideals. In the sixteenth century Thomas More's *Utopia* was one such, though the name has been taken over for the other kind. The American Edward Bellamy in his *Looking Backward* of 1888 wrote of a capitalistic paradise. And Rudyard Kipling wrote just a couple of true science fiction stories which carried to extremes the hierarchical rulership he preferred, 'With the Night Mail' of 1905, and 'As Easy as A.B.C.' of 1912.

Both stories tell of the same society, though one is set in AD 2000, the other in AD 2065. Electronics and aerial traffic are both fully developed, and it is a shock on first reading to realize that all the craft of the earlier story – the passenger ships, mail boats, sporting boats, tramps – are not winged aircraft but airships, with the mail boats travelling at 16 miles a second. This world (population 600 million and steadily falling) is ruled by the semi-elected, semi-nominated Aerial Board of Control (the A.B.C.), its motto being 'Transportation is Civilisation'. 'With the Night Mail' is not really a story, but rather a piece of imaginary reportage, a journey with the night mail in 'Postal Packet 162' from the despatching-caisson outside London to the Heights Receiving Towers at Quebec.

This earlier story is simple fun: the SF part of it is properly inventive, and the twenty-six pages that go with it from a specialist aeronautical magazine are charmingly ingenious. By the time of the second story, sixty-five years later, we learn that the principle on which the world is now governed is everyone's utter detestation of invasion of privacy, and hence of crowds. But in the backwoods district of Illinois, the citizens of small-town Chicago are singing MacDonagh's Song, the long-forbidden song:

> Once there was The People – Terror gave it birth;
> Once there was The People and it made a hell of earth!
> Earth arose and crushed it. Listen, oh, ye slain!
> Once there was The People – it shall never be again!

It is night and the citizens cannot see each other, and so they mass and scream, ready to lynch. The A.B.C. arrives, subdues them with searing light and intolerable noise, and then the Mayor of Chicago explains. A local group, the Serviles, want Democracy back, and the Chicagoans won't stand for it. So the A.B.C. lifts the Serviles away to the world's capital, London, where they will go through their risible procedures of voting and suchlike on a huge music-hall stage to audiences that will, presumably, explode in Kiplingesque laughter. There is something dark and unpleasant about this story. The kinds of humans exalted, the kinds derided, are not derived from a humanistic view of our kind.

The only other future-set story was the moralistic 'The Army of a Dream'. But its plea for conscription need imply no specifically political viewpoint, and the story should not count as science fiction, since only new organization, not new technology, is needed to fulfil the dream.

*   *   *

Kipling worked by far the better, in both verse and in prose, in the past rather than the future.

In fiction, he uses two basic forms. In one, we are plunged directly into the past with no intervening Narrator: such stories are 'The Manner of Men' and 'The Eye of Allah', *(see pages 85 and 83–4)*. Perhaps we should put the *Just So Stories* into this category, though as historical fiction we need hardly take them seriously; yet many a child may (as I did) read 'How the First Letter was Written' and 'How the Alphabet was Made', and think that this is what Neolithic people were really like, and that this is how the first alphabet really came to be made.

In the other kind of time-past story, the Narrator intervenes between the reader and the past, sometimes to aesthetic satisfaction, but least happily, surely, in the Puck stories. 'The tales had to be read by children, before people realized they were meant for grown-ups,' Kipling wrote,[1] and those dull children, Dan and Una, based on John and Elsie Kipling, were there to entice the children to Puck 'the oldest Old Thing in England'. But even a child can reject the magicking of the children out of any recollection of their experiences between one story and the next. What's the use, any sensible child will ask, of learning, encountering, experiencing our past if it has no continuous place in shaping our memories and therefore ourselves?

This cavil apart, and forgetting about the children (and best to do so), there is no story in these two books that is not at least good, at best excellent. The accompanying poems vary more in quality, but if some are commonplace, others are very fine indeed. One of these, for the story 'Weland's Sword', is written in the manner of its time, which is before the Conquest but after the Dark Ages when the Old Thing Weland, smith to the gods, had come down in the world and, as Puck had prophesied, was plying his trade for hire by the wayside, never to be released till some human wished him well. This a surly farmer is forced to do by an unruly novice, and in gratitude Weland makes a sword for the novice, who is not the stuff for a monk, as his Abbot sees. On the sword Weland carves his prophetic runes:

> A Smith makes me
> To betray my Man
> In my first fight...

Such pastiches in the manner of other people, other times, were attractive to Kipling, as to every clever rhymster. (Some others will be found here on pages 63 and 177.) But without *copying* a precise manner or time, Kipling could still well convey its flavour. 'Harp Song of the Dane Women' is a lament of Viking women, left behind each spring in the *viks* or creeks, of Scandinavia while their men go out in the long-boats, desperate for the plunder that can help them to survive on their insufficient lands. This poem's shape, though modern, is impressively appropriate, with its almost total avoidance of words derived from the Latin, and its compound nouns and epithets characteristic of Northern poetry of the period:

> What is a woman that you forsake her,
> And the hearth-fire and the home-acre,
> To go with the old grey Widow-maker?...
>
> She has no strong white arms to fold you,
> But the ten-times-fingering weed to hold you –
> Out on the rocks where the tide has rolled you...

In putting together, as I did, a series of BBC radio programmes called *Kipling's English History*, the two Puck books provided much of the material, but there were other works to draw on. One was *The History of England* of 1911, in which Kipling collaborated with the historian C.R.L. Fletcher. Not all Kipling's poems for this book were historical. They included 'Big Steamers' – 'Oh, where are you going to all you Big Steamers...?' and the even better known verses called 'The Glory of the Garden' – 'Our England is a garden, and such gardens are not made/By singing:–"Oh, how beautiful! and sitting in the shade..."' But there were historical verses too. There was the jingly, moral 'What Dane-geld means', based on King Ethelred the Unready who paid the Danes cash to go away:

> And that is called paying the Dane-geld;
>   But we've proved it again and again,
> That if once you have paid him the Dane-geld
>   You never get rid of the Dane...

Another worthy set of verses used the voice of an English sailor to tell of 1667, when the Dutch fleet sailed cheekily up the Medway, spent three days off Chatham burning our ships, and sailed away unscathed; because King Charles II had squandered the Navy's money 'in merriment/And revel at Whitehall':

> The moneys that should feed us
>   You spend on your delight,
> How can you then have sailor-men
>   To aid you in your fight?
> Our fish and cheese are rotten,
>   Which makes the scurvy grow –
> We cannot serve you if we starve,
>   *And this the Dutchmen know!*...
>   from 'The Dutch in the Medway'

Not even Kipling could write about everything, but some of his historical omissions are perhaps surprising. There is a cunning astrological story called 'A Doctor of Medicine' about Nicholas Culpeper coping with plague as the Civil War ends but Kipling wrote nothing about the Commonwealth that followed, one of the most important periods of our history and surely the most neglected by popular literature after the picturesque Cavaliers had left the scene. He wrote nothing whatsoever about the Industrial Revolution and its artefacts, despite his delight in machines. But perhaps these gaps are merely fortuitous. He wrote, after all, nothing about the Field of the Cloth of Gold.

*   *   *

Kipling's explorations beyond his own living space were not only forwards and backwards in time. Sometimes the teller (not Narrator, for he is not in the story) used the eye-view not of men but of gods or, at least, half-gods. The most interesting of the Indian stories thus is 'The Children of the Zodiac' of 1891, an allegory to do with creativity and service. This is almost a prose poem, and a tragic one. For the Zodiac's six children turn to service and servitude and die, one by one, the special deaths destined to them by the Zodiac's six Houses. 'Does Death hurt?' Leo, the Singer asks the Bull, who replies, 'No, but dying does', as he dies his death from the Scorpion. For the Girl, whom he loves, and for Leo himself are destined death from the Crab, whom Kipling always feared. First the Girl's – 'she laid his hand upon her breast, and the breast that he knew so well was hard as stone' – and then his own, 'In the middle of his singing he felt the cold touch of the Crab's claw on the apple of his throat.' The death of gods was a theme of the times, and Kipling would surely have read Richard Garnett's brilliant but now almost forgotten stories in *The Twilight of the Gods* of 1888; his own story has some faint echoes of the first story there.

The divine hierarchy of the Westerners was his theme in 'On the Gate: A Tale of '16' published in 1926, in which Death and St Peter, with a reformed Iscariot, J., strive frenetically in the manner of a modern Civil Service to wangle whomever they can into heaven. This story has its admirers and so do some of the poems written in the same mode; notably the poem called 'L'Envoi' of 1893. Kipling wrote six different poems with this title. The one in question is the Envoi to *The Seven Seas*, the one that begins 'When Earth's last picture is painted and the tubes are twisted and dried' and ends:

> And only The Master shall praise us, and only The Master shall blame;
> And no one shall work for money, and no one shall work for fame,
> But each for the joy of the working, and each, in his separate star,
> Shall draw the Thing as he sees It for the God of Things as They are!

This poem was frequently reproduced as an illuminated broadsheet.

Heaven was also the locale of a popular but rather embarrassing poem called 'Jane's Marriage'. (It goes with a popular but rather embarrassing story called 'The Janeites'.) In this poem, Jane Austen dies and goes to Paradise. She is welcomed by the greatest writers and asked what she most desires. 'Jane said: "Love,"' and Love turns out to be a Hampshire gentleman, the original of Captain Wentworth in *Persuasion*, swept from limbo to Paradise for Jane.

*   *   *

Far better in terms of broadening the bounds of the actual were Kipling's many stories in which the supernatural comes in, or appears to. He himself seemed to be in the position of many unbelievers, doubtful of all orthodoxies, attached to none, yet conscious of some inexplicable 'otherness'. Sometimes his seeming tales of the supernatural dissolved – in some measure – their terrors in rational explanation, as in 'The Return of Imray' of 1891, where the ceiling cloth of an apparently haunted bungalow gives up a horrible real-life, or, rather, real-death occupant.

It is possible and perhaps right to treat Kipling's strangely beautiful story '"Wireless"' of 1902 as of similar kind. The Narrator is spending the evening in a chemist's shop, where the proprietor's nephew is hoping to be able to let him hear

'Marconi signals' – 'eavesdropping across half South England'. In the chemist's shop too is the consumptive assistant, Mr Shaynor, passionately enamoured of an opulently attractive girl called Fanny Brand. It is bitterly cold: the fur of the hare hanging outside the shop next door is blown apart to show the bluish skin underneath; the great red, green, and blue glass jars of the chemist reflect their colours on to the corseted young lady in the advertisement on the wall; and while young Mr Caskell tinkers with his batteries and his coherer, young Mr Shaynor, entranced, struggles to write the poetry of John Keats, whom he has never heard of – John Keats who was, like him, the son of a small job-master; who was, like him, a chemist (Keats trained as an apothecary before he decided to be a surgeon), who was consumptive and loved a girl called Fanny Brawne, who wrote of a hare in a bitter-cold night, and of red light falling through glass on to a girl's breast. Must like causes beget like effects, the Narrator desperately asks himself, and nearly like causes–? Or is he in the presence of something stranger than wireless was in 1902?

Often, however, Kipling's 'otherness' stories are of entirely inexplicable horrors, like 'The Mark of the Beast', about a white man cursed by an Indian leper. The manuscript of this early story was sent, in 1886, by a friend of Kipling's, to two English editors. One of them, Andrew Lang, wrote that 'this poisonous stuff' had left an extremely disagreeable impression on his mind. The other, William Sharp, strongly recommended burning 'this detestable piece of work'; he guessed that the writer was young, and that he would die mad before he was thirty.

It is not easy to be sure now what so much shocked Sharp and Lang. It was not, surely, that a white man should be effectively cursed by an Indian leper but rather the horror of man becoming beast, and the power with which this was portrayed.

Kipling did not, as Sharp had predicted, die mad, but madness, like cancer, he feared, and no doubt rightly, with his inherited poor health, his extraordinary imaginative sensitivity. More than once he was on the verge of breakdown, and more than once his sister Trix toppled over the edge of sanity. It is for her care of her husband's health, including his mental health, that we owe Carrie gratitude, though her own frequent swings into depressiveness must have been another burden for him, in his turn, to bear.

In 1879, before Rudyard went back to India, Madame Blavatsky had visited Lahore, with her Theosophy and its accompanying seances and 'miracles'. Lockwood had been robustly sceptical, but Trix was later dangerously drawn to Theosophy, and it appears that Rudyard himself was not altogether immune to it. Some years ago I asked Professor Carrington what was the significance in the story '"They"' of the mystical 'Colours' and of 'the Egg which it is given to very few of us to see', and he told me that these were theosophical symbols. Rudyard was once asked if he thought there was anything in spiritualism, and he replied with a shudder that he knew that there was, and that it should at all costs be avoided.

It is said that after her son's death in 1915, Carrie Kipling, like so many bereaved women at that time, wanted to try to 'get into touch'. Rudyard would have nothing

Left: At Simla, Rudyard's circle still talked credulously of 'the aftermaths of Theosophy as taught by Madame Blavatsky', despite Lockwood's assertion that she was 'one of the most interesting and unscrupulous imposters' he had ever met.

Right: The cover of the first English edition of 1890. There are four frightening stories here, of which only the first, the name story, depends finally on the supernatural for its effect.

of it. His dreadfully impressive poem 'En-dor 1914–19–?' was published in 1919, its reference being to the woman we know as the Witch of En-dor, the woman, who, in II Samuel 27 was consulted by Saul because she had 'a familiar spirit', and could call up the dead. Its full title suggests it was written before the end of the war:

> The road to En-dor is easy to tread
>   For Mother or yearning Wife.
> There, it is sure, we shall meet our Dead
>   As they were even in life...
>
> Whispers shall comfort us out of the dark –
>   Hands – ah, God! – that we knew!
> Visions and voices – look and hark! –
>   Shall prove that the tale is true,
> And that those who have passed to the further shore
> May be hailed – at a price – on the road to En-dor...

158

Oh, the road to En-dor is the oldest road
  And the craziest road of all!
Straight it runs to the Witch's abode,
  As it did in the days of Saul.
And nothing has changed of the sorrow in store
  For such as go down on the road to En-dor!

Good as are some of the earlier works of the supernatural ('The Phantom Rickshaw' of 1885 should not pass without mention), the best is work of Kipling's last years. 'The Madonna of the Trenches' *(see pages 96–7)* is one of these stories. At least as great is a story first published in 1924, 'The Wish House'.

Two old Sussex women, Liz Fetley and Grace Ashcroft, meet in the village where Mrs Ashcroft, retired from London service, now lives. They are old friends. Each knows more of the other than anyone else does. Mrs Ashcroft will soon die of cancer. She has chosen her ordeal to save from the same the cruel, casual lover of her youth. For the London charwoman's little girl, who had it from a gypsy girl, had shown her that by means of a wish house, 'a house which 'ad stood unlet an' empty, long enough for Some One, like, to come an in'abit there' one could take on another's pain.

The stoical old women are impressively true, and the wish house is horrible, as much as anything because it is so damnably ordinary, and so is the Some One who inhabits there:

Fourteen, Wadloes Road, was the place – a liddle basement-kitchen 'ouse, in a row of twenty-thirty such... I ringed the front-door bell. She pealed loud, like it do in an empty house. When she'd all ceased, I 'eard a cheer, like, pushed back on de floor o' the kitchen. Then I 'eard feet on de kitchen-stairs, like it might ha' been a heavy woman in slippers... an' at de front-door dey stopped. I stooped to the letter-box slit, an' I says: 'Let me take everythin' bad that's in store for my man, 'Arry Mockler, for love's sake.'... Then the steps went back an' downstairs to the kitchen – all draggy – an' I heard the cheer drawed up again.

In his writing persona, as in his life, Kipling knew, on the pulse (as Keats put it) what fear was; not only fear of the real, but fear, too, of what seemed sometimes to lie beyond it.

CHAPTER THIRTEEN

VIA DOLOROSA:
THE GREAT WAR

A tinker out of Bedford,
    A vagrant oft in quod,
A private under Fairfax,
    A minister of God –
Two hundred years and thirty
    Ere Armageddon came
His single hand portrayed it,
    And Bunyan was his name!

from 'The Holy War'

N 4 August 1914 England entered the Great War. On one side, the Central Powers of Germany and Austria-Hungary, with such smaller allies as Turkey and Bulgaria; on the other, the Western Powers, the Allies – Russia, France, and in 1915 Italy, Great Britain with her Dominions and Colonies, and some smaller countries like Brave Little Belgium (as she was often referred to) whose invasion by the Germans had triggered the war in the West.

Not the most horrible war in all these nations' histories, but certainly in England's and the very horrors inspired some great English war poets – Siegfried Sassoon, Wilfred Owen, Isaac Rosenberg, Rupert Brooke. All were soldiers and all but Sassoon died. Rudyard Kipling, nearly fifty when the war began, was too old to fight, and he is not usually thought of as one of the war poets of the Great War. But he was a war poet and at times a painfully fine one.

Kipling's first poem of the war, which was published in *The Times* on 2 September 1914, was quietly dignified, a reflection of the best of the nation's mood:

For all we have and are,
For all our children's fate,
Stand up and take the war.
The Hun is at the gate!...

There is but one task for all –
One life for each to give.
What stands if Freedom fall?
Who dies if England live?

from '"For All We Have and Are"'

Kipling went to France to report on the war before ever his son left England. He saw ruined towns and cathedrals, and a countryside of yellowed grass, poisoned by German gas.

Kipling's calm was not to persist. Soon the atrocity stories, the reports of the Germans' brutal and callous behaviour in the territories they occupied, roused Kipling to a hatred which had no room for such respect as he had been able to retain for Piet, the Boer fighting man. Poets have, however, no duty to make measured judgments, and Kipling's political judgment was never very sound. A rumour that he was off to propagandize the Americans led Sir Edward Grey, the Liberal Foreign Secretary, to say that if anything of the kind happened, he, Grey, would resign. In fact, Kipling had not thought of going, and in the event the British Government made sensible use of such services as he could offer. His first task, however, was a personal one: to help his son John into the war.

When war broke out, John, not yet seventeen, straightway left his crammer's and tried to enlist, first as an officer, then as a private. He was rejected on both applications for his poor eyesight. So his father asked for help from the aged Field-Marshal Lord Roberts – once Bobs of Kandahar. Roberts, when Commander-in-Chief in India in the later 1880s had not been too proud to ask young Kipling's views on the common soldiers, and had known how to use Kipling's

161

talents *(see page 137)* when he took over from Sir Redvers Buller in South Africa in 1900. Now in 1914 Roberts was appointed Colonel-in-Chief of the first British Expeditionary Force sent out to France. He responded to Kipling's request by obtaining for John a nomination to his own regiment, the Irish Guards, which John joined as a Second Lieutenant on 14 September. It is ironical to think that only a month later Lord Roberts would not have been there to help, for on 14 November, he died of a chill at St Omer, among his troops. But no doubt the Kiplings would have found some other way to wangle their boy into the Army. It was clearly unthinkable that Rudyard Kipling's son should not be in khaki, and this was what John himself wanted. A friend reportedly asked Carrie why John did join up, since, with his poor eyesight, he clearly didn't have to, and Carrie said proudly that John went *because* he didn't have to, a reply characteristic of the British matron she had now become, who 'gave' her son for England.

In the event, Rudyard Kipling went to France just before his son did, in the summer of 1915. He had steadfastly refused to write 'official' war propaganda, and, as usual with him, it was not the direct reporting of what he had seen that was of value, but the creative reworking of the material.

Until he went to France, Kipling had been visiting hospitals and training camps at home and by 1915 his creative war-writing had begun to come on stream. His visit to the Navy led to two much-quoted poems:

> 'Have you news of my boy Jack?'
> *Not this tide*
> 'When d'you think that he'll come back?'
> *Not with this wind blowing and this tide . . .*

> 'Oh, dear, what comfort can I find?'
> *None this tide*
> *Nor any tide,*
> *Except he did not shame his kind –*

This is not a woman asking for her lover, but a mother for her son:

> *Then hold your head up all the more . . .*
> *Because he was the son you bore,*
> *And gave to that wind blowing and that tide!*

from 'My Boy Jack'

It is moving, especially when read aloud as dialogue, but it is flawed. To most of us today, the concept of the young men killed in war being 'given' by their mothers is nauseating, and though such a phrase as 'he did not shame his kind' met the mood of the moment, there is a touch of the jelly-bellied flag-flapper about it. There are some things better left unsaid, even by poets, and it is because Kipling too often said such things that he has been denied the highest standing by critics who failed to notice the rarer occasions when he obliterated his own personality and transmuted the occasion's temporality: as he did in 'Mine Sweepers', which is perfect, not least because of its simple language, with hardly a word from the Latin; and in its choice of proper names, a skill in which Kipling excelled.

> Dawn off the Foreland – the young flood making
>> Jumbled and short and steep –
> Black in the hollows and bright where it's breaking –
>> Awkward water to sweep.
>> 'Mines reported in the fairway,
>> 'Warn all traffic and detain.
> ''Sent up *Unity, Claribel, Assyrian, Stormcock,* and *Golden Gain.*'
>
> Noon off the Foreland – the first ebb making
>> Lumpy and strong in the bight.
> Boom after boom, and the golf-hut shaking
>> And the jackdaws wild with fright!
>> 'Mines located in the fairway,
>> 'Boats now working up the chain,
> 'Sweepers – *Unity, Claribel, Assyrian, Stormcock* and *Golden Gain.*'
>
> Dusk off the Foreland – the last light going
>> And the traffic crowding through,
> And five damned trawlers with their syreens blowing
>> Heading the whole review!
>> 'Sweep completed in the fairway.
>> 'No more mines remain.
> ''Sent back *Unity, Claribel, Assyrian, Stormcock,* and *Golden Gain.*'

Short stories about the war also began to be published in 1915. 'Swept and Garnished' appeared in January, a fantasy about a complacent German *Hausfrau* seeing, in delirium, children starving and dying through German actions. 'Sea Constables', already noticed, (*see page 149*), appeared in October. 'Mary Postgate', the harshest of Kipling's war-stories, was already being written in March, and the date is significant, because it was before John went to France.

Mary Postgate is a forty-year-old rather stupid lady-companion, interrupted in her task of burning in the garden all the childhood possessions of Wynn, the nephew her employer had brought up, killed while in training for the Flying Corps. The interruption comes from a broken man in uniform who has fallen to the ground through an oak-tree. 'Cassée,' 'It' moans, and, 'Le médecin, Toctor!'

It is this creature's plane, Mary assumes, which has just dropped a bomb on the village and killed a child, and, she assumes, too, that he knows what he has done. It was, she had felt, a great pity that Wynn hadn't killed somebody before he died. For whatever confusion of reasons, Mary replies to Its request for help, 'Nein' and again, 'Nein, I tell you! Ich haben der todt Kinder gesehen.' A woman, she feels, can be more useful in a situation like this than a man, who would fetch help, would bring It into the house. So she waits, 'while an increasing rapture laid hold on her. She

Mary Postgate confronts the dying German airman. In this illustration for the story's first publication in Nash's Magazine, *September, 1915, Matania creates an enemy both hateful and pitiable.*

ceased to think. She gave herself up to feel.' At last It dies, and Mary goes into the house, having enjoyed, Kipling intimates, sexual climax. She looked, her employer noticed, when she saw Mary, lying relaxed on the sofa, 'quite handsome!'

'Mary Postgate' has poetic truth. It would be improper to try to relate it to anything that Kipling was 'really' like; with his best work, there is hardly any justification for drawing inferences from the work to the man who made it. Its date of composition makes it certain that it had nothing to do with the loss of John Kipling, reported wounded and missing in September 1915 after the Battle of Loos. He was just eighteen years old, and by all accounts, a promising and well-liked young officer. 'It's something to have bred a man,' Kipling wrote to Colonel Dunsterville, his old friend Stalky.

Thereafter, Kipling's war poems were acrid with bitterness, and more, now, than against the Germans, against the Government and the old men in power. 'Mesopotamia' was typical. In late 1915, the British Cabinet had persuaded the Indian Government to send a Brigade under General Townsend to drive the Turks out of Basra on the Persian Gulf. This achieved, Townsend, for no good reason, pushed inland towards Baghdad. The force was entrapped, besieged in the crumbling mud-fort of Kut-el-Amara on the Tigris river, and after a five-month siege, General Townsend surrendered unconditionally to the Turks. He went into comfortable internment, his officers into endurable prison-camps. The men were herded across the desert, flogged, raped, tortured, and murdered; two-thirds of them were dead before the war ended.

> They shall not return to us, the resolute, the young,
>   The eager and whole-hearted whom we gave:
> But the men who left them thriftily to die in their own dung,
>   Shall they come with years and honour to the grave?...
>
> Shall we only threaten and be angry for an hour?
>   When the storm is ended shall we find
> How softly but how swiftly they have sidled back to power
>   By the favour and contrivance of their kind?...
>
> from 'Mesopotamia'

This bitter mood was not transient. Kipling's 'Epitaphs of the War' were not published until 1919. A few were calm, but most were not:

> If any question why we died,
> Tell them, because our fathers lied.
>
> 'Common Form'

> I could not dig: I dared not rob,
> Therefore I lied to please the mob.
> Now all my lies are proved untrue
> And I must face the men I slew.
> What tale shall serve me here among
> Mine angry and defrauded young?
>
> 'A Dead Statesman'

> If any mourn us in the workshop, say
> We died because the shift kept holiday.
>
> 'Batteries Out Of Ammunition'

and nearest, perhaps, to his own condition:

> My son was killed while laughing at some jest. I would I knew
> What it was, and it might serve me in a time when jests are few.
>
> 'A Son'

165

The poem that seems to bear most directly on John's death is 'The Children', published in 1917, a most painful poem, and yet one for which Kipling avoided directness by weaving a complicated convolution of rhyme-scheme and imagery:

> These were our children who died for our lands: they were dear in our sight.
> We have only the memory left of their home-treasured sayings and laughter.
> The price of our loss shall be paid to our hands, not another's hereafter.
> Neither the Alien nor Priest shall decide on it. That is our right.
> *But who shall return us the children?...*
>
> They bought us anew with their blood, forbearing to blame us,
> Those hours which we had not made good when the Judgment o'ercame us.
> They believed us and perished for it. Our statecraft, our learning
> Delivered them bound to the Pit and alive to the burning...
>
> That flesh we had nursed from the first in all cleanness was given
> To corruption unveiled and assailed by the malice of Heaven –
> By the heart-shaking jests of Decay where it lolled on the wires –
> To be blanched or gay-painted by fumes – to be cindered by fires –
> To be senselessly tossed and retossed in stale mutilation
> From crater to crater. For this we shall take expiation.
> *But who shall return us our children?*

The language of his Minister forebears, a language of justification and redemption by blood, came often to Kipling in the war years. He used it to greatest effect in an argument which can fairly be called theological: an argument addressed to the still neutral Americans who were, said President Wilson, 'too proud to fight':

> Brethren, how shall it fare with me
>   When the war is laid aside,
> If it be proven that I am he
>   For whom a world has died?
>
> If it be proven that all my good,
>   And the greater good I will make,
> Were purchased me by a multitude
>   Who suffered for my sake?...
>
> Brethren, how must it fare with me,
>   Or how am I justified,
> If it be proven that I am he
>   For whom mankind has died –
> If it be proven that I am he
>   Who, being questioned, denied?
>
> from 'The Question'

The Americans entered the war on the Allied side on 6 April 1917.

The New Testament also provided the imagery for the poem 'Gethsemane', which was not published until 1919. Its subject is the Germans' use of poison-gas –

which Kipling seems to have pronounced with a long 'a' to rhyme with the Southern English pronunciation of pass:

> The Garden called Gethsemane
> In Picardy it was,
> And there the people came to see
> The English soldiers pass.
> We used to pass – we used to pass
> Or halt, as it might be,
> And ship our masks in case of gas
> Beyond Gethsemane...
>
> The officer sat on the chair,
> The men lay on the grass,
> And all the time we halted there
> I prayed my cup might pass.
>
> It didn't pass – it didn't pass –
> It didn't pass from me.
> I drank it when we met the gas
> Beyond Gethsemane!

From the autumn of 1915, the Kiplings were, of course, in despair. Like almost everyone else, they could only continue doggedly with the war work they had chosen or that had come their way. Their offer of their Sussex house for a war hospital was not accepted, but they still spent much of their time in London, usually staying at Brown's Hotel. For Rudyard, probably his most satisfying work came from an invitation to write the war history of John's regiment. *The Irish Guards in the Great War* was published in 1923, in two volumes illustrated with pretty maps. On page 12 of the second volume we read of the foray from Chalk-Pit Wood on 27 September 1915: 'Here 2nd Lieutenant Clifford was shot and wounded or killed – the body was found later – and 2nd Lieutenant Kipling was wounded and missing.' John Kipling's body was not found.

This may have influenced Kipling's acceptance, in 1917, of an invitation to become one of the War Graves Commissioners. In Western Europe alone there were literally millions of bodies to be reburied in the official war cemeteries and some three-quarters of a million of them were British. For the rest of his life Kipling worked devotedly for the Commission, and suggested almost all the commemorative words used, like 'Their name liveth for evermore', engraved on the Stone of Sacrifice at the entrance to each cemetery. Carrington says that Kipling was one of the originators of the proposal to bury an Unknown Soldier in Westminster Abbey and of the nightly ceremony of the Last Post at the Menin Gate by Ypres.

Kipling's most important war-story, 'The Gardener', must have found its source in this work: most important, because of the comfort it gave to many women, yet of all his serious stories one of the hardest to enter into now, to feel as well as to read of its intended effect.

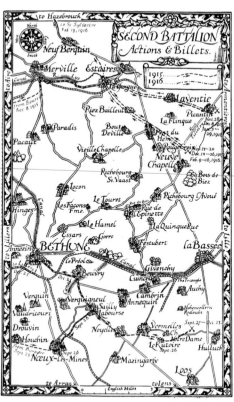

Left: John Kipling, 2nd Lieutenant in the Second Irish Guards. He looked, his mother said, 'very smart and straight and young and brave' when he said goodbye at Bateman's on his birthday, 17 August 1915.
Right: This map from Kipling's The Irish Guards in the Great War *carries many names still painfully reverberative – Laventie, Festubert, Béthune, and, of course, Loos where John was lost.*

In this story, Helen Turrell, a spinster living in a Hampshire village, goes soon after the war to France, to see the grave of the boy she had brought up as her nephew. There were many relatives of the dead on this same melancholy pilgrimage, a sadly common one for at least the next decade. At the Authority's office in a board-and-tar-paper shed, a Lancashire woman collapses in hysteria for fear she should fail to find her son's grave before her Cook's Tourist Ticket runs out. At tea in a wooden hut, another woman chums up with Helen, tells her she comes regularly to photograph graves for people who cannot make the journey; but later, in Helen's bedroom, she confesses that why she really comes is to see one grave, the grave of someone who was everything to her and should have been nothing. Next morning Helen goes to the cemetery, Hagenzeele Third, and is bewildered among the 21,000 graves already occupied, the many others still in the making. She sees, as she thinks, a gardener, who asks her whom she is looking for. My nephew, she replies, words she had said 'many thousands of times in her life'.

'"Come with me," he said, "and I will show you where your son lies."' So Helen visits her grave and leaves the cemetery, turning backwards for a last look. 'In the distance she saw the man bending over his young plants; and she went away, supposing him to be the gardener.'

It could be that Kipling came to understand that there were worse ends than dying in that war. It might be worse to live:

> I have a dream – a dreadful dream –
>   A dream that is never done.
> I watch a man go out of his mind,
>   And he is My Mother's Son.
>
> They pushed him into a Mental Home,
>   And that is like the grave:
> For they do not let you sleep upstairs,
>   And you aren't allowed to shave.
>
> And it was *not* disease or crime
>   Which got him landed there,
> But because They laid on My Mother's Son
>   More than a man could bear.
>
> What with noise, and fear of death,
>   Waking, and wounds and cold,
> They filled the Cup for My Mother's Son
>   Fuller than it could hold.
>
> They broke his body and his mind
>   And yet They made him live,
> And They asked more of My Mother's Son
>   Than any man could give.
>
> For, just because he had not died,
>   Nor been discharged nor sick,
> They dragged it out with My Mother's Son
>   Longer than he could stick.
>
> And no one knows when he'll get well –
>   So, there he'll have to be:
> And, 'spite of the beard in the looking-glass,
>   I know that man is me!
>
> 'The Mother's Son'

To try to rank Kipling among the war poets I named on page 160 would be a thankless task, for he is in a different class and of a different kind. What can be said with assurance is that his almost uncategorizable talents rose to the heights required for the interpretation by poetry of the filthiest war we ever fought.

CHAPTER FOURTEEN

AT HOME IN SUSSEX

God gives all men all earth to love,
But, since man's heart is small,
Ordains for each one spot shall prove
Belovèd over all.
Each to his choice, and I rejoice
The lot has fallen to me
In a fair ground – in a fair ground –
Yea, Sussex by the sea!

from 'Sussex', 1902

OR their return to England in 1896 after the disastrous ending to their sojourn in Vermont, the Kiplings rented a house in a pretty cove near Torquay. For nearly a year, all went well. The scenery was lovely, the Navy at Dartmouth sent Kipling their first invitation; Rudyard and Carrie, who had learned to ride bicycles in Brattleboro, tried to master a tandem, each persisting in the belief the other enjoyed it; and Lockwood came to stay and work on the clay bas-reliefs that were to illustrate *Kim*. But the muggy, enervating winter climate did not suit them, and the house came to feel as depressingly hostile to them as the M'Leods's house would in the story 'The House Surgeon'.

Although Rudyard was in the middle of the Stalky stories, and Carrie was pregnant, in the late spring of 1897 they precipitately left Devonshire and stayed for a time in a London hotel, for a time in a rented house in Brighton. Then Georgie Burne-Jones offered to lend her Rottingdean house for the birth, though it seems improbable she or Ned used the pompous sentence that Rudyard thought he recollected, nearly thirty years later: 'Let the child that is coming to you be born in our house.' But however the invitation was worded, the Burne-Joneses moved out of North End House and the Kiplings moved in.

This was Diamond Jubilee Year, and several people, including the Editor of *The Times*, had been pressing Kipling for a poem appropriate to the occasion. He was not unwilling, being disturbed by the contrast between the cocky optimism of the English people and the clouds he saw gathering on the horizon, not least in South Africa. For a long time the poem would not 'come', and when, in mid-July, it did, Kipling was still dissatisfied and tossed it into the waste-paper basket, and only the

The Diamond Jubilee Procession in London: a Sikh detachment of 'The men an' the 'orses what makes up the forces/O' Missis Victorier's sons'. ('The Widow at Windsor')

urgings of family and friends persuaded him that this, at last, was the right version to work on. The title he gave to this poem, 'Recessional', is that of the hymn sung at the end of the church service as the clergy and the choir leave the chancel. The poem was intended, Kipling said much later, as a charm to avert the evil eye:

> God of our fathers, known of old,
>   Lord of our far-flung battle-line,
> Beneath whose awful Hand we hold
>   Dominion over palm and pine –
> Lord God of Hosts, be with us yet,
> Lest we forget – lest we forget!
>
> The tumult and the shouting dies;
>   The Captains and the Kings depart:
> Still stands Thine ancient sacrifice,
>   An humble and a contrite heart.
> Lord God of Hosts, be with us yet,
> Lest we forget – lest we forget!

The Elms at Rottingdean. After the Kiplings left, it was owned by Sir William Nicolson (who collaborated with Kipling in An Almanac of Twelve Sports *of 1898) and then by Enid Bagnold.*

Far-called, our navies melt away;
   On dune and headland sinks the fire:
Lo, all our pomp of yesterday
   Is one with Nineveh and Tyre!
Judge of the Nations, spare us yet,
Lest we forget – lest we forget!

If, drunk with sight of power, we loose
   Wild tongues that have not Thee in awe,
Such boastings as the Gentiles use,
   Or lesser breeds without the Law –
Lord God of Hosts, be with us yet,
Lest we forget – lest we forget!. . .

Providentially, as it seemed then, The Elms, a house on the village green, fell vacant, and the Kiplings took it. The Ridsdales, the family of Stanley Baldwin's wife Lucy, also had a house on the green, and the Kiplings had a few good years there, with summer beach parties for all the families, and then, winters at the Cape; winters in England they were determined to avoid.

But Rottingdean did not prove satisfactory. The Sussex coast's gimcrack development was already under way, and Rudyard hankered for 'real' country. And his own fame was burdensome. Sightseers would cluster around The Elms.

The Kiplings were not, however, sure yet where they wanted to live, and with the help of motor-cars they began searching from Kent to Dorset. Then family troubles supervened. Ned Burne-Jones died in the summer of 1898. Rudyard had once been very fond of him, but sorrow at his loss must have been mitigated on the Macdonald side of the family by unavoidable knowledge of his flagrant infidelities to Georgie.

Lockwood, with a CIE already awarded in the New Year Honours of 1887, had retired with Alice to Tisbury in Wiltshire; but in 1898 they had to bear the burden of Trix's first mental breakdown, for one of its symptoms was aversion from her husband. In early 1899 came the death of Josephine Kipling, and then the Boer War, and it was not until a couple of years had passed that Rudyard and Carrie took up house-hunting again.

They first saw Bateman's in 1900. In the chapter in *Something of Myself* called 'The Very-Own House', Kipling recollected Carrie exclaiming, 'That's Her! The Only She! Make an honest woman of her – quick!' But the house had been let for a year, and it was not until June 1902 that the contract was signed, the house and forge and 33 acres of land bought for £9,300, a low price because the deep valley in which it stood was nearly inaccessible to light horse-traffic. By a stroke of good fortune, on the two occasions the Kiplings had visited Bateman's before purchase, their steam motor-car, the Locomobile, had broken down, and they had come to the house from the station by fly, the horse finding the steep slope down and the climb back very hard going. The former owner said later that if he had realized, as Mr Kipling did, that motor-cars had come to stay, he would have asked twice as much.

Bateman's is a handsome early seventeenth-century house, almost certainly built by a prosperous ironmaster. Kipling assumed this was so, and in the final version of his endearing and evocative poem, 'Puck's Song', which travels backwards in time, three consecutive verses are about the iron works:

> And mark you where the ivy clings
> To Bayham's mouldering walls?
> O there we cast the stout railings
> That stand around St. Paul's.
>
> See you the dimpled track that runs
> All hollow through the wheat?
> O that was where they hauled the guns
> That smote King Philip's fleet.
>
> (Out of the Weald, the secret Weald,
> Men sent in ancient years
> The horse-shoes red at Flodden Field,
> The arrows at Poitiers!)...

The interior of the old house could have been made attractive and comfortable, but even today, under the care of the National Trust and deodorized of the 'blue haze of smoke' with which Kipling liked to surround himself, it is a cheerless place to which Lord Birkenhead's epithet 'clammy' seems fairly applied. It lacks simple conveniences such as might have been expected of a wealthy couple and one of them American: no bathroom, for instance, or even running water near the Kiplings' bedroom. The general style is an early example of the one Osbert

Bateman's: 'Sooner or later,' wrote Kipling, 'all sorts of men cast up at our house. From India . . . from the Cape . . . Australia . . . Canada . . . each with his life-tale, grievance, idea, ideal, or warning.'

Lancaster later dubbed Stockbroker Tudor. But *de gustibus* – It is fair to record that Martin Fido, in 1974, thought the interior was in 'almost perfect taste'.

The gardens are successful. For a part of them Kipling earmarked his Nobel Prize money of 1907, and the gardens of the blind woman's house in '"They"' are a not too idealized transmutation of them:

> – my fore-wheels took the turf of a great still lawn from which sprang horsemen ten feet high with levelled lances, monstrous peacocks, and sleek round-headed maids of honour – blue, black, and glistening – all of clipped yew. Across the lawn – the marshalled woods besieged it on three sides – stood an ancient house of lichened and weather-worn stone, with mullioned windows and roofs of rose-red tile. It was flanked by semi-circular walls, also rose-red, that closed the lawn on the fourth side, and at their feet a box hedge grew man-high. There were doves on the roof above the slim brick chimneys, and I caught a glimpse of an octagonal dove-house behind the screening wall.

It has been said that Bateman's was the model for the house of 'An Habitation Enforced' *(see page 119)*, but this is clearly wrong. Bateman's is down by a stream in the Weald, the wooded country between the North and South Downs, as the ironmasters' houses all were, and it was built in the seventeenth century, their period of greatest prosperity. The prosperity of the fictional Pardons was founded on wool and wheat, so it was built up on the Downs and in the late eighteenth century, the right period for grand houses built from money so made. Kipling's enchanting description of Pardons's interior and furnishings – two Hepplewhite couches for the drawing-room, a mirror over the mantelpiece, a spinet – suggests that, left to himself, he would have done better by Bateman's.

The Mill at Bateman's: 'See you our little mill that clacks,/So busy by the brook?/She has ground her corn and paid her tax/Ever since Domesday Book.' (from 'Puck's Song', 1906)

The years between 1902 and 1914 were probably the best of Kipling's life. 'At last I'm one of the gentry,' he wrote to C. E. Norton in 1902, but of course he was not, as the making of such a statement showed, and the obligations of the country gentry were not those he was prepared to take on. But he was now, at last, finally at home, able – when Carrie allowed it – to receive his friends and talk and smoke until she told him it was time to go to bed.

From 1902 the presence of Sussex is constantly in Kipling's work, and never more so than in the Puck stories, almost all set at Bateman's or radiating out from it. It was by the Long Pool near the weir that Dan and Una first met Sir Richard Dalyngridge, the Norman Knight who was given the Saxon manor that stood where Bateman's now stands. Slave-rings, like the one Sir Huon's boy fastened round his own neck, were made at the old forge, and the worn stone the chickens used for a drinking-trough was the plague-stone set on the village boundary, where the people from the infected villages left money and the outsiders left victuals. And in Kipling's best story of prehistory, 'The Knife and the Naked Chalk', the man from the chalk uplands ventures into the fever-haunted weald, and sacrifices an eye for the iron knife with which his people can fight the wolves and keep the sheep safe.

There were more Sussex creations in the good years than only the Puck stories. 'Below the Mill Dam' of 1902 was one of the first fruits of Bateman's. It told of the harnessing of the mill stream, the Dudwell, to supply Bateman's electric light, from the eye-view of the Black Rat, one of the last of the old English breed, who lives in the mill. A more serious story and an oddly neglected one is 'The Friendly Brook' of 1914, where the brook does a murderously good turn to the countryman Jim Wickenden who had adopted Mary, a Barnardo's child from London (and a

175

stuck-up piece she grew up to be, says the hedger who tells the tale). So, the brook having been a good friend to him by disposing of Mary's troublesome father, 'if she be minded to have a snatch at my hay, *I* ain't settin' out to withstand her,' says Jim when the waters rise.

Though all the stories of *Puck* and *Rewards* are closely connected with Sussex, this is not necessarily true of their accompanying poems. The famous 'If –', for instance, which appears in *Rewards*, is clearly intended to have a wider application than to Sussex boys only. Similarly, 'A Smuggler's Song' from *Puck* could have applied anywhere along the English coastline where smuggling was (as it still is) profitable; but the story it goes with, 'Hal o' the Draft' is to do with a complicated smuggling of guns in late fifteenth-century Sussex. 'A Smuggler's Song' is one of the best known and best loved of Kipling's popular poems:

> If you wake at midnight, and hear a horse's feet,
> Don't go drawing back the blind, or looking in the street,
> Them that asks no questions isn't told a lie.
> Watch the wall, my darling, while the Gentlemen go by!
>> Five and twenty ponies
>> Trotting through the dark –
>> Brandy for the Parson,
>> 'Baccy for the Clerk;
>> Laces for a lady, letters for a spy,
> And watch the wall, my darling, while the Gentlemen go by! . . .

Another model of popular poetry at its best is 'The Land' of 1911. Where 'Puck's Song' harks backward in time, 'The Land' goes forward, each verse a dialogue between the rustic, Hobden, and the land's owners, from Julius Fabricius in the days of Diocletian, through Ogier the Dane and the Norman William of Warenne to – it might be – Kipling himself:

> *Georgii Quinti Anno Sexto*, I, who own the River-field,
> Am fortified with title-deeds, attested, signed and sealed,
> Guaranteeing me, my assigns, my executors and heirs
> All sorts of powers and profits which – are neither mine nor theirs.
>
> I have rights of chase and warren, as my dignity requires.
> I can fish – but Hobden tickles. I can shoot – but Hobden wires.
> I repair, but he reopens, certain gaps which, men allege,
> Have been used by every Hobden since a Hobden swapped a hedge . . .
>
> His dead are in the churchyard – thirty generations laid.
> Their names were old in history when Domesday Book was made;
> And the passion and the piety and prowess of his line
> Have seeded, rooted, fruited in some land the Law calls mine . . .
>
> 'Hob, what about that River-bit?' I turn to him again,
> With Fabricius and Ogier and William of Warenne.

> 'Hev it jest as you've a mind to, *but*' – and here he takes command.
> For whoever pays the taxes old Mus' Hobden owns the land.

By the time that Kipling went to Bateman's, his fame was such that to honour him publicly seemed proper. Already in the 1890s, after Lord Tennyson had died, Kipling had been considered for Poet Laureate. But on being sounded, he refused, as he did all subsequent honours from the State, even, in 1924, the Order of Merit, though this honour is a personal gift from the Monarch, and between King George V and Kipling there was then some friendly acquaintance. But it was thirty years earlier, before he had been offered anything at all, that Kipling wrote 'The Last Rhyme of True Thomas', in which the King offers

> To dub True Thomas a belted knight,
>   And all for the sake of the songs he made . . .

It is an overlong ballad, but its ending is decisive:

> 'I ha' harpit ye up to the Throne o' God,
>   'I ha' harpit your midmost soul in three.
> 'I ha' harpit ye down to the Hinges o' Hell,
>   'And – ye – would – make – a Knight o' me!'

All that Kipling would accept of honours were academic ones, for there were no possible strings attached to these, and perhaps he felt them some compensation for the university education he had missed. He had much pleasure in being elected Lord Rector of St Andrews University in 1923; in 1931 he accepted the pleasant duty of serving on the management committee of the British Institute in Paris but he went to only one meeting, in London, and did not speak.

Not all, of course, could be carefree during the pre-war years at Bateman's. Agnes Poynter died of cancer in 1906, and Louisa's husband, Alfred Baldwin, died suddenly in 1908. In 1910 Alice Kipling died, and Lockwood a year later. Their retirement had not been wholly happy. There had been the sad burden of Trix's derangement. The English climate was hard on them, as on most Anglo-Indians, and Alice, with a ginger wig and too-bright vivacity, had not taken old age well. But her marriage with Lockwood had been a good one, and Alice was still writing poetry up to the night before she died. Their son's literary debt to them both was immeasurable.

For Rudyard, all these deaths were in the course of nature and could be endured. He did not, perhaps, then realize that his parents' death would mean that the care of Trix in breakdown would now fall on him, as it did during the war when it was a hard duty. (After the war, Trix recovered and went to live in Edinburgh, where she would talk to the animals in the Zoo. She died in 1948.) Neither Rudyard nor Carrie was ever in robust health. Already in the later 1890s Carrie was subject to deep depressions, apt especially to strike her when Rud was away from her, with the Navy, or in the field in South Africa; while to his own constant fears of cancer and

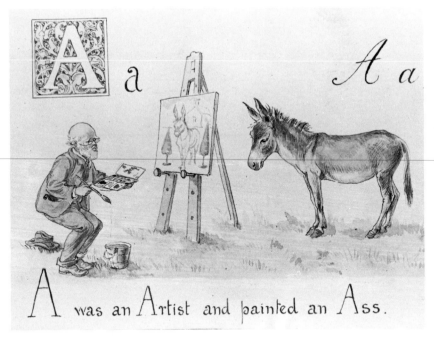

A was an Artist and painted an Ass.

To commemorate the death of John Lockwood Kipling, a new beginning feels proper, and here is the start of the alphabet he made to amuse the children at Rottingdean.

madness were added digestive troubles which grew steadily worse and which no English doctor seemed able to diagnose or alleviate.

Still, there was the 'very-own' home. There were the children, Elsie and John. There were, from 1909 till the war, winter-sports holidays in Switzerland every January at St Moritz or at Engelberg, and then, after the children had gone back to school, a February sojourn in a warm climate, though seldom, now, further afield than the Mediterranean. Travel always made Kipling feel better. Increasingly, it made Carrie feel worse.

After the war, there was not much in the way of good times. Two children were irrevocably lost, and as well as the usual guilt that follows death, the Kiplings must have been aware that here were two deaths that their own actions had helped to bring about. If only Carrie had listened to her mother-in-law on the risks of taking the children to America in mid-winter – If only Rudyard had put his foot down – If only they had left John to discover his own right place in war work suited to his physical disabilities –. In 1924 Elsie married Captain George Bambridge, and the gap this left in family life hit the Kiplings harder than a child's marriage should.

Some happiness in his own strange marriage Kipling had undoubtedly found. At the end of 1897 he added to the diary that Carrie kept throughout her married life. 'The sixth year of our life together. In all ways the richest to us personally. "She shall do him good and not evil in the days of her life."'[1]

178

Four years later Rudyard wrote to Carrie's mother, Mrs Henry Balestier,

You have no notion what a sweet and winning little woman your Carrie has grown into. Her face gets more beautiful year by year, and her character deepens and broadens with every demand upon it. She is near an angel...[2]

At this time, Carrie, who had never been a pretty girl, was, to impartial eyes, settling into fleshy middle age. The most attractive picture of her is Philip Burne-Jones's portrait which still hangs in the study at Bateman's. The household keys hanging at her waist are significant; she wanted them painted out, but Philip insisted on keeping them. The nickname 'The Committee of Ways and Means', thought up by Rudyard in Yokohama for the young couple in economic confabulation when they discovered they were broke, came to be used by him more and more to indicate Carrie taking decisions.

In the 1920s, Carrie made Rudyard's life more unhappy than it need have been. Her parsimony was now extreme; of the comparatively few people she would welcome at Bateman's, none has ever spoken of generous hospitality there, and when she and her husband went away, the electricity was turned off and the candles and the very matches counted out to the servants. Her possessiveness became obsessive. Except in London at his clubs, and that rarely, Rudyard had no life he could call his own, and the old friends he was at ease with were becoming fewer. In 1919, his American friend, Theodore Roosevelt, died. It had been to Roosevelt, just elected Vice-President of the United States, that Kipling sent the first copy of his poem 'The White Man's Burden', its occasion being the American annexation of the Philippines at the end of 1898. Rider Haggard, one of the best friends since the early days in London, died in 1925. Of the older generation, the beloved Aunt Georgie caught a cold and died of it in 1920, and in 1925 Aunt Louie Baldwin, the only religious Macdonald sister.

There were other losses than by death. 'Stalky' Dunsterville, whom Kipling had helped to a billet in the war, could never be close after he had associated himself with the putative formation of a Kipling Society in 1922, become its President when it was formally set up in 1927, and taken money for talking and writing about his old school friend. Worse was the alienation from Stanley Baldwin who in 1923 had become Prime Minister. Rudyard's now outdated and impracticable conservatism, together with his lack of political sense made him see his cousin's now necessary empiricism as a betrayal. He wrote to a friend, '...S.B. is a Socialist at heart. It came out of the early years when he was in that sort of milieu among some of the academic Socialist crowd...'[3] The efforts of Stanley's son Oliver had unearthed Sergeant Farrell who had been with John Kipling in Chalk-Pit Wood, the last person to see John alive, but this counted for nothing when Oliver joined the Labour Party; Kipling was far more outraged by Oliver's unfilial behaviour than Oliver's own father was.

Changes in his own personality must have lost him new friends he would have liked to make. Few people who had endured the war wanted to speak of it afterwards, but Kipling, in company even with people who had suffered near losses, would insist on bringing the subject up. It sometimes seemed as if in old age he had reverted to the boorishness that had repelled people in the club at Lahore, and those who met him newly in the last years were apt to be struck less by the once-famous shy charm than by the insensitive coarseness with which he would talk about the kinds of people he disliked: Jews, Germans, all except the most conservative of English politicians. His lifelong habit of seeking to draw what special information he could from anyone he met now passed the bounds of courtesy. 'Does this man take me for a camel dealer?' asked King Feisal of Iraq after an intensive interrogation about camel branding in the Hejaz.

Yet for all the miseries and their exacerbation by the increasingly poor health of both husband and wife, Kipling went on writing. Almost all the better poems of the post-war years were, not surprisingly, melancholy: 'The Mother's Son'; 'Dayspring Mishandled'; and 'Rahere', about Henry I's jester who suffered from the Deadly Sin of Accidia, or Wanhope, or Despair. In one of his agonies, Rahere wandered 'to reeking Smithfield where the crowded gallows are' and saw that

> . . . beneath the wry-necked dead,
> Sat a leper and his woman, very merry, breaking bread.

> He was cloaked from chin to ankle – faceless, fingerless, obscene –
> Mere corruption swaddled man-wise, but the woman whole and clean;
> And she waited on him crooning, and Rahere beheld the twain,
> Each delighting in the other . . .

The poem ends with Rahere consoled by the redemptive power of love.

Much of the best work of that last period consisted of sombre short stories, like 'The Wish House' and the Chaucer story, called, like its poem, 'Dayspring Mishandled'. But there were some embarrassingly determined farces too: 'Aunt Ellen' about an eiderdown and 'Beauty Spots' about a pig, and both on the old theme of humiliation. Of the two post-war collections of short stories, *Debits and Credits* of 1926, and *Limits and Renewals* of 1932, the story nearest to popular taste was 'The Woman in his Life' in the latter volume, about a war-shocked officer whose sanity was saved by an Aberdeen terrier. (This had first been published in 1928 before *Thy Servant a Dog* of 1930.) The Kiplings themselves owned two Aberdeens, James or Jimmy, and Mike, and the death of Jimmy was yet another unhappy loss.

Of the work of the very last years, it is interesting that the autobiography, *Something of Myself*, and the rearrangement of the collected poems show clear signs of failing capacity, whereas the last short story, 'Proofs of Holy Writ' *(discussed on pages 68–9)*, is diamond sharp.

In the early 1920s all Kipling's teeth had been taken out, then something of folk-magic medicine for undiagnosed pain. A little later he had been X-rayed and then opened up and told that he had not got cancer, though he could not believe this. It was not until 1933 that a French doctor in Paris correctly diagnosed his

Left: Caroline Kipling's portrait in the study at Bateman's, painted by Philip Burne-Jones in 1899, a companion picture to the portrait of Rudyard painted in the same year.
Right: Said to be the last photograph of Rudyard Kipling, this was taken in Paris by G.L. Manuel Frères in 1935, on condition it was not published till after Kipling's death.

persistent, often agonizing pain as duodenal ulcers. Earlier something could have been done, but now he was not strong enough for an operation.

It was courageous indeed of him to keep on working, hurting and unhappy. Nothing consoled him for old age, and why should it? – 'such an ugly and lonesome place,' he wrote to a friend on his seventieth birthday in December 1935. Yet in the same month he wrote to his Aunt Edie – she nearly ninety and good for another year after him – that: 'He who puts us into this life does not abandon His work for *any* reason or default at the end of it. That is all I have come to learn out of my life. So there is *no* fear!'

We must hope there was not. Three weeks after his birthday, on 18 January 1936, Rudyard Kipling died of a perforated duodenum in a London nursing-home. His ashes were laid in Poet's Corner. On the day Kipling died, King George V fell ill, and his death two days later robbed Kipling of most of the public tributes and substantial assessments that were his due. But they would have been of historic interest only. It is still too early to be sure where, in English literature, Rudyard Kipling's work will finally stand.

CHAPTER FIFTEEN

CONCLUSION

For to admire an' for to see,
    For to be'old this world so wide –
It never done no good to me,
    But I can't drop it if I tried!

from '"For To Admire"'

UDYARD Kipling was very much widely travelled indeed. But no matter how widely travelled a story-teller may be, we do not read him primarily for his travels but for his stories. Certainly what Dickens has to tell us about America in *Martin Chuzzlewit* adds to the interest of that novel as Somerset Maugham's exotic backgrounds do to his tales. But the story (or, as it might be, the poem) comes first, and Kipling's greatness is not that he travelled so widely and wrote about so many places but that wherever he was, he wrote – or could write – so well.

But it has to be granted that Kipling has been read and is still read for more than the quality of his writing. Both in his fiction and in his verse he was saying things that no one had put into words before. To the middle classes in India and at Home, as to the soldiers and the common people, he was able to verbalize what they – but not everyone else – wanted to feel about the British Empire.

When Kipling was writing and for a long time after his death, there was widespread rejection of his interpretation of the white Englishman's role in his Empire. One man may steal a horse where another cannot look over the hedge, and it might well seem at first sight unjust that where Shakespeare could celebrate English greatness, English glory, and the unparalleled qualities of Englishmen, Rudyard Kipling, as proud of his country and his countrymen, has been and still is widely reviled for doing the same. These differences in public response do not depend on differences in the writers' quality, but on the fact that our historical situation at the turn of the sixteenth century differed from that of the time when Kipling was writing: the last decades of the nineteenth century until the mid-1930s. Shakespeare was writing at the beginning of a period of flaming national pride, Kipling towards the end of it, when thinking people were already aware that on dune and headland the fire was sinking; and what national pride we have today is largely unfocused and certainly unsympathetic to a man who came to believe that white men, and preferably white Englishmen, shouldering their right burden of

182

responsibility, must constitute the greatest force for good that the world had yet seen.

But already by the time that Kipling was first writing, his views were unacceptable to the people who were, in the event, to be the most influential in shaping the future for good. The Indian Civil Service had already rejected the view preferred by Kipling and many of his white middle-grade colleagues, that Indians would never be fit to govern themselves. And as the Indians progressed towards, finally achieved self-government and independence, it was hardly to be expected that they would think well of a writer so contemptuously sceptical of their capacity for civilized government at home and a world role abroad. It is only within the past decade or so that Indians have been able to discount the often frantic boasts and foolish words, and to claim that in Kipling they have one of *their* finest writers; and not only for his work on the Indians themselves, but on the English in India too, and the role they played during a few centuries of India's long history.

Similarly, for the liberally inclined people in England, trying to make a new social world which Kipling could only revile, outrage at his views is now nearly historic, and there is some recognition of the fact that we have to begin to work on the right ways to judge Kipling's contribution to English literature.

This is not easy, and even for those concerned more with literature than with politics, there is much in the way of adequately dispassionate judgment. No other writer whom we may have to admit among our greatest has received such widespread popular acclaim together with almost unanimous rejection by the literary establishment, and again, as much for the views as for the quality of the work. At the same time, few other writers' lives and views can have been so totally irrelevant to the work at its best.

It would seem reasonable to suppose that in the near future, literary criticism will find itself able to approach Kipling primarily as artist, with no more and no less attention to his political views than is proper in the context. Already much valuable work has been and is being done. But we are still a very long way from any more or less lasting assessment of Kipling's standing among English writers, and in the meantime, as it seems to me, any of us who chooses to write about Kipling's life and work has something of a duty to say where we think Kipling stands in English Literature now. This, then, is my assessment:

Granting the need to discard, both in prose and verse, a great deal of dross, what remains may be judged in three categories.

In the category where we count poetry great when it touches sublimity, Kipling can offer only a very few poems worth serious consideration; and most of these few will be better considered in the category below.

What it is to be a popular poet has not been seriously defined, since apart from Kipling there has hardly been a popular poet who could justify the category as worth literary (as opposed to sociological) consideration. Some part of an adequate definition must include poetry with a wide appeal to people outside the world of literary art, but with the capacity to reverberate with such profound ambiguities that the more the cultural knowledge, the greater the possible appreciation; together with the quality of being readable-aloud with gain not loss. Were a class of popular poetry to be defined and accepted as within the proper bounds of art, then Rudyard Kipling would be virtually its only practitioner worth serious consideration.

Finally, the stories. As a short-story writer Kipling can stand among the few who count as the best in the world; and as written by those few, the short-story is not to be regarded as an art form inferior to that of the novel. It was a part of Kipling's misfortunes with the critics that the short-story has been so regarded, and Kipling's failure as a novelist has been taken, and to some extent by himself, as a measure of his failure to count among great writers of fiction.

The last tribute here can come from another of the great short-story writers, from Jorge Luis Borges who in 1986 wrote of Kipling – in a short-story – that 'the whole of India – and in a way the whole world – may be found in his pages.'

This dying beast with the waiting crows ends Lockwood Kipling's Beast and Man in India. *To me, it says something about Rudyard and his cruelly assailed genius, and so I use it too for 'The End'.*

KIPLING'S LIFE: A BRIEF CHRONOLOGY

1865 Birth of Rudyard Kipling in Bombay
1868 Birth of sister Alice (Trix)
1871–7 Boarded at Southsea
1878–82 At school at Westward Ho!
1882–9 A journalist in India
1889–91 In London
1892 Marriage of Kipling to Caroline Balestier
1892–6 Living in Vermont
1892 Birth of daughter Josephine
1896 Birth of daughter Elsie
1896–1902 Living in Torquay, then in Rottingdean, Sussex

1897 Birth of son John
1899 Death of Josephine Kipling
1899–1902 The Boer War
1900–8 Winter months spent in South Africa
1902 **onward** Living at Bateman's, Burwash, Sussex
1907 Kipling receives the Nobel Prize
1914–18 The Great War
1915 Death of John Kipling
1924 Marriage of Elsie Kipling
1936 Death of Rudyard Kipling
1939 Death of Kipling's widow

KIPLING'S MAJOR TRAVELS

1868 From India to England, and back
1871 From India to England
1878 First visit to France
1882 From England to India
1889 March-October: From India to England, *via* Burma, Malaya, Hong Kong, Japan, the United States, with a side trip to Canada
From England to France, and back
1890 From England to Italy, and back
To New York and back
1891–2 To South Africa *via* Madeira; to New Zealand, Australia, Ceylon, India, and back to England
1892 To Vermont, Vancouver, Yokohama; back to Vermont
1894 From Vermont to Bermuda and to England, and back
1895 From Vermont to England, and back
1896 From Vermont to England
1897 First outing with the Royal Navy
1898 Four months in South Africa; back to England
Autumn: out with the Navy; only visit to Ireland

1899 From England to New York; last visit to the United States
To Scotland
1900–8 Winter months spent in South Africa
1907 To Stockholm and back
1908–14 Winter sports holidays in Switzerland
Several motor tours in France
1912 To Venice
1913 To Egypt
1915–18 Visits to the Navy in England and in Scotland; to the Army in France and Italy
1920 **onwards** Visits to war cemeteries on the Continent
Motor tours in France
Holidays, mostly in winter, on the French Riviera and elsewhere in the Mediterranean basin, including Spain, Sicily, Egypt, Palestine, Algiers
1927 From England to Rio de Janeiro, and back
1930 From England to Bermuda, and back *via* Canada; last transatlantic journey
1935 To Marienbad and back

KIPLING'S MORE IMPORTANT WORKS

Unless otherwise indicated the dates are of first publication in England. An asterisk after the title indicates books that were in print at the time of writing – 1986; but more reprints are likely soon.

1886 *Departmental Ditties and Other Verses* (India)

1886 *Plain Tales from the Hills** (India)

1890 *The Light that Failed**

1891 *Life's Handicap**

1892 *Soldiers Three**/*The Story of the Gadsbys**/*In Black and White** (Three of the Indian Railway Books of 1888) *Wee Willie Winkie**/*Under the Deodars**/*The Phantom Rickshaw, and Other Stories** (The other three Indian Railway Books of 1888) *Barrack-Room Ballads and Other Verses* *The Naulahka** (with Wolcott Balestier)

1893 *Many Inventions**

1894 *The Jungle Book**

1895 *The Second Jungle Book**

1896 *The Seven Seas* (verse)

1897 *Captains Courageous**

1898 *An Almanac of Twelve Sports* (verses, with illustrations by William Nicholson) *The Day's Work** *A Fleet in Being**

1899 *Stalky & Co.** *From Sea to Sea* (US edition, including *Letters of Marque* of 1891; UK edition published 1900)

1901 *Kim**

1902 *Just So Stories For Little Children**

1903 *The Five Nations* (verses)

1904 *Traffics and Discoveries**

1906 *Puck of Pook's Hill**

1909 *Actions and Reactions**

1910 *Rewards and Fairies**

1911 *A History of England* (with C. R. L. Fletcher: verses)

1915 *France at War*

1916 *Sea Warfare* (including *The Fringes of the Fleet* of 1915)

1917 *A Diversity of Creatures**

1919 *The Years Between* (verses)

1920 *Letters of Travel* (including *From Tideway to Tideway* of 1892; *Letters to the Family* of 1908; *Egypt of the Magicians*) *Q. Horati Flacci Carminum Librum Quintum* (with Charles Graves)

1923 *The Irish Guards in the Great War* *Land and Sea Tales for Scouts and Guides*

1926 *Debits and Credits**

1930 *Thy Servant a Dog**

1932 *Limits and Renewals**

1933 *Souvenirs of France*

1937 *Something of Myself** (posthumous)

The latest edition of Kipling's collected verse is the Definitive Edition*, first issued in 1940; this is incomplete and in other ways unsatisfactory. *Early Verse by Rudyard Kipling** edited by Andrew Rutherford (1986) contains verse from 1879 to 1889, not in the Definitive Edition. Some prose pieces from the Indian period were published as *Abaft the Funnel* in 1909, others in 1986 as *Kipling's India** edited by Thomas Pinney. Kipling's letters to his children are in *O Beloved Kids* of 1983, edited by Elliot L. Gilbert.

Lockwood Kipling's *Beast and Man in India* was published in 1891.

A Brief Bibliography

There are hundreds of books about Rudyard Kipling, about his life and his works, and most of them have something useful to offer. With one exception, I list here only those I have cited, of which the first two have been invaluable; anyone who wants to read more about Kipling will find guidance in their bibliographies. The penultimate book in this list I add because it is an important introduction to criticism of Kipling's stories, and any reader who wants to go further will be glad to know of it.

Lord Birkenhead: *Rudyard Kipling* (Weidenfeld & Nicolson, London, 1978)
Charles Carrington: *Rudyard Kipling, his Life and Work* (Macmillan, London, 1955)
Martin Fido: *Rudyard Kipling* (Hamlyn, Feltham, Middlesex, 1974)
R. L. Green ed.: *Kipling, The Critical Heritage* (Routledge & Kegan Paul, London, 1971)
John Gross ed.: *Rudyard Kipling, The Man, His Work, and His World* (Weidenfeld & Nicolson, London, 1972)
J. L. Kipling: *Beast and Man in India* (Macmillan, London, 1891)
Philip Mason: *Kipling; The Glass, The Shadow and the Fire* (Jonathan Cape, London, 1975)
Murray's *Guide to the Punjab and Rajputana* (London, 1882)
Murray's *Handbook for India, Burma, and Ceylon* (London, 4th edn. 1903)
J. M. S. Tompkins: *The Art of Rudyard Kipling* (Methuen, London, 1959)
Angus Wilson: *The Strange Ride of Rudyard Kipling* (Secker & Warburg, London, 1977)

There is one more book that is indispensable to anyone who wants to pursue a serious interest in Kipling's work, though hard to come by, and best consulted in or borrowed from libraries. This is:

James MacG. Stewart: *Rudyard Kipling, A Bibliographical Catalogue*, edited by A. W. Yeats (Dalhousie University & University of Toronto Press, Toronto, 1959)
Virtually everything ever published by Kipling is listed in this book, with date and place of every publication, and even, where relevant, names of Kipling's illustrators of material published in newspapers and periodicals as well as in books; together with lists of the unauthorized editions, and of all the known musical settings of his verse.

The calligraphic tiger that decorates the dedication 'To the Other Three' of Lockwood Kipling's Beast and Man in India. *It is by Mūnshi Sher Muhammad, I think a teacher at the Lahore Art School.*

NOTES

Chapter One: The Child in His Family
1. *Something of Myself*, chap. 4, p.89
2. Pinney, Thomas, *Kipling's India*, p.276
3. Baldwin, A. W., *The Macdonald Sisters*, chap. 7, p. 114 (Peter Davies Ltd, London, 1960)
4. Baldwin, chap. 7, p.115

Chapter Two: Kipling's Own India
1. Baldwin, chap. 7, p. 115
2. *Something of Myself*, chap. 3, p.41
3. *Something of Myself*, chap. 4, p.103
4. Pinney, p. 191
5. Allen, Charles, *A Glimpse of the Burning Plain*, chap. 9, p.136
6. Carrington, Charles, *Rudyard Kipling*, chap. 4, pp.64–5
7. Quoted in Green, R. L., *Kipling, The Critical Heritage*, p.34
8. *Something of Myself*, chap. 3, p. 55
9. Pinney, p.73
10. Pinney, p.28
11. *Letters of Marque, From Sea to Sea*, vol. 1, chap. 18, p.188

Chapter Three: The Craftsman
1. *Something of Myself*, chap. 8, p.205
2. *Something of Myself*, chap. 8. p.229
3. *Something of Myself*, chap. 3, p.119
4. Carrington, chap. 5, p.104
5. *Something of Myself*, chap. 5, p.141
6. *Something of Myself*, chap. 2, p.25
7. *Something of Myself*, chap. 8, p.210
8. *Something of Myself*, chap. 8, p.185
9. *Something of Myself*, chap. 3, p.43
10. *Something of Myself*, chap. 7, p.188
11. *Something of Myself*, chap. 8, p.210
12. *Something of Myself*, chap. 8, p.209
13. *Something of Myself*, chap. 5, p.113
14. *Something of Myself*, chap. 8, p.210
15. *Something of Myself*, chap. 8, p.208

Chapter Four: A Long Way East of Suez
1. *From Sea to Sea*, vol. 1, chap. 5, p.256
2. *From Sea to Sea*, vol. 1, chap. 7, p.275
3. *From Sea to Sea*, vol. 1, chap. 7, p.274
4. *From Sea to Sea*, vol. 1, chap. 11, p.325
5. *From Sea to Sea*, vol. 1, chap. 19, p. 427

Chapter Five: Kipling in Europe
1. *Something of Myself*, chap. 1, p.11
2. *Something of Myself*, chap. 1, p.20
3. *Nineteenth Century*, September 1890
4. *Something of Myself*, chap. 4, p. 80
5. *Souvenirs of France*, chap. 1, p.12

Chapter Six: Le Pays de Tendre: I Men and Women
1. *Something of Myself*, chap. 1, p.13
2. *Something of Myself*, chap. 4, pp.77–8
3. Carrington, chap. 3, p.41
4. Pinney, p.10
5. Carrington, chap. 8, p.194
6. Gross, John, *Rudyard Kipling, The Man, His Work, and His World*, p.16

Chapter Seven: From Australasia to South America
1. Primrose, J. B., *Kipling's Visit to Australia and New Zealand* (in *Kipling Society Journal*, 1963, vol. 30, March, pp.11–16)
2. *Something of Myself*, chap. 4, p.101
3. *Something of Myself*, chap. 4, p.98
4. *Something of Myself*, chap. 4, p.102

Chapter Eight: North America
1. *From Sea to Sea*, vol. 1, let. 6, p.262
2. *From Sea to Sea*, vol. 1, let. 21, p.451
3. *From Sea to Sea*, vol. 1, let. 23, pp.471–2
4. *Letters to the Family*, p.119 of *Letters of Travel*
5. Carrington, chap. 6, p.138
6. *From Sea to Sea*, vol. 1, let. 36, p.177
7. *From Sea to Sea*, vol. 2, let. 37, p.193
8. *Something of Myself*, chap. 5, p.130
9. Lord Birkenhead, *Rudyard Kipling*, chap. 13, p.201

Chapter Nine: Le Pays de Tendre: II Animals and Children
1. *Times Literary Supplement*, 4 Nov., 1983, p.1203

Chapter Ten: Africa
1. *Something of Myself*, chap. 4, p.95
2. *Something of Myself*, chap. 4, p.97
3. Primrose, *op. cit.*
4. *Something of Myself*, chap. 1, p.4
5. *Letters of Travel*, p.237

Chapter Twelve: Travels in Time and Space
1. *Something of Myself*, chap. 7, p.190

Chapter Fourteen: At Home in Sussex
1. Carrington, chap. 11, p.270
2. Carrington, chap. 13, p.318
3. Birkenhead, chap. 25, p.341
4. Carrington, chap. 20, p.404

INDEX

ILLUSTRATION ACKNOWLEDGMENTS

Author's collection: half-title, 22 (top), 34 (left), 59, 61 (left), 78, 93, 122, 124, 135, 168 (right), 184, 187 (photos: Eileen Tweedy); Earl Baldwin of Bewdley and Weidenfeld & Nicolson Archives: 14 (left); BBC Hulton Picture Library: 17, 54, 71, 99, 108, 112, 117, 137 (left and right), 139, 171; Culver Pictures Inc, New York: 111; Peter Davies Ltd: 13 (left and right), 87; Douglas Dickins FRPS: 42; ET Archive: 74; Mary Evans Picture Library: 110, 152 (left), 158 (left); Haileybury and Weidenfeld & Nicolson Archives: 18; F. Cabot Holbrook & Howard C. Rice Junior and Weidenfeld & Nicolson Archives: 113, 114; The Illustrated London News Picture Library: 75, 133; India Office Library: 22 (bottom), 27, 53, 91, 143; Kipling Society: 34 (right), 64, 66 (left), 84, 116, 125, 145, 147 (left and right) (photos: Eileen Tweedy); Kipling Society and Weidenfeld & Nicolson Archives: 89, 158 (right) (photos: John Freeman); Kobal

Collection: 131; Hammersmith and Fulham Archives: 28; Billie Love Historical Collection: 73; Mansell Collection: title page, 14 (right), 24 (right), 61 (right), 82, 95 (left), 104, 172; National Portrait Gallery: 16; The National Trust (Tunbridge Wells): 46, 181 (left) (photos: David Fawcett); The National Trust (University of Susex Library): 10, 66 (right), 95 (right), 123, 128, 178, 181 (right); The National Trust Photographic Library: 57 (photo: The Times), 174 (photo: John Bethell); The National Trust and Weidenfeld & Nicolson Archives: 168 (left); Popperfoto: 49, 175; Roger-Viollet: 161; Royal Commonwealth Society: 21 (photo: Brian Spearpoint); The Salvation Army Archives and Research Centre: 24 (left); La Trobe Collection, State Library of Victoria: 100.

The extract from Les Silences du Colonel Bramble by André Maurois on p. 81 is quoted by kind permission of Editions Bernard Grasset, Paris.